Sydney, 05/03/06

From the midst of a
wonderful exploration that
is spanning the world,
its maps and much more.

With many loving kisses,

KT

THE EXPLORER'S EYE

THE EXPLORER'S EYE

First-hand Accounts of Adventure and Exploration

EDITED BY FERGUS FLEMING & ANNABEL MERULLO

INTRODUCTION BY MICHAEL PALIN

DESIGNED BY DAVID ROWLEY

WEIDENFELD & NICOLSON

CONTENTS

PREFACE

THE 18TH CENTURY marked a watershed in the history of exploration. Hitherto, discovery had entailed finding gold or spices and then conquering the lands that produced them. As Enlightenment scholars pondered the workings of the world, however, greed gave way to a spirit of inquiry. The old concerns of wealth, territorial acquisition and national prestige still pertained; but it was now accepted that the purpose of exploration was to increase humankind's understanding of the globe. Those who left for the unknown were no longer buccaneers but investigators; they were expected to provide a full and accurate account of their journeys; and, for the first time, they were to supplement their prose with pictures. They were to be proper pictures, too: not the dragon-filled maps, blowy oceans, sketchy diagrams and romanticized woodcuts of previous centuries, but images as lifelike as was within the artist's power.

Captain James Cook was among the first to supply the goods. Between 1768 and 1779 he undertook three great voyages spanning Antarctica, the Arctic, Australia, New Zealand and Polynesia. His journals not only described new and exotic lands but, thanks to the expeditions' draughtsmen, showed what they looked like. The authorities were agog and so was the public: nothing like it had been seen before. Thereafter no explorer dared come home without surpassing Cook's benchmark or at least attempting to match it.

It is hard to over-emphasize the impact these early journals made. They arrived at a time when literacy was reasonably widespread, when wild landscapes and 'noble savages' were all the rage, and when science was not yet so far advanced that dream could be divorced from reality. Indeed, reality abetted the dream. Romantics such as Byron, Keats, Shelley and Coleridge produced much of their best work under the influence of exploration literature. (Samuel Taylor Coleridge's *Ryme of the Ancient Mariner* (1798), Mary Shelley's *Frankenstein* (1818) and Edgar Allen Poe's *Narrative of Arthur Gordon Pym* (1850) were all inspired by polar narratives.) By the 1820s explorers had become men of the moment: their journals were best-sellers; strangers crossed the street to shake hands with them; they were showered with honours and encouraged to do it again – which they often did because there was always more to be discovered and because the public liked an exciting read with nice pictures.

This was not the birth of travel writing but it was the start of its popularization. Over succeeding decades it became an established genre, one that had all the attributes of fiction – narrative progression, suspense, development of character, vivid descriptions of places and people – but with the advantage of being based on fact. Not that fact was necessarily separable from fiction. As late as the 1830s, Charles Darwin remarked: 'The limit of man's [sic] knowledge in every subject possesses a high interest, which is perhaps increased by its close-ness to the imagination.' The proximity was exploited by authors such as Jules Verne whose novels not only had their roots in exploration literature but at times were indistinguishable from it. In a curious game of literary leap-frog some of the most apparently outlandish examples of science fiction later became exploration fact.

Explorers, no less than novelists, saw the money-spinning potential of a ripping yarn. Sometimes they played up their experiences: elaborating dangers, exaggerating quarrels, falsifying records and occasionally lying from start to finish. A prime example of the last was Frederick Cook, who vanished in the Canadian Arctic for a year then announced in 1909 that he had been to the North Pole, assuming confidently that nobody could prove he hadn't. (His expectations were dashed.) Few were as crooked as Cook – with the possible exception of his rival Robert Peary – but as the globe's mysteries were gradually uncovered, explorers' journals changed noticeably in character. From being factual records of sights seen and countries visited, they evolved into dramatized narratives and then contemplative essays on the nature of exploration, the world and humanity itself. The manner in which explorers recorded their experiences changed, too. Pen, paper and watercolours were gradually replaced by typewriters and cameras, which in turn were superceded by computers and films. Regardless of medium, century or mind-set, each explorer fulfilled the original Enlightenment remit: to give as vivid a picture of new worlds as they could.

This anthology, in words and pictures, is a record of their achievements. The subjects have been chosen partly because they were historically important, partly because they were fascinating chroniclers and partly because they were expert painters or photographers. In some cases the words are stronger than the images; in others the pictures are more impressive than the text. The proportion does not really matter because, whatever their individual strengths, each entry provides a snapshot of one person's journey into the unknown. In choosing between primary and 'remembered' sources we have made the final selection on merit alone. Thus, the diaries of Robert Scott have been reproduced verbatim, whereas those of Ernest Shackleton – which can be paraphrased (more or less) as 'Nothing much happened today' – have not.

There arises, inevitably, the question of who is or is not an explorer. A commonly accepted definition is someone who discovers new lands. Yet what is discovery, and what new lands? A geographical purist would say that, with a few exceptions, very little new has been discovered: all that has happened is that people from one place have announced that other places exist, thereby confirming a suspicion long held by those who inhabited them. In the same vein it is hard to distinguish between exploration and 'mere' travel, one person's death-defying odyssey being another's old hat. We have therefore determined that an explorer is someone who charts the unknown, who does so for reasons of inquiry rather than reportage, and with priority given to those who did so first – reserving always the editorial privileges of favoritism and inconsistency.

FERGUS FLEMING & ANNABEL MERULLO

INTRODUCTION *by Michael Palin*

It was not until I was twelve or thirteen that I finally gave up hope of becoming an explorer. Since about the age of eight, I had been aware of a strong, and at times almost desperate need to see parts of the world before anyone else did. I've never been quite sure where this urge came from, but reading *The Explorer's Eye* has reminded me. I was absolutely entranced by the tales the great explorers told. The frostbite, the gangrene, the cannibalism, the curses, the naked fear and total exhaustion, the whole panoply of horrors seemed so much more attractive than playing French cricket and drinking Horlicks.

My imagination fed greedily on accounts of appalling suffering and insane bravery, like Captain Scott's doomed but grippingly documented South Pole expedition, Livingstone's defiance of death and disease to reach the towering waters of the Victoria Falls, Mallory and Irvine vanishing into a cloud 800 feet from the top of Everest, never to be seen again.

For a would-be explorer the 1940s and early 1950s were difficult times. Both Poles had gone, as well as the North West and North East Passages, the source of the Nile and most of Saudi Arabia. The great Himalayan peaks, on which I'd pinned my hopes, were going down like flies. Annapurna, Everest and then K2, all conquered, and I hadn't even reached puberty.

On 29 May 1953, Edmund Hillary and Tenzing Norgay struggled to the top of Everest, the first people ever to do so. I was proud of them. We all were. And maybe I was a little disappointed too. Maybe I had a hint even then of what I feel looking back now, that this was literally and metaphorically the high point of a golden age of exploration which had enthralled the western world for a century and a half.

After Everest most of the iconic extremes had been conquered. But it was not only that. The Everest expedition, well-financed, well-equipped and media conscious, seemed to suggest that we had got the measure of the difficult and dangerous. Something of the mystique of exploration had gone. Technology was becoming more sophisticated, reducing both human risk and human achievement. There were great challenges left, but few of them captured the public imagination in the same way as the search for the source of the Nile or the crossing of Australia. Four years after Hillary and Tenzing's triumph, Vivian Fuchs led the first-ever crossing of Antarctica, but as Fergus Fleming points out, 'After so many glamorous failures at the South Pole, it seemed that victory had become a non-event..nobody died, everything went more or less according to plan.' At the time of writing Ranulph Fiennes is doing his best to keep the traditions of exploring alive and well, setting himself ever-harder targets and ever-more punishing challenges. But the achievement of 'being the First' is no longer as evocative and resounding as it once was. The fact remains that, as I had reluctantly to admit, before I was even out of short trousers, most of the world has been explored.

The only exploration that captured international attention in my adult life was when the *Eagle* landed on the moon on 20 July 1969 and Neil Armstrong became the first man to set foot on a surface beyond our earth. But, if it's not too facetious to say so, even this was different from the classic feats of exploration. Neil Armstrong was hurled at the moon at the cutting edge of a massive investment programme, he didn't have to part the bushes and dodge the blowpipes, face a third year on the ice like John Ross in the 1830s or see his fingers and toes removed one-by-one like Maurice Herzog as he descended Annapurna.

Fergus Fleming and Annabel Merullo have put together an enormously attractive and comprehensive guide to the whole heroic, tragic and triumphant history of the great years of exploration. Using the explorers' own words wherever possible, and accompanying them with a priceless collection of visual records, they have brought extraordinary adventures back to life. It's impossible to look through this book without being dazzled by the scale and scope of these giant steps for mankind and thankfully Fergus Fleming's commentary keeps the essential human perspective, celebrating the fearless and the foolhardy alike and relishing the follies as much as the successes.

It's difficult to know which plums to pick out. I was pleased to be reminded that one of the greatest, and least known Firsts belongs to the expedition led by the seriously un-catchy Jules-Sébastien-César Dumont D'Urville, the first man ever to set foot on the Antarctic continent, in 1837. No pemmican for them, being French they celebrated with a bottle of good Bordeaux, well-chilled, I suppose. The Scandinavians come out particularly well, the inspirational and inventive Fridtjof Nansen creating an egg-shaped hull for his polar expedition, to avoid being trapped by the ice. And it worked. Amundsen, a career explorer, almost scoring a sensational trio, first to the South Pole, first through the North West Passage and quite possibly, first to the North Pole.

The exploration of the North Pole turns out to have a murky history. I had thought it an incontrovertible fact the American Admiral Peary reached it in 1909, but it turns out that he may have only got within 60 miles of it, and Fleming suggests that the first man to 'indisputably' reach the North Pole on foot was Wally Herbert in 1968. I was 25 then, dammit, and could have done it after all. As it is, I had to wait until 1991. *(Stop showing off – ed.)*

What typified this era of post-Enlightenment journeys was the need to write everything down. We learn that Freya Stark, one of only two lady explorers to make the book, wrote an average of ten letters for every day she travelled. Richard Burton, who spoke 27 languages, wrote copious journals, but, in one of the most tragic episodes recorded in these pages, his wife Isabella burnt them all on his death for being too rude. Scott's expedition to the South Pole may have been a failure but his diaries are surely the most moving of any quoted here. Trapped by a tremendous blizzard, crippled by frostbite, Scott continues with daily entries, until the very end, when the mundane becomes unbearably poignant.

'It seems a pity, but I do not think I can write more.'

Scott's expedition moves us particularly, accompanied as it is by some of the great photographs of the exploration age. Frank Hurley's striking images remain among the most powerful polar images ever taken, as unsurpassed as Wilfred Thesiger's photographs of The Empty Quarter in Arabia.

Designer David Rowley has made full use of these and other examples of the explorer's eye, enriching the stories with terrific illustrations ranging from the pure Indiana Jones of the cave John Stephens discovered at Bolonchén, one of the lost cities of Central America, to the delightfully batty aero-helmets worn by Auguste Piccard and his crew when they became the first men ever to ascend into the stratosphere.

The Explorer's Eye is a treasure trove. Like Hiram Bingham unearthing Macchu Picchu or Charles Darwin landing on the Galapagos, untold wonders are about to unfold before you.

MICHAEL PALIN LONDON MAY 2005

JOSEPH BANKS 1743–1820
To the Great Barrier Reef and beyond

BANKS WAS THE 18TH CENTURY'S *Natural Philosopher par excellence. Although trained as a botanist, he applied himself with unquenchable curiosity to practically every branch of the sciences. At one moment he could be investigating the weather patterns of Tierra del Fuego, at another pondering the existence of Antarctica, and at another examining (with reference to the oil in his household lamps) how a warm spell might affect the composition of whale blubber. His 1768-71 journey with James Cook aboard the* Endeavour *took him to the South Pacific via South America, New Zealand and Australia and resulted in the discovery of so many new plants that the findings are still being analyzed today. It also saw the charting of a bay on the Australian coast that Banks subsequently recommended as an ideal site for a penal colony. Now known as Sydney, its settlement inaugurated the colonization of the entire continent. Later, as President of the Royal Society, Banks established himself as an authority on African and Arctic exploration, his house in Soho Square a focal point for Britain's scientists and explorers.*

WHILE SAILING UP THE EAST COAST OF AUSTRALIA, THE ENDEAVOUR BECAME THE FIRST EUROPEAN SHIP TO NAVIGATE THE GREAT BARRIER REEF.

August 1770 For the first time these three months we were this day out of sight of Land to our no small satisfaction: that very Ocean which had formerly been look'd on with terror by (maybe) all of us was now the Assylum we had long wishd for and at last found. Satisfaction was clearly painted in every mans face...The Captn fearfull of going too far from the Land...steerd the ship west right in for the land....but just at night fall found himself in a manner embayd in the reef so that it was a moot Point whether or not he could weather it on either tack; we stood however to the Northward and at dark it was concluded that she would go clear of every thing we could see. The night however was not the most agreable: all the dangers we had escaped were little in comparison of being thrown upon this reef if that should be our lot. A Reef such a one as I now speak of is a thing scarcely known in Europe or indeed any where but in these seas: it is a wall of Coral rock rising almost perpendicularly out of the unfathomable ocean, always overflown at high water commonly 7 or 8 feet, and generally bare at low water; the large waves of the ocean meeting with so sudden a resistance make here a most terrible surf breaking mountain high...

At three O'Clock this morn it dropd calm on a sudden which did not at all better our situation: we judged ourselves not more than 4 or 5 l'gs from the reef, maybe much less, and the swell of the sea which drive right in upon it carried the ship towards it fast...Every method had been taken since we first saw our danger to get the boats out in hopes that they might tow us off but it was not yet accomplishd...All the while we were approaching and came I beleive before this could be effected within 40 yards of the breaker; the same sea that washed the side of the ship rose in a breaker enormously high the very next time it did rise, so between us and it was only a dismal valley the breadth of our wave...Now was our case truly desperate, no man I beleive but who gave himself himself intirely over, a speedy death was all we had to hope for and that from the vastness of the Breakers which must quickly dash the ship all to peices was scarce to be doubted...At this critical

Bromelia bracteata.

Sydney Parkinson pinxt 1760.

A Brazilian bromeliad (a relative of the pineappple) as depicted by Sydney Parkinson, one of the two official draughtsmen who sailed aboard the Endeavour. An expert botanical illustrator, Parkinson's job was to record the specimens collected by Banks and his fellow naturalist Daniel Solander. Captain Cook recalled Parkinson's tribulations with the insect population in Tahiti, 'The flies…made it almost impossible for Mr Parkinson…to work; for they not only covered his subject so that no part of its surface could be seen, but even ate the colour off the paper as fast as he could lay it on.' Although Parkinson died on the voyage he left behind a total of 1332 drawings.

juncture, at this I may say terrible moment, when all assistance seemd too little to save even our miserable lives, a small air of wind sprang up, so small that at any other time in a calm we should not have observed it. We however plainly saw that it instantly checkd our progress; every sail was therefore put in a proper direction to catch it and we just observd the ship to move in a slaunting direction off from the breakers...The ship still movd a little off but in less than 10 minutes our little Breeze died away into as flat a calm as ever... Now was our anxiety again renewd: innumerable small peices of paper &c were thrown over the ships side to find whither the boats really movd her ahead or not and so little did she move that it remaind almost every other time a matter of dispute. Our little freindly Breeze now visited us again and lasted about as long as before, thrusting us possibly 100 yards from the breakers: we were still however in the very jaws of destruction. A small opening had been seen in the reef a furlong from us, its breadth was scarce the length of the ship, into this however it was resolved to push her if possible. Within was no surf, therefore we might save our lives: the doubt was only whether we could get the ship so far: our little breeze however a third time visited us and pushd us almost there. The fear of Death is Bitter: the prospect we now had before us of saving our lives tho at the expence of every thing we had made my heart set much lighter on its throne, and I suppose there were none but what felt the same sensation...By 4 we came to an anchor happy once more to encounter those shoals which but two days before we thought ourselves supreamly happy to have escap'd from. How little do men know what is for their real advantage: two days ago our utmost wishes were crownd by getting without the reef and today we were made again happy by geting within it.

J. BEAGLEHOLE (ED.), *The Endeavour, Journal of Joseph Banks. Vol. II, 1962.*

ON THE ABORIGINES

Thus live these I had almost said happy people, content with little nay almost nothing. Far enough removd from the anxieties attending upon riches, or even the possession of what we Europeans call common necessities: anxieties intended maybe by Providence to counterbalance the pleasure arising from the Posession of wishd for attainments, consequently increasing with increasing wealth, and in some measure keeping up the balance of hapiness between the rich and the poor. From them appear how small are the real wants of human nature, which we Europeans have increased to an excess which would certainly seem incredible to these people could they be told it. Nor shall we cease to increase them as long as Luxuries can be invented and riches found for the purchase of them; and how soon these Luxuries degenerate into necessaries may be sufficiently evincd by the universal use of strong liquors, Tobacco, spices, Tea &c. &c. In this instance again providence seems to act the part of a leveler, doing much towards putting all ranks into an equal state of wants and consequently of real poverty: the Great and Magnificent want as much and may be more than the midling: they again in proportion more than the inferior: each rank still looking higher than his station but confining itself to a certain point above which it knows not how to wish, not knowing at least perfectly what is there enjoyed.

The Endeavour, Journal of Joseph Banks, Vol. II.

Barter commences in New Zealand with a tentatively proferred lobster. Probably painted by Banks himself, this image casts a rosy glow on relations with the Maoris. A war-like race, who occasionally indulged in cannibalism, they did not take kindly to intruders. In the rare instances when trade was possible the Endeavour's crew sought not lobsters but partially gnawed human bones as souvenirs. '[They] constantly ask for and purchase them for whatever trifles they have', wrote Banks.

JAMES COOK 1728–1779

Epic voyages to the South Seas

COOK WAS ONE OF THE 18TH *century's great seafarers. In the course of four ground-breaking voyages – one of them with Joseph Banks – he circumnavigated Antarctica, charted the South Pacific, New Zealand, the east coast of Australia, and attempted the North West Passage. He was aided by the first-ever chronometer, which allowed him to determine longitude – the holy grail of navigation – and by an innovatory diet, rich in vegetables, that kept scurvy at bay and thereby enabled him to stay at sea longer than any of his predecessors. His career ended in 1779 when, commanding the* Resolution *and* Discovery, *he became the first European to land on Hawaii. Unfortunately his arrival coincided with a major fertility ritual and, mistaken for a god, he was bludgeoned to death. Explorers of all nations stood in awe of his achievements; and in Britain he became a demi-god, the public paying outrageous prices for even the smallest personal memento.*

COOK REPORTED WITH ALARM THAT THE MAORIS WERE PRONE TO CANNIBALISM.

21 February [1777]...From my own observations, the information of Tiarooa and others, the New Zealanders must live under perpetual apprehinsions of being destroyed by each other. There being few Tribes that have not received some injury or another from some other, which they are continually upon the watch to revenge and perhaps the idea of a good meal may be no small incitement. I am told that many years will sometimes elapse before a favourable opportunity happens, and that the Son never loses sight of an injury that has been done his Father.

There method of executing these horrible designs is by stealing upon the party in the night, and if they find them unguarded (which however I beleive is very seldom the case) they kill every soul that falls in their way, not even sparing the Women and Children, and then either feast or gorge themselves on the spot or carry off as many of the dead as they can and do it at home with acts of brutality horrible to relate. If they are discovered before they can put their designs into execution, they generally steal off again, some times they are persued and attacked by the other party; they neither give quarter nor take prisoners, so that the Vanquish'd can only save their lives by flight.

This method of makeing War keeps them continually upon their guard so that one hardly ever finds a New Zealander of his guard either day or night. Indeed, no man can have such powerful reasons, having both body and Soul to preserve, for they tell us that the Soul of the Man who falls into the hand and whose flesh is eat by the Enimy, goes to Hell, that is descends down to a perpetual fire, but the Soul of him who is killed whose body is rescued from the Enemy goes to Heaven, that is it ascends upwards to the habitations of the Gods, as also the Souls of all those who die a natural death.

I asked if they eat the flesh of such of their friends as was killed by the enemy, but whose bodies was rescued or saved from falling into their hand; they seemed surprised at the question and answered no, and express'd some abhorrence at the very idea. The dead they bury in the earth, but if they have more of their enemies than they can eat, they throw them into the Sea.

J. BEAGLEHOLE (ED.), *The Voyage of the Resolution and Discovery, 1999.*

A VIEW of the *ENDEAVOUR'S* Watering-place in the Bay of GOOD SUCCESS

CHARLES CLERKE, FIRST LIEUTENANT ABOARD COOK'S SHIP, WAS IMPRESSED BY THE INHABITANTS OF NEW CALEDONIA.

These people are of a dark mahogony colour – well featur'd – Woolly headed – well form'd bodies, and of the middling Stature - the Features both of the men and women are remarkably good, exceeding by far, any woolly Headed Nation we ever met with – their benevolence when they find an opportunity, can be exceeded by nothing but their assiduity in finding it – they're absolutely unhappy unless they can suggest some means of making themselves serviceable and agreeable – when Wooding or Watering – they wou'd either cut or carry – fill the Casks or rowl – and if you interrupted them in this business, they seem'd uneasy that they cou'd not render their best endeavours worthy your accept-ance. We have all the reason in the World to suppose ourselves the first Europeans they ever beheld, and that unlimited confidence they immediately plac'd in us, I think speaks greatly in favour of their Honesty and Goodness of Heart...the dress of these our good friends is somewhat singular – when we found them, they were totally naked to the Penis, which was wrapt up in leaves, and whatever you gave them, or they, by any means attain'd; was immediately apply'd there; nor wou'd they care one farthing for any article of dress, that cou'd not in some form, be made to contribute, to the decorating that favourite part. I gave one of them one day a stocking – he very deliberately pull'd it on there – I then presented him with a medal, which he immediately hung to it – in short let

OVERLEAF
The young landscape artist William Hodges painted this panorama of Tahiti on Cook's second voyage to the South Pacific. By the time of Cook's third visit the island had become so familiar and its hospitality so legendary that he had difficulty prising his men away. Charles Clerke, his First Lieutenant, wrote, 'I must own that 'tis with some reluctance I bid adieu to these happy isles where I've spent so many happy times.'

A Tahitian priest cuts a rakish slant on Cook's first voyage. Among the wonders that Cook encountered on the island was a temple platform whose stones were squared and fitted with remarkable precision. He was baffled as to how Tahitians could have fashioned such a structure in the absence of iron tools and European masonry skills.

that noble part be well decorated and fine, they're perfectly happy, and totally indifferent about the state of all the rest of the Body. The Womens dress consists of a long string, from which suspends Hemp, work'd into small distinct Ends about 8 inches long – in general dy'd black – this they wrap 4 or 5 times round them, the turns immediately upon each other, just below the Hips; which as perfectly secretes all they want to hide, as all the Petty-Coats &c. &c. I ever saw upon a Woman in my life.

DAVID SAMWELL, SURGEON ABOARD THE DISCOVERY, RECORDED THE AFTERMATH OF COOK'S DEATH ON HAWAII.

Saturday Febry 20th...Between ten and eleven o'Clock we saw a great Number of people coming down the hills in a kind of procession, every one of them carrying a Sugar Cane or two on his Shoulders & about as many breadfruit, Taroo root, or Plantains in his Hand. Two Drummers who accompanyed them sat down on the Beach by a white Flag & beat their Drums, while the Indians came one by one, laid down their Sugar Cane &c., and then retired; another party came along the Beach, in the same order, & laid down their Presents or peace offerings upon the others and then withdrew. Another white Flag with one Man sitting by it was flying about midway on the Beach. In a short time we saw Eeapo in his feathered Cloak standing on a rock waving to us for a boat to come on shore, on which Captn. Clerke went to him in the pinnace attended by the 1st. Lieut. in the large Cutter. They did not land, for Eeapo attended by Taweno-ora came into the Pinnace, and a large bundle was handed in covered with a black feathered Cloak, in which was contained the remains of Capt. Cook decently wrapped up in a large quantity of fine new Cloth. Eeapo did not stay long on board either Ship, but soon returned on shore with the presents that were made to him, a fine new Cloak was given to him on board the Discovery made of red Bays with a border of green. In the Afternoon the Bundle was opened on board the Resolution in the Cabinn, we found in it the following bones with some flesh upon them which had the marks of fire. The Thighs & Legs joined together but not the feet, both Arms with the Hands seperated from them, the Skull with all the bones that form the face wanting with the Scalp seperated from it, which was also in the bundle with the hair on it cut short, both Hands whole with the Skin of the fore Arms joined to them, the hands had not been in the fire, but were salted, several Gashes being cut in them to take the Salt in. Tho we had no doubt concerning the Identity of any of the parts contained in the bundle, every one must be perfectly satisfied as to that of the hands, for we all knew the right by a large Scar on it seperating for about an inch the Thumb from the fore-finger. The Ears adhered to the Scalp, which had a cut in it about an inch long, probably made by the first blow he received with the Club, but the Skull was not fractured so that it was likely that the stroke was not mortal. Such was the Condition in which those, who looked upon Captn. Cook as their father & whose great Qualities they venerated almost to adoration, were doomed to behold his Remains; what their feelings were upon the Occasion is not to be described.

The Voyage of the Resolution and Discovery.

Plate XI.

S. Parkinson del.

J. Chambers Sculp.

An Heiva, or kind of Priest of Yoolee-Etea, & the Neighbouring Islands.

LOUIS-ANTOINE DE BOUGAINVILLE 1729–1811

Passage to Tahiti

BOUGAINVILLE WAS, IN SOME RESPECTS, a martial version of Joseph Banks. Having trained as a lawyer and mathematician in Paris, he served as an army officer before transferring at the age of 34 to the navy. Such was his capability that within just three years he found himself in command of an expedition to circumnavigate the globe. With two ships, La Boudeuse *and the* Étoile, *he sailed down the South American coast and made a brief investigation of the South Pacific – where he waxed lyrical on the delights of Tahiti, but failed to locate Australia – before continuing on his way. He was not the first European to visit the region: Dutch explorers had long ago annexed the East Indies; and a Briton had beaten him to Tahiti the year before. But the narrative of his 1766-69 voyage thrilled the public with its accounts of paradisical islands; its description of 'Noble Savagery' was discussed in many an academic salon. Like Banks, he collected numerous specimens of plant and marine life and, following the French Revolution, devoted himself to science, becoming one of France's most influential savants. His original journal was not published until 1977.*

IN 1768 BOUGAINVILLE REACHED THE ISLAND OF TAHITI.

Thursday 7 [April] We worked on clearing our water casks and in the afternoon I went to set up a camp on land. The Indians seemed at first pleased to see us, then the cacique came, he had a kind of meeting with the leading men. The outcome was to tell me that we had to go and sleep on board and return in the morning. I explained that we were coming to sleep ashore in order to obtain water and wood, and that for this I needed 18 days after which we would leave. I gave him a number of stones equal to the number of days I expected to stay. Deliberations of the council, they wanted to remove 9 stones. I did not agree. In the end everything was settled, the Indians however still displaying a great deal of mistrust. I had supper in my tent with the cacique and part of his family, each kitchen having supplied its dishes; we did not eat much, His Majesty and the princes of the blood having an appetite that we could not emulate. After supper I had 12 rockets fired on land in front of the guests. Their terror was indescribable...Towards the middle of the night...there was a loud altercation between the king, his brothers and people who appear to be their servants, over some opera glasses that had been stolen from my pocket during the supper. The king was accusing his subjects and threatening to kill them; the poor devils were, I think, less responsible for this theft than he was. It all quietened down and the end of the night was more peaceful. During the following day, several Frenchmen had cause to praise the country's customs. As they went into houses, they were presented with young girls, greenery was placed on the ground and with a large number of Indians, men and women, making a circle around them, hospitality was celebrated, while one of the assistants was singing a hymn to happiness accompanied by the sounds of the flute...Married women are faithful to their husbands, they would pay with their lives any unfaithfulness, but we are offered all the young girls. Our white skin delights them, they express their admiration in this regard in the most expressive manner. Furthermore, the race is superb, with men 5 feet 10 inches tall, many reaching six foot, a few exceeding this. Their features are very handsome. They have a fine head of hair which they wear in

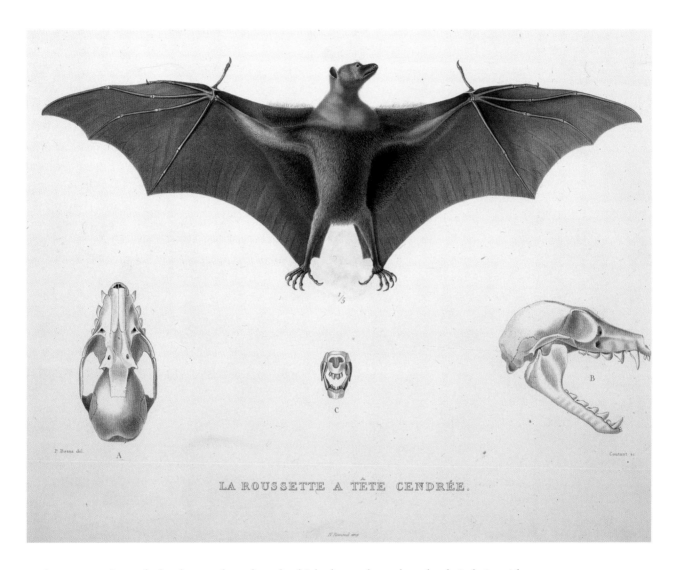

P. Bessa del.   A   C   B   Coutant sc.

LA ROUSSETTE A TÊTE CENDRÉE.

N. Remond imp.

various ways. Several also have a long beard which they rub as they do their hair with coconut oil. The women are pretty and, something that is due to the climate, their food and the water, men and women and even old men have the finest teeth in the world. These people breathe only rest and sensual pleasures. Venus is the goddess they worship. The mildness of the climate, the beauty of the scenery, the fertility of the soil everywhere watered by rivers and cascades, the pure air unspoiled by even those legions of insects that are the curse of hot countries, everything inspires sensual pleasure. And so I have named it New Cythera and the protection of Minerva is as necessary here as in the ancient Cythera to defend one against the influence both of the climate and of the people's morals.

I cannot as yet describe their form of government, their differences in rank and their distinctive marks. The cacique, we see this constantly, rules despotically, drives them away with a stick when they bother us, even saw to the return of items stolen from us even though he is himself a great thief, but he wants to be the only one to steal in his kingdom. As for indications of social differences, I believe (and this is not a joke) that the first one,

A parrot from the South Pacific. Of all the places he visited Bougainville was most charmed by Tahiti, or New Cythera as he called it. 'This morning three lords from a neighbouring district came up with a present of cloth. Their size and girth are gigantic. I gave them an axe, some nails and some gimlets. We fired a pistol in their presence, the shot piercing a plank. Their heavy highnesses fell backwards and it took us some time to persuade them to get up again. We had to repay their visit in the after-noon. The chief offered me one of his wives, young and fairly pretty, and the whole village sang the wedding anthem. What a country! What a people!'

the one that distinguishes free men from slaves, is that free men have their buttocks painted...I shall write things down as I discover them.

The Pacific Journal of Louis-Antoine De Bougainville, 1767-68.

WITH FOOD RUNNING LOW, AND SCURVY THREATENING, BOUGAINVILLE WAS ALERTED TO AN UNEXPECTED CHANGE IN THE ÉTOILE'S ROSTER.

Saturday 28 to Sunday 29 [May] We had courses brailed up and the main topsail shivering to wait for the Étoile which sails worse than ever. Nevertheless we are compelled not to lose one instant. The state and condition of our food stocks require us to reach some European establishment. We have been for a long time on the same rations as the crew. We have only a few poultry left that are reserved for the sick and three turkeys that will do for three Sundays. We are eating one at midday today and it is a great cause of rejoicing for us. These large beans, called horse beans, bacon and salt beef almost three years old make up such sad meals!...

Yesterday I checked a rather peculiar event on board the Étoile. For some time, a rumour had been circulating on the two ships that Mr de Commercon's servant, named Bare, was a woman. His build, his caution in never changing his clothes or carrying out any natural function in the presence of anyone else, the sound of his voice, his beardless chin, and several other indications have given rise to this suspicion and reinforced it. It seemed to have been changed into a certainty by a scene that took place on the island of Cythera [Tahitit]. Mr de Commercon had gone ashore with Bare who followed him in all his botanizing, [and] carried weapons, food, plant notebooks with a courage and strength which had earned for him from our botanist the title of his beast of burden. Hardly had the servant landed than the Cytherans surround him, shout that he is a woman and offer to pay her the honours of the island. The officer in charge had to come and free her. I was therefore obliged, in accordance with the King's ordinances, to verify whether the suspicion was correct. Bare, with tears in her eyes, admitted that she was a girl, that she had misled her master by appearing before him in men's clothing at Rochefort at the time of boarding, that she had already worked for a Genevan as a valet, that, born in Burgundy and orphaned, the loss of a lawsuit had reduced her to penury and that she had decided to disguise her sex, that moreover, she knew when she came on board that it was a question of circumnavigating the world and that this voyage had excited her curiosity. She will be the only one of her sex [to have done this] and I admire her determination all the more because she has always behaved with the most scrupulous correctness. I have taken steps to ensure that she suffers no unpleasantness. The Court will, I think, forgive her for this infraction of the ordinances. Her example will hardly be contagious. She is neither ugly nor pretty and is not yet 25.

THE PACIFIC JOURNAL OF LOUIS-ANTOINE DE BOUGAINVILLE, 1767–68.

Pl. 39

G. N.

Bessa del.

Coriant sc.

LE CALLOCEPHALE AUSTRAL, Mâle.

ALEXANDER VON HUMBOLDT 1769–1859

Botanical studies in South America

A GERMAN ARISTOCRAT *who was disappointed in love and disenchanted with his job as an inspector of mines, Humboldt decided to become an explorer. In 1799 he arrived in South America with a sizeable personal fortune and a single, grand ambition: to learn everything about everything. For the next five years, accompanied by the French botanist, Aime Bonpland, he travelled widely throughout the Americas and amassed so much scientific information that it took him another thirty years to collate it. (The final volume of his* Travels to the Equinoctial Regions of the New World *did not come out until 1834.) He spent the remainder of his dwindling fortune on expeditions to the Alps, the Urals and Central Asia, then settled down to write* Kosmos, *a philosophical treatise that attempted to explain the world's workings. It was still unfinished when he died in 1859, by which time he had become so famous that he had to place an advertisement asking fans to leave him in peace. His journals are remarkable not only for their exuberant inquisitiveness but also for the skill and precision of their illustrations.*

Humboldt allowed nothing to impede his quest for knowledge. Despite having no climbing experience he scaled some of the Andes' most impressive mountains, just to see what was there, and on 23 June 1802 he attempted what was then the world's highest known peak, Mt Chimborazo, reaching an altitude of 5790 metres, a skywards record for any human to date and one that would not be broken for several decades. He was forever clambering into volcanic craters, retreating only when his clothes started to singe or when the air became unbreathable. Unlike other mountaineers, who dwelled on the difficulties and terrors of height, Humboldt treated it all as a magnificent game. Having been mildly sizzled in one crater, he wrote, 'What a fantastic place! What fun we had!'

Between them, Humboldt and Bonpland collected more than 60,000 plants of which more than half were species unknown to Europe. Transporting the specimens across the mountains and rivers of South America became a major problem. 'The conveyance of these objects, and the minute care they required, occasioned us such embarassments as would scarcely be conceived', Humboldt wrote. 'Our progress was often retarded by the three-fold necessity of dragging after us, during expeditions of five or six months, twelve, fifteen and sometimes twenty loaded mules, exchanging these animals every eight or ten days, and superintending the Indians who were employed in leading so numerous a caravan.' Against their loss, he recorded each item in his journal, using rough sketches that he later elaborated into detailed illustrations. And against the loss of his journal he made three painstaking copies, two of which he forwarded to France and Britain, the other being cached in Havana. In the event, he need not have bothered because all three versions were retrieved safely.

ACQUIRING AN ELECTRIC EEL.

The dread of the shocks caused by the gymnoti [electric eels] is so great, and so exaggerated among the common people, that during three days we could not obtain one, though they are easily caught, and we had promised the Indians two piastres for every strong and vigorous fish. This fear of the Indians is the more extraordinary, as they do not attempt to adopt precautions in which they profess to have great confidence. When interrogated

on the effect of the [eels], they never fail to tell the Whites that they may be touched with impunity while you are chewing tobacco. This supposed influence of tobacco on animal electricty is as general on the continent of South America, as the belief among mariners of the effect of garlic and tallow on the magnetic needle.

Impatient of waiting, and having obtained very uncertain results from an electric eel which had been brought to us alive, but much enfeebled, we repaired to the Cano de Bera, to make our experiments in the open air, and at the edge of the water. We set off on the 19th of March, at a very early hour, for the village of Rastro; thence we were conducted by the Indians to a stream, which, in times of drought, forms a basin of muddy water, surrounded by fine trees, the clusia, the amyris, and the mimosa with fragrant flowers. To catch the gymnoti with nets is very difficult, on acount of the extreme agility of the fish, which bury themselves in the mud...The Indians therefore told us that they would 'fish with horses'. We found it difficult to form an idea of this extraordinary manner of fishing; but we soon saw our guides return from the savannah, which they had been scouring for wild horses and mules. They brought about thirty with them, which they forced to enter the pool.

The extraordinary noise caused by the horses' hoofs, makes the fish issue from the mud, and excites them to the attack. These yellowish and livid eels, resembling large

Pl. XXX.

Simia ursina.

Huet, fils 1807.   De l'Imprimerie de Langlois.   Bouquet sculpsit.

aquatic serpents, swim on the surface of the water, and crowd under the bellies of the horses and mules...The Indians, provided with harpoons and long slender reeds, surround the pool closely; and some climb up the trees, the branches of which extend horizontally over the surface of the water. By their wild cries, and the length of their reeds, they prevent the horses from running away and reaching the bank of the pool. The eels, stunned by the noise, defend themselves by the repeated discharge of their electric batteries. For a long interval they seem likely to prove victorious. Several horses sink beneath the violence of the invisible strokes which they receive from all sides, in organs the most essential to life; and stunned by the force and frequency of the shocks, they disappear under the water. Others, panting, with mane erect, and haggard eyes expressing anguish and dismay, raise themselves, and endeavour to flee from the storm by which they are overtaken. They are driven back by the Indians into the middle of the water; but a small number succeed in eluding the active vigilance of the fishermen. These regain the shore, stumbling at every step, and stretch themselves on the sand, exhausted with fatigue, and with limbs benumbed by the electric shocks of the gymnoti.

In less than five minutes two of our horses were drowned. The eel being five feet long, and pressing itself against the belly of the horses, makes a discharge along the whole extent of its electric organ. It attacks at once the heart, the intestines, and the caeliac fold of the abdominal nerves. It is natural that the effect felt by the horses should be more powerful than that produced upon man by the touch of the same fish at only one of his extremities. The horses are probably not killed, but only stunned. They are drowned from the impossibility of rising amid the prolonged struggle between the other horses and the eels.

We had little doubt that the fishing would terminate by killing successively all the animals engaged; but by degrees the impetuosity of this unequal contest diminished, and the wearied gymnoti dispersed. They require a long rest, and abundant nourishment, to repair the galvanic force which they have lost. The mules and horses appear less frightened; their manes are no longer bristled, and their eyes express less dread. The gymnoti approach timidly the edge of the marsh, where they are taken by means of small harpoons fastened to long cords. When the cords are very dry the Indians feel no shock in raising the fish into the air. In a few minutes we had five large eels, most of which were but slightly wounded. Some others were taken, by the same means, towards evening...

It would be temerity to expose ourselves to the first shocks of a very large and strongly irritated gymnotus. If by chance a stroke be received before the fish is wounded or wearied by long pursuit, the pain and numbness are so violent that it is impossible to describe the nature of the feeling they excite. I do not remember having ever received from the discharge of a large Leyden jar, a more dreadful shock than that which I experienced by imprudently placing both my feet on a gymnotus just taken out of the water. I was affected during the rest of the day with a violent pain in the knees, and in almost every joint...

In Dutch Guiana, at Demerara for instance, electric eels were formerly employed to cure paralytic affections. At a time when the physicians of Europe had great confidence in the effects of electricity, a surgeon of Essequibo, named Van der Lott, published in Holland a treatise on the medical properties of the gymnotus. These electric remedies are practised among the savages of America...I did not hear of this mode of treatment in the Spanish colonies which I visited; and I can assert that, after having made several experiments during four hours successively with gymnoti, M. Bonpland and myself felt, till the next day, a debility in the muscles, a pain in the joints, and a general uneasiness, the effect of a strong irritation of the nervous system.

A. VON HUMBOLDT, *Personal Narrative to the Equinoctial Regions of America, 1852, Vol. 2.*

This red howler monkey, one of the largest primates in South America, was just one of the many discoveries that Humboldt sketched in his journal.

MERIWETHER LEWIS 1774-1809
WILLIAM CLARK 1770-1838

Into the wilderness of North America

LEWIS WAS SECRETARY to US president Jefferson, Clark an officer whom he had befriended in the army. They were far from being scientists but, as Jefferson remarked shrewdly, they had 'the firmness of constitution & character, prudence, habits adapted to the woods & familiarity with the Indian manners and character, requisite for this undertaking'. The undertaking was to lead an expedition from one side of North America to the other and back again. Between 1803 and 1806, they travelled up the Mississippi, across the Rockies and down the Columbia to the Pacific, through territories that were completely unmapped and which had been visited, if at all, only by occasional traders from Canada. Belittled by some as no more than a prolonged trek, it was a political and scientific fact-finding mission that had far-reaching consequences. Lewis and Clark opened the continent to a horde of colonists in much the same way that Livingstone, Stanley and others did in Africa. But whereas Europeans were eventually removed from Africa, the US settlers remained, displacing an entire race by force of arms and disease. It was one of the most calculated and far-sighted moves in the history of empire.

LEWIS RECORDS HIS EXCITEMENT AT THE START OF THE EXPEDITION.

Our vessels consisted of six small canoes, and two large pirogues. This little fleet altho' not quite so rispictable as those of Columbus or Capt. Cook, were still viewed by us with as much pleasure as those deservedly famed adventurers ever beheld theirs; and I dare say with quite as much anxiety for their safety and preservation. We were now about to penetrate a country at least two thousand miles in width, on which the foot of civilized man had never trodden; the good or evil it had in store for us was for experiment yet to determine, and these little vessels contained every article by which we were to expect to subsist or defend ourselves...enterta[in]ing as I do the most confident hope of succeeding in a voyage which had formed a da[r]ling project of mine for the last ten years, I could not but esteem this moment of my departure as among the most happy of my life. The party are in excellent health and sperits, zealously attached to the enterprise, and anxious to proceed; not a whisper or murmur of discontent to be heard among them, but all act in unison, and with the most perfect harmony. I took an early supper this evening and went to bed.

E.OSGOOD (ED.), *The Field Notes of Captain William Clark*, 1964.

ON THE PACIFIC COAST, WITH PROVISIONS LOW, THE EXPEDITION WAS ALERTED TO THE PRESENCE OF A WHALE THAT HAD WASHED ASHORE.

January 5th. Two of the of the five men who had been dispatched to make salt returned. They had carefully examined the coast, but it was not till the fifth day after their departure that they discovered a convenient situation for their manufacture...The Indians treated them very kindly, and made them a present of the blubber of the whale, some of which the men brought home. It was white and not unlike the fat of pork, though of a coarser and more spongy texture, and on being cooked was found to be tender and palatable, in flavor resembling the beaver. The men also brought with them a gallon of salt,

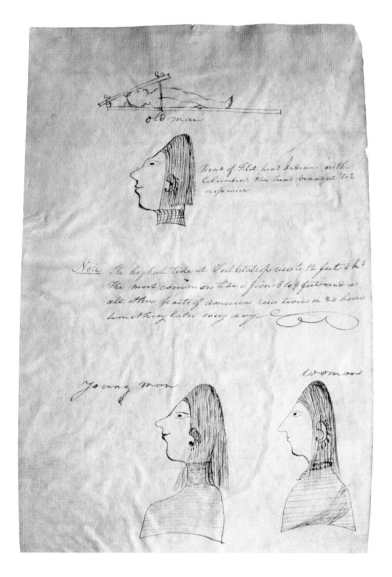

A page from Clark's illuminated elkskin journal shows how the Flathead tribe gained their name. When pressed between two boards an infant's skull would assume the desired (and distinctive) shape. 'This is done in order to give a greater width to the forehead, which they much admire', Lewis wrote. This cosmetic privilege marked superior status: slaves were not permitted to flatten their heads.

which was white, fine, and very good, but not so strong as the rock-salt common in the western parts of the United States...

The appearance of the whale seemed to be a matter of importance to all the neighbouring Indians, and as we might be able to procure some of it for ourselves, or at least purchase blubber from the Indians, a small parcel of merchandise was prepared, and a party of the men held in readiness to set out in the morning. As soon as this resolution was known, Chabonneau and his [Indian] wife requested that they accompany us. The poor woman stated very earnestly that she had traveled a great way with us to see the great water, yet she had never been down to the coast, and now that this monstrous fish was also to be seen, it seemed hard that she should not be permitted to see nether the ocean nor the whale. So reasonable a request could not be denied; they were therefore suffered to accompany Captain Clark, who January 6th, after an early breakfast, set out with twelve men in two canoes... [On their return] The weather was beautiful, the sky clear, and the moon shone brightly, a circumstance the more agreeable as this is the first fair evening we have enjoyed for two months.

E. COUES (ED.), *History of the Expedition under the Command of Lewis and Clark, Vol. II, 1965.*

MUNGO PARK 1771–1806
Voyage to the Niger

In a scene from his Travels in the Interior Districts of Africa, Mungo Park observes smelting furnaces at the Gambian village of Kamalia. Following his death explorers made determined attempts to locate his journal. All they found was a book of logarithms containing a tailor's bill and an invitation to dine with Mr and Mrs Watson of the Strand.

A SCOTTISH SURGEON, *recently returned from a posting to Sumatra, Park was chosen by Joseph Banks to lead an expedition to the Niger. European geographers were much exercised by this fabled river. They knew it existed – probably – but had no idea where it went. Some said it joined the Nile, others the Congo; one theory had it flowing westwards and another northwards. As for its mouth, many authorities believed it didn't have one, simply vanishing somewhere in the Sahara. In 1795, Park sailed from Portsmouth to settle the matter. After a hazardous solo journey through equatorial Africa he eventually found the Niger, but was prevented by illness and lack of supplies from following it to its termination. He returned in 1805 with a complement of redcoats to finish the job. Most of the company perished from disease before they even reached the Niger and the remainder were killed in an ambush on the river. Park became a cause celebre, several expeditions being sent to locate his remains and complete his task but it would be 25 years before the riddle of the Niger was finally solved.*

IN 1796, PARK REACHED THE NIGER.

July 20 – ...We passed several large villages, where I was constantly taken for a Moor, and became the subject of much merriment to the Bambarrans, who, seeing me drive my horse before me, laughed heartily at my appearance...He has been at Mecca, says one, you may see that by his clothes: another asked me if my horse was sick: a third wished to purchase it, &c. – so that, I believe the very slaves were ashamed to be seen in my company. Just before it was dark we took up our lodging for the night at a small village, where I procured some victuals for myself and some corn for my horse, at the moderate price of a button; and was told that I should see the Niger (which the negroes call Joliba, or the Great Water) early the next day. The lions here are very numerous: the gates are shut a little after sunset, and nobody allowed to go out. The thoughts of seeing the Niger in the morning, and the troublesome buzzing of mosquitoes, prevented me from shutting my eyes during the night; and I had saddled my horse, and was in readiness before daylight - but, on account of the wild beasts, we were obliged to wait until the people were stirring and the gates opened...

As we approached the town [of Sego], I was fortunate enough to overtake the fugitive Kaartans, to whose kindness I had been so much indebted in my journey through Bambarra. They readily agreed to introduce me to the king; and we rode together through some marshy ground, where, as I was anxiously looking around for the river, one of them called out, Geo affilli! ('See the water!') and, looking forwards, I saw with infinite pleasure the great object of my mission - the long-sought-for majestic Niger, glittering to the morning sun, as broad as the Thames at Westminster, and flowing slowly to the eastward. I hastened to the brink, and having drunk of the water, lifted up my fervent thanks in prayer to the Great Ruler of all things, for having thus far crowned my endeavour with success.

M. PARK, *The Life and Travels of Mungo Park, 1870.*

I am very sorry to say that of forty-four Europeans who left the Gambia in perfect health,
five only are at present alive – namely, three soldiers, (one deranged in his mind,)
Lieutenant Martyn, and myself. From this account I am afraid that your lordship will be
apt to consider matters as in a very hopeless state; but I assure you I am far from
despairing. With the assistance of one of the soldiers, I have changed a large canoe into a
tolerably good schooner, on board of which I this day hoisted the British flag, and shall
set sail to the east, with the fixed resolution to discover the termination of the Niger, or
perish in the attempt. I have heard nothing that I can depend on respecting the remote
course of this mighty stream, but I am more and more inclined to think it can end nowe-
here but in the sea.

My dear friend Mr Anderson, and likewise Mr Scott, are both dead; but though all
the Europeans who are with me should die, and though I myself were half-dead, I would
still persevere, and if I could not succeed in the object of my journey, I would at last die
on the Niger.

The Life and Travels of Mungo Park

GEORGE LYON 1795–1832
Saharan experiences

IN 1818, BRITAIN'S JOSEPH RITCHIE *landed at Tripoli with the object of crossing the Sahara to the Niger. With him came Lyon, an extrovert young naval officer whose avowed interests were 'balls, riding, dining & making a fool of myself'. The two men achieved little and Ritchie died a year after his arrival, leaving Lyon to produce a journal of their exploits. He approached the task with vigour, commenting on subjects as wide-ranging as sandstorms, slavery, mirages, the type of spiders he encountered in the desert and a species of oasis worm that tasted like caviar. He later went on several expeditions to the Arctic where, although failing to make any momentous geographical discovery, he proved himself a successful – if idiosyncratic – amateur anthropologist. An accomplished artist and draughtsman, Lyon had an eye for what the public wanted to see. Although not a best-seller in Britain, his journal became so famous in Africa that subsequent travellers to the Sahara were pestered continually by people who wanted to see the pictures Lyon had painted of them. It is one of the few recorded instances of an explorer's journal being of greater interest to the 'explored' than to the domestic market.*

OF A DESERT INFATUATION.

March 31st...A boy who accompanied us from Tripoli came to me, full of the praises of Lilla Fatima, the fat wife of Sheikh Barood, a white woman, who, he said, was the most beautiful creature he had ever seen, and so fat that she could scarcely walk: 'her arm is as big as my body,' continued he, 'and she says she should like to see you and Sidi Yussuf [Ritchie]'. Such a hint was not to be rejected, and I therefore immediately paid her a visit, the boy acting as my Interpreter. On my entrance she so veiled herself as to exhibit to advantage her arm, with all its gay ornaments; and on my requesting to be favoured with a view of her face, she, with very little reluctance, gratified me. Her chin, the tip of her nose, and the space between her eyebrows, were marked with black lines; she was much rouged; her neck, arms, and legs, were covered with tattooed flowers, open hands, circles, the names of God, and of her numerous male friends. She had a multitude of gold ear-rings and ornaments, set with very bad and counterfeit jewels, and weighing all together, I should think, two or three pounds. Her shirt was of striped silk; and she had a rich purple silk barracan, or mantle, gracefully thrown around her, and fastened at the breast by a gold pin, with ornaments of the same metal suspended from it: all the other articles of finery which she possessed were displayed around the tent, whilst a multitude of poor thin wretches, resembling witches, sat around her in astonishment, never having in their lives seen such a paragon of perfection. Like all other Arabs, they touched whatever pleased them most, one admiring this object, another something near it, so that our poor belle was sometimes poked by a dozen fingers at once; all, however, agreeing on one point, that she was beautifully and excessively fat, and I must say I never before beheld such a monstrous mass of human flesh. One of her legs, of enormous size, was uncovered as high as the calf, and every one pressed it, admiring its solidity, and praising God for blessing them with such a sight. I was received most graciously, and invited to sit close to her, when one of the first questions she asked me was, if in my country the ladies were as fat and handsome as herself? For the plumpness of my countrywomen, I owned, with shame, that

I never had seen one possessed of half such an admirable rotundity, which she took as a great compliment; but I did not attempt to carry the comparison farther, though she was really very handsome in face and features. She amused herself while speaking with playing on a kind of drum, made of clay, called Derbooka, by beating with one hand, and playing with the fingers of the other; and perceiving that that I was amused by it, she ordered an old man to get up and dance. The females sang and clapped their hands in good time, and the dancer went through a variety of figures, all equally indelicate. A woman then succeeded him, and in this respect quite threw him in the shade; but as I know it to be the general mode of dancing in this part of Barbary, I of course applauded it. Lilla Fatima herself then thought it proper to honour us with a few graceful attitudes in the same style; but Mr. Ritchie's entrance into the tent soon put a stop to the exhibition, and the ceremony of veiling took place in the same manner as before. Fatima soon discovered a likeness between her late husband and Mr. Ritchie, from their being both very slender; but unfortunately the resemblance failed in all other points, her former spouse being, at the time she was obliged to leave him by an order of the Bashaw, fifty years old, with a grey beard; while on the other hand, Mr. Ritchie was but twenty-seven, and of a very fair

complexion. She was at all events determined to be pleased with us; and having sprinkled us with rose-water, allowed us to take our leave. On returning to our tent, we sent her some coffee, and a few lumps of sugar.

G. LYON, *A Narrative of Travels in Northern Africa, 1821.*

ON AFRICAN HOSPITALITY:

January 16th...We set out at ten for Murzouk...About noon, we heard the firing of the Ghrazzie's people on entering Beedan, a village near Zaizow, and soon after, arriving at the latter place, we alighted at the residence of the Kaid Saad. We found him lying on the ground, most amusingly drunk and communicative, and surrounded by fowls and breads, eggs, cakes, soup, sweet and sour lackbi, and dates.

He was all generosity, and would have given us his whole house, and into the bargain, even his old wife, who waited on us during the meal, and was most highly oiled for the occasion. We soon discovered, as he was not in condition to keep a secret, why he had recourse to such large draughts of lackbi. He had boasted, all the time he was with me, of his second wife, and had promised I should be treated with a sight of her, if he could prevail upon so beautiful and bashful a creature to show her face to any other than her husband: no sooner, however, had he left Zaizow to accompany me a month before, than this charming person decamped. She first collected as much corn as she could find, and a dollar or two which were hoarded up; and after abusing her house-mate, the elder wife, set out for Murzouk. Report spoke unfavourably of her conduct there, and the old man was endeavouring, in consequence, to drown his sorrows in his favourite liquor. The lady of the house presented me with a bowl of Soudan manufacture.

This afternoon, a man came to me for medicine, for a pain in his chest, and opening his shirt, displayed the most sickening sight I ever beheld: he had been so burnt over the whole of his breast, that it had festered, and become a sore above a foot in diameter, and had so eaten into his skin, that I imagined he could not survive many days. I had nothing with me which would relieve him, but advised that his sore should be kept clean, a precaution which had never entered his head. His friend, who brought him to me, said, that for all the world he would not suffer him to be washed, as he had read in a book, that using water to a burn occasioned certain death. Thus, owing to their ignorance and prejudice, this poor man probably lost his life. After being nearly killed with kindness, we set out. The Kaid, though almost incapable of sitting on his own poor lean horse, amused himself by riding at full speed before and across mine, screeching and discharging his gun out of compliment to me; but happily for his own neck, and I may add for mine also, in about half an hour his powder failed him.

A Narrative of Travels in Northern Africa.

Lyon painted this picture of an Eskimo woman during an 1821–23 voyage to Foxe Basin. He participated enthusiastically in every aspect of Eskimo life, living in igloos, learning how to handle a dog sled, and eating their food – manfully, he commented that a slice of deer's windpipe was very tasty; and the contents of its stomach reminded him of 'a mixture of sorrel and radish leaves'. He pursued his research with such gusto that, when the expedition departed, two pregnant sisters waved him goodbye.

JOHN FRANKLIN 1786–1847

The quest for the North West Passage

FRANKLIN WAS A MAN *whose life could be described charitably as mismanaged. He was overweight, had circulation problems, could not move without frequent stops for tea, and had to be carried on treks of any appreciable distance. In 1819, he was sent on an over-land journey through Canada's most inhospitable territory to find the North West Passage. He became lost in the Badlands north of Hudson Bay: half his party either starved or were eaten by the others; the survivors lived off carrion, lichen (tripes de roche), and eventually their own shoes. That any of them came home alive was a miracle. Remarkably, he was ordered to go back and finish the job. This time none of his men died – but he stripped the region of so much food that several hundred Indians starved as a result. In 1845, after a disastrous period as governor of a penal colony, he led yet another expedition to the North West Passage. Neither he, his ships, nor the 133 men under his command were ever seen again.*

ON HIS RETREAT THROUGH THE BADLANDS, FRANKLIN LEFT HIS SECOND-IN-COMMAND, DR RICHARDSON, TO FEND FOR THE STARVING MEN WHILE HE WENT AHEAD TO GET FOOD FROM THEIR LAST-YEAR'S CAMP, FORT ENTERPRISE.

October 4 – Our shoes and garments were stiffened by the frost, and we walked in great pain...There was no tripes de roche [rock lichen], and we drank tea and ate some of our shoes for supper. Next morning, after taking the usual repast of tea, we proceeded to the house. Musing on what we were likely to find there, our minds were agitated between hope and fear, and, contrary to the custom we had kept up, of supporting our spirits by conversation, we went silently forward.

At length we reached Fort Enterprise, and to our infinite disappointment and grief found it a perfectly desolate habitation. There was no deposit of provision, no trace of the Indians, no letter from Mr. Wentzel to point out where the Indians might be found. It would be impossible for me to describe our sensations after entering this miserable abode, and discovering how we had been neglected: the whole party shed tears, not so much for our own fate, as for that of our friends in the rear, whose lives depended entirely on our sending immediate relief from this place...

We now looked round for the means of subsistence, and were gratified to find several deer-skins, which had been thrown away during our former residence. The bones were gathered from the heap of ashes; these with the skins, and the addition of tripes de roche, we considered would support us tolerably well for a time. As to the house, the parchment being torn from the windows, the apartment we selected for our abode was exposed to all the rigours of the season. We endeavoured to exclude the wind as much as possible, by placing loose boards against the apertures. The temperature was now between 15° and 20° below zero. We procured fuel by pulling up the flooring of the other rooms, and water for the purpose of cooking, by melting the snow...

When I arose the following morning, my body and limbs were so swollen that I was unable to walk more than a few yards. Adam was in a still worse condition, being absolutely icapable of arising without assistance. My other companions fortunately expe-rienced this inconvenience in a less degree, and went to collect bones, and some tripes de

roche which supplied us with two meals. The bones were quite acrid, and the soup
extracted from them excoriated the mouth if taken alone, but it was somewhat milder
when boiled with tripes de roche, and we even thought the mixture palatable, with the
addition of salt, of which a cask had been fortunately left here in the spring..

[October 22] – I undertook the office of cooking, and insisted they should eat twice
a-day whenever food could be procured; but as I was too weak to pound the bones, Peltier
agreed to do that in addition to his more fatiguing task of getting wood. We had a violent
snow storm all the next day, and this gloomy weather contributed to the depression of
spirits under which Adam and Samandre were labouring. Neither of them would quit
their beds, and they scarcely ceased from shedding tears all day; in vain did Peltier and
myself endeavour to cheer them. We even had to use much entreaty before we prevailed
upon them to take the meals we had prepared. Our situation was indeed distressing,
but in comparison with that of our friends in the rear, we considered it happy...

[October 26] – We perceived our strength decline every day, and every exertion began
to be irksome; when we were once seated the greatest effort was necessary in order to rise,
and we frequently had to lift each other from our seats...Having expended all the wood
which we could procure from our present dwelling, without endangering its falling, Peltier

began this day to pull down the partitions of the adjoining houses. Though these were only distant about twenty yards, yet the increase of labour in carrying the wood fatigued him so much, that by evening he was exhausted. On the next day his weakness was such...that he with difficulty lifted the hatchet: still he persevered, Samandre and myself assisting him...but our united strength could only collect sufficient to replenish the fire four times in the course of the day. As the insides of our mouths had become sore from eating the bone-soup, we relinquished the use of it, and now boiled our [hide blanket], which mode of dressing we found more palatable than frying it, as we had hitherto done...

29 October – [When Richardson's party reached Fort Enterprise] We were all shocked at beholding the emaciated countenances of the Doctor and Hepburn, as they strongly evidenced their extremely debilitated state. The alteration in our appearance was equally distressing to them, for since the swellings had subsided we were little more than skin and bone. The Doctor particularly remarked the sepulchral tone of our voices, which he requested us to make more cheerful if possible, unconscious that his own partook of the same key...

November 1 – Peltier was so much exhausted, that he sat up with difficulty, and looked piteously; at length he slided from his stool upon his bed, as we supposed to sleep, and in this composed state he remained upwards of two hours, without our apprehending any danger. We were then alarmed by hearing a rattling in his throat, and on the Doctor's examining him, he was found to be speechless. He died in the course of the night. Samandre...began to complain of cold and stiffness of joints. Being unable to keep up a sufficient fire to warm him, we laid him down and covered him with several blankets. He did not, however, appear to get better, and I deeply lament to say that he also died before daybreak. We removed the bodies of the deceased into the opposite part of the house, but our united strength was inadequate to the task of interring them, or even carrying them down to the river.

[November 6] – I observed, that in proportion as our strength decayed, our minds exhibited symptoms of weakness, evinced by a kind of unreasonable pettishness with each other. Each of us thought the other weaker in intellect than himself, and more in need of advice and assistance. So trifling a circumstance as a change of place, recommended by one as being warmer and more comfortable, and refused by the other from a dread of motion, frequently called forth fretful expressions which were no sooner uttered than atoned for, to be repeated perhaps in the course of a few minutes. The same thing often occurred when we endeavoured to assist each other in carrying wood to the fire; none of us were willing to receive assistance, although the task was disproportionate to our strength. On one of these occasions Hepburn was so convinced of his waywardness that he exclaimed, 'Dear me, if we are spared to return to England, I wonder if we shall recover our understandings.'

November 7 – Dr. Richardson came in to communicate the joyful intelligence that relief had arrived. He and myself immediately addressed thanksgiving to the throne of mercy for this deliverance, but poor Adam was in so low a state that he could scarcely comprehend the information. When the Indians entered, he attempted to rise but sank down again. But for this seasonable interposition of Providence, his existence must have terminated in a few hours, and that of the rest probably in not many days... Dr. Richardson, Hepburn, and I, eagerly devoured the food, which they imprudently presented to us, in too great abundance, and in consequence suffered dreadfully from indigestion, and had no rest the whole night...We were perfectly aware of the danger, and Dr. Richardson repeatedly cautioned us to be moderate; but he was himself unable to practise the caution he so judiciously recommended..

November 8 – In the evening they brought in a pile of dried wood, which was lying on the river-side, and on which we had often cast a wishful eye, being unable to drag it up the bank. The Indians set about everything with an activity that amazed us. Indeed, contrasted with our emaciated figures and extreme debility, their frames appeared to us gigantic, and their strength supernatural. These kind creatures next turned their attention to our personal appearance, and prevailed upon us to shave and wash ourselves. The beards of the Doctor and Hepburn had been untouched since they left the sea-coast, and were become of a hideous length, and peculiarly offensive to the Indians. The doctor and I suffered extremely from distension and therefore ate sparingly.

J. FRANKLIN, *Narrative of a Journey to the Shores of the Polar Sea, 1823.*

An unlikely couple of heroes, Sir John Franklin (right) and Lieutenant Francis Crozier pose for the camera on the eve of their departure aboard HMS Erebus and HMS Terror for the North West Passage in 1845. At the time, many people questioned the wisdom of Franklin's appointment because of his age (60) and his obvious ill health. However, he and his fellow officers were idolized after their disappearance.

DIXON DENHAM 1786–1828
HUGH CLAPPERTON 1788–1826
WALTER OUDNEY 1790–1824

The slave trail to Chad

Clapperton, the least tutored member of the expedition, laboured to produce this painting of a Saharan oasis. Such a bounteous sight was rare: typically they had to dig for several hours to find the smallest trickle. As Denham recorded of one stop, 'The wells were so choked up with sand, that several cart-loads of it were removed previous to finding sufficient water; and even then the animals could not drink until near ten at night.'

IN 1822 DENHAM, CLAPPERTON AND OUDNEY, *accompanied by a seaman named Hillman, attempted to cross the Sahara with a view to finding the Niger. They caught a caravan through the desert and on 24 February 1823 became the first Europeans to see Lake Chad. It had been a quarrelsome journey, both Denham and Oudney disputing leadership of the group: at one point Denham felt so aggrieved that he quit the expedition; Clapperton and Oudney were extremely disappointed when he later rejoined them. At Lake Chad the anatagonists went their separate ways: Denham to explore the surrounding region (and become inadvertently involved in a slave raid); Clapperton and Oudney to strike west towards Sokoto, where they hoped not only to glean information concerning the Niger's whereabouts but also to learn about the mysterious city of Timbuctoo. They regrouped in 1824, neither party having found the Niger and Oudney having died of tuberculosis. Within three months of their return Clapperton was off again, this time attacking the Niger from the south. He died of fever in Sokoto in 1826, still without success. His manservant, Richard Lemon Lander, successfully traced the course of the Niger in 1831.*

THEIR WAY SOUTH TOOK THEM ALONG ANCIENT TRANS-SAHARAN TRADE ROUTES. DENHAM WAS UNSETTLED TO DISCOVER HOW MUCH HUMAN DEBRIS SLAVE CARAVANS LEFT IN THEIR WAKE.

Dec. 22 – We moved before daylight, passing some rough sand hills, mixed with red stone, to the west, over a plain of fine gravel, and halted at the maten, called El-Hammar, close under a bluff head, which had been in view since quitting our encampment in the morning. Strict orders had been given this day for the camels to keep close up, and for the Arabs not to straggle – the Tibboo Arabs having been seen on the look-out. During the last two days, we had passed on an average from sixty to eighty or ninety skeletons each day; but the numbers that lay about the wells at El-Hammar were countless: those of two women, whose perfect and regular teeth bespoke them young, were particularly shocking; their arms still remained clasped around each other as they had expired; although the flesh had long since perished by being exposed to the burning rays of the sun, and the blackened bones only left: the nails of the fingers, and some of the sinews of the hand, also remained; and part of the tongue of one of them still appeared through the teeth. We had now passed six days of desert without the slightest appearance of vegetation, and a little branch of the souak was brought me here as a comfort and curiosity. On the following day we had alternately plains of sand and loose gravel, and had a distant view of some hills to the west. While I was dozing on my horse about noon, overcome by the heat of the sun, which at that time of the day always shone with great power, I was suddenly awakened by a crashing under his feet, which startled me excessively. I found that my steed had, without any sensation of shame or alarm, stepped upon the perfect skeletons of two human beings, cracking their brittle bones under his feet, and, by one trip of his

foot, separating a skull from the trunk, which rolled on like a ball before him. This event gave me a sensation which it took some time to remove. My horse was for many days not looked upon with the same regard as formerly.

D. Denham, H. Clapperton, W. Oudney, *A Narrative of Travels and Discoveries in Northern and Central Africa, 1828.*

AN UNEXPECTED OUTCOME TO A SLAVE RAID.

I now for the first time, as I saw Barca Gana on a fresh horse, lamented my own folly in so exposing myself, badly prepared as I was for accidents. If either of my horse's wounds were from poisoned arrows, I felt that nothing could save me: however there was not much time for reflection; we instantly became a flying mass, and plunged, in the greatest disorder, into that wood we had but a few hours before moved through with order, and very different feelings. I had got a little to the westward of Barca Gana, in the confusion which took place on our passing the ravine which had been left just in our rear, and where upwards of one hundred of the Bornowy were speared by the Felatahs, and was following at a round gallop the steps of one of the Mandara eunuchs, who, I observed, kept a good look out, his head being constantly turned over his left shoulder, with a face expressive of the greatest dismay – when the cries behind, of the Felatah horse pursuing, made us both quicken our paces. The spur, however, had the effect of incapacitating my beast altogether, as the arrow, I found afterwards, had reached the shoulder-bone, and in passing over some rough ground, he stumbled and fell. Almost before I was on my legs, the Felatahs were

upon me; I had, however, kept hold of the bridle, and seizing a pistol from the holsters, I presented it at two of the ferocious savages, who were pressing me with their spears; they instantly went off; but another who came on me more boldly, just as I was endeavouring to mount, received the contents somewhere in his left shoulder, and again I was enable to place my foot in the stirrup. Remounted, I again pushed my retreat; I had not, however, proceeded many hundred yards, when my horse again came down, with such violence as to throw me against a tree at considerable distance; and alarmed at the horses behind him, he quickly got up and escaped, leaving me on foot and unarmed.

The eunuch and his four followers were here butchered, after a very slight resistance, and stripped within a few yards of me: their cries were dreadful; and even now the feelings of that moment are fresh in my memory: my hopes of life were too faint to deserve the name. I was almost instantly surrounded, and incapable of making the least resistance, as I was unarmed – was as speedily stripped, and whilst attempting first to save my shirt and then my trousers, I was thrown to the ground. My pursuers made several thrusts at me with their spears, that badly wounded my hands in two places, and slightly my body, just under my ribs on the right side: indeed, I saw nothing before me but the same cruel death I had seen unmercifully inflicted on the few who had fallen into the powers of those who now had possession of me; and they were alone prevented from murdering me, in the first instance, I am persuaded, by the fear of injuring the value of my clothes, which appeared to them a rich booty – but it was otherwise ordained.

My shirt was now absolutely torn off my back, and I was left perfectly naked. When my plunderers began to quarrel for the spoil, the idea of escape came like lightening across my mind, and without a moment's hesitation or reflecting I crept under the belly of the horse nearest to me, and started as fast as my legs could carry me for the thickest part of the wood: two of the Felatahs followed, and I ran on to the eastward, knowing that our stragglers would be in that direction, but still almost s much afraid of friends as foes. My persuers gained on me, for the prickly underwood not only obstructed my passage, but tore my flesh miserably; and the delight with which I saw a mountain-stream gliding along at the bottom of a deep ravine cannot be imagined. My strength had almost left me, and I seized the young branches issuing from the stump of a large tree which overhung the ravine, for the purpose of letting myself down into the water, as the sides were precipitous, when, under my hand, as the branch yielded to the weight of my body, a large liffa, the worst kind of serpent this country produces, rose from its coil, as if in the very act of striking. I was horror-struck, and deprived for a moment of all recollection – the branch slipped from my hand, and I tumbled headlong into the water beneath; this shock, however, revived me and with three stroked of my arms I reached the opposite bank, which, with difficulty, I crawled up; and then, for the first time, felt myself safe from my pursuers.

A Narrative of Travels and Discoveries in Northern and Central Africa.

A bodyguard in service to the Sheikh of Bornu exudes an air of menace, as depicted by Dixon Denham. The Sheikh, whose kingdom lay to the west of Lake Chad, was hospitable in the extreme. His subjects, however, were less accommodating. Of one village Denham recorded that the inhabitants considered Christians, 'the worst people in the world, and probably, until they saw me, scarcely believed them to be human'.

RENÉ CAILLÉ 1799–1838
Finding the fabled city of Timbuctoo

Caillié's sketch of
Timbuctoo disenchanted
many Europeans. It was
popularly held to be a
city of fantastic wealth,
a centre of civilization
whose streets were
paved with gold and
whose libraries were the
repository of ancient
wisdom. In fact it was
just a drab entrepot in
an even drabber desert.
'The city presented, at
first view, nothing but a
mass of ill-looking
houses, built of earth',
Caillié wrote. 'Nothing
was to be seen in all
directions but immense
plains of quicksand of a
yellowish white colour.
The sky was a pale red
as far as the horizon: all
nature wore a dreary
aspect, and the most
profound silence
prevailed; not even the
warbling of a bird was
to be heard...the
difficulties surmounted
by its founders cannot
fail to excite the
admiration.'

CAILLIÉ HAD ALWAYS *wanted to explore Africa and in the mid-1820s he set his cap at the fabled city of Timbuctoo. The only European to have seen it was a Briton, Gordon Laing, who had been murdered in 1826 by Touareg tribesmen before he could bring home the news of his discovery. Caillié resolved that a Frenchman could do better. In 1827, having learnt Arabic, and undertaken a brief course of religious instruction, he left West Africa on a caravan bound for Timbuctoo, posing as a Muslim slave who wanted to find his way home to Egypt. He suffered from fever, was crippled by an infected foot and contracted such bad scurvy that his palate crumbled onto his tongue. Nevertheless, he persevered until he eventually reached his goal on 20 April 1828. He left within two weeks, preferring to catch a trans-Saharan caravan to Morocco rather than retrace his steps to West Africa because his 'many enemies, would pretend to doubt the fact of my journey and of my residence at Timbuctoo, whereas, by returning though the Barbary states, the mere mention of the point at which I had arrived would reduce the most malignant to silence.' He was rewarded handsomely by the Geographical Society of Paris, but never returned to Africa, dying of tuberculosis on 17 May 1838.*

ON HIS HOMEWARD JOURNEY CAILLIÉ ENCOUNTERED A SANDSTORM.

What distressed us most during this horrible day was the pillars of sand, which threatened every moment to bury us in their course. One of the largest of these pillars crossed our camp, overset all the tents, and whirling us about like straws, threw us one upon another in the utmost confusion; we knew not where we were, and could distinguish nothing at the distance of a foot. The sand wrapped us in darkness like a thick fog, and heaven and earth seemed confounded and blended into one.

In this commotion of nature, the consternation was general; nothing was heard on all sides but lamentation, and most of my companions recommended themselves to heaven, crying out with all their might, 'There is no God but God, and Mahomet is his prophet!' Through these shouts and prayers, and the roaring of the wind, I could distinguish at intervals, the low plaintive moan of the camels, who were so much alarmed as their masters, and more to be pitied, as they had not tasted food for four days. Whilst this frightful tempest lasted, we remained stretched on the ground, motionless, dying of thirst, burned by the heat of the sand, and buffetted by the wind. We suffered nothing, however, from the sun, whose disk, almost concealed by the cloud of sand, appeared dim and shorn of its beams. We durst not use our water, for fear the wells should be dry, and I know not what would have become of us if, about three o'clock, the wind had not abated. As soon as it became calm, we prepared to set off, and the dokhnou was mixed and distributed. It is difficult to describe with what impatience we longed for this moment; to enhance the pleasure which I expected from my portion, I thrust my head into the vessel and sucked up the water in long draughts. When I had drunk, I had an unpleasant sensation all over me, which was quickly succeeded by fresh thirst.

About half past four in the afternoon, we left the place where we had experienced this terrible hurricane, and proceeded on our way towards the north. The camels walked slowly and with effort, for they were almost exhausted; the poor beasts looked jaded and

dejected. The sight of this numerous caravan, destitute of water, and condemned to die of thirst, scattered over the arid land, was truly dismal. The camels gently shaking their heads, or ruminating, took their course towards the north, without requiring any direction. We advanced over a sandy soil covered with rocks, rising about five feet above its surface. Wrapped in my own reflections, I thought of the wisdom of divine Providence, which has anticipated all our wants. What a masterpiece of nature's workmanship, said I, is the camel! If it were not for this wonderful animal, who could exist for a week without food, how could these deserts be traversed? No mortal would dare attempt it, or if any were rash enough to venture upon such an undertaking, certain death would be the reward of his temerity. These reflections are trite; but they were natural in the situation in which I was placed, and I wish to give an account of my thoughts as well as of my sensations and sufferings.

R. Caillié, *Travels through Central Africa to Timbuctoo, 1830.*

JOHN ROSS 1777–1856

Icebound in the Arctic

The inhabitants of Boothia – the only landmass in the world to be named after a brand of gin – flee from the interlopers. Later, however, they came aboard the Victory to draw maps of the terrain and to advise Ross on how best to survive the Arctic winter. In return, Ross ordered the Victory's carpenter to make a wooden leg for a man who had lost his own to a polar bear. Far ahead of his time, Ross kept his crew scurvy-free by the adoption of an Eskimo diet rich in fresh meat and fish.

HAVING BEEN CASTIGATED *for his failure to locate the North West Passage on an 1818 expedition to Baffin Bay, Ross sought to restore his reputation. In 1829 he sailed for the Arctic aboard a tiny steam ship,* Victory, *sponsored by the gin magnate Felix Booth. He spent a record four years trapped in the Passage. A cantankerous man, he used the many spare hours to vent his opinions on the Arctic, its inhabitants, its climate, his ship, his crew and life in general. In his less irritable moments he also painted watercolours of naive immediacy that gave the outside world its first glimpse (in colour) of the long, Arctic night. Although disliked by the majority of the crew - including his nephew James Clark Ross who discovered the North Magnetic Pole in 1832 - his ingenuity and forcefulness brought them safely home in one of the first, great, boat escapes from the polar ice.*

ON ESKIMOS.

23 August 1831 It being the King's birthday, the flags were all displayed; an exhibition which seemed much to delight our native friends; while the men had extra allowance, and so forth, according to custom. One of the natives, being invited into the cabin, informed us of some of the affairs of his coterie. The widow of the dead man had immediately obtained a new husband; because she had five children. The because would not be a very good reason in England, it is certain; the ready made family of another is not often a source of much comfort; and that it is not a valuable property needs not be said. But here, the five children were a commodity of price...a source of profit instead of loss, and of happiness instead of vexation and torment. Even at eight they begin to be serviceable: in a few years they are able to maintain more than themselves; and when the parents are old, be they step-children, or entirely and absolutely adopted, as is also here the usage, it is on them that the helpless depend for that support which is a matter of course. There are no poor-rates in this country...It is a Utopian state of things when she of five children is the best of wives, and can take her choice of the young men: it is more than Utopian, when population is not poverty, but wealth: when men really will labour, and when the labour of a man will...support, not only himself, but those who must depend on him till they can, and will, labour for themselves. Let the wise of wiser lands travel hither and take lessons of wisdom from the savages in seal-skins, who drink oil, and eat their fish raw.

Of another portion of their political economy I must not speak with approbation: yet there is some philosophical fitness in it too, when coupled with that which has preceded. We must not pull a system of legislation to pieces, and then say that this or the other law is a bad one. Let the whole be contemplated in a mass...before we presume to decide what is right... It is the custom to interchange wives. If the Romans did the same, under very other civilization, I fear their reasons are indefensible, though I need not here inquire what those were. In this country, the views of the citizens may be physiologically philosophical, for aught that I know to the contrary, though it remained to discover whether they proved sound in practice. The people thus considered that they should have more children: it is a good thing to have good reasons for doing what may not be very right.

J. ROSS, *Narrative of a Second Voyage in Search of a North West Passage, 1835.*

13 August 1831 The party returned, wives, children, and all, to the amount of twenty-three, and were regaled by us with a dinner of fish and fat. We purchased some clothing, and accompanied them to their tents; glad even of their society, under our present dearth of variety or amusement. Is there any thing that can convey in a stronger manner our utter destitution of all that can interest men, whether in occupation or amusement, than to confess that we found a relief from the self-converse of our own minds and the society of each other, from the eternal wearisome iteration of thermometrical registers and winds, and tides, and ice, and boats, and rigging, and eating, in the company of these greasy gourmandizing specimens of humanity, whose language we could scarcely comprehend, yet whose ideas were, I believe, more than sufficiently comprehended without any language at all. Let no one suppose that we had not felt all this, during months, first, and during years, afterwards, if I have not told it, if I have passed it all by, as if we had never felt it. There were evils of cold, and evils of hunger, and evils of toil; and though we did not die nor lose our limbs, as men have done in those lands, we had to share with the rest of the world, those evils of petty sickness which are sufficiently grievous while they exist, though they make but a small figure in the history of life, and would make a much smaller one in that of such an expedition as ours. Had we not also undergone abundance of anxiety and care; of the sufferings of disappointed hope; of more than all this, and of not less than all, those longings after our far-distant friends and our native land, from which who that has voyaged far from that home and those friends has ever been exempt? And who more than we, to whom it could not but often have occurred, that we might never again see those friends and that home? Yet there was a pain even beyond all this; and that

OVERLEAF
On a trip to Baffin Bay in 1818, Ross's ships encounter what he described aptly as 'A Remarkable Iceberg'. During the voyage he discovered the world's northernmost community at Etah, on the west coast of Greenland. The Eskimos had, '[no] tradition how they came to this spot, or from whence they came; having until the moment of our arrival believed themselves to be the only inhabitants of the universe'. They wanted to know what kind of a bird his ship was, who lived behind a mirror, and what a watch tasted like.

grievance seldom ceased. We were weary for want of occupation, for want of variety, for want of the means of mental exertion, for want of thought, and (why should I not say it?) for want of society. To-day was as yesterday, and as was to-day, so would be tomorrow: while if there was no variety, as no hope of better, is it wonderful that even the visits of barbarians were welcome, or can anything more strongly show the nature of our pleasures, than the confession that these were delightful; even as the society of London might be amid the business of London?'

THIRD YEAR IN THE ICE.

31 August 1831 It was an unpleasing circumstance to know, that although we had no men absolutely sick, and there had been no scurvy, the health of our crew in general was not what it had been; as they had also proved that they were incapable of bearing fatigue, and especially the travelling among ice.

That it had been a dull month, on the whole, to us, I need scarcely to say. I fear that this meagre journal bears but too evident marks of it, and on no more occasions than the present. But what can the journalist do, more than the navigator? If this was a durance of few events, and those of little variety, even these had no longer aught to mark a difference among them, nothing to attract attention or excite thought. The sameness of every thing weighed on the spirits, and the mind itself flagged under the want of excitement; while even such as there was, proved but a wearisome iteration of what had often occurred before. On no occasion, even when all was new, had there been much to interest; far less was there, now that we had been so long imprisoned to almost one spot: and, with as little to see as to reflect on, there were not materials from which any thought, keeping clear of the equal hazards of falsity or romance, could have constructed an interesting narrative. On the land there was nothing of picturesque to admit of description: the hills displayed no character, the rocks were rarely possessed of any, and the lakes and rivers were without beauty. Vegetation there was hardly any, and trees there were none; while, had there even existed a beauty of scenery, every thing was suffocated and deformed by the endless, wearisome, heart-sinking, uniform, cold load of ice and snow. On the sea there was no variety; for here, equally, all was ice during the far greater part of the year, and it was thus indifferent what was water and what land. Rarely did the sky show aught to replace this dearth of beauty and variety below; all the means of the picturesque display were wintry, and when we turned to the moral picture, what was it but the rare sight of men whose miserable peculiarities were too limited to interest us long, and whose ideas were exhausted at almost the first meeting. Who, confined to materials as these, shall hope to produce a book of interest and amusement? It is worse than the condemnation to 'make bricks without straw...

14 September The new ice was thick enough to skate on; but it was an amusement that we would gladly have dispensed with...

To us, the sight of ice was a plague, a vexation, a torment, an evil, a matter of despair. Could we have skated the whole country over, it would not have been an amusement; for there was no object to gain, no society to contend with in the race of fame, no one to admire us, no rivalry, no encouragement, no object. We had exercise enough without this addition; and worst of all, the ice which bound us and our ship in fetters of worse than iron, which surrounded us, obstructed us, annoyed us in every possible manner, and thus haunted and vexed us for ten months of the year, had long become so odious to our sight, that I doubt if all the occupation which the skating on it could have afforded us, would not rather have been a grievance than an enjoyment. We hated its sight, because we hated its effects; and every thing that belonged to it, every idea associated with it was hateful.

Is there any one who loves the sight of ice and snow? I imagine, now, that I always doubted this; I am quite sure of it at present...

These are the objections to a snow landscape, which even the experience of a day may furnish: how much more, when, for more than half the year, all the element above head is snow, when the gale is a gale of snow, the fog a fog of snow, when the sun shines but to glitter on snow which is, yet does not fall, when the breath of the mouth is snow, when snow settles on the hair, the dress, the eyelashes, where snow falls around us and fills our chambers, our beds, our dishes, should we open a door, should the external air get access to our 'penetralia;' where the 'crystal stream' in which we must quench our thirst is a kettle of snow with a lamp of oil, where our sofas are of snow, and our houses of snow; when snow was our decks, snow our awnings, snow our observatories, snow our larder, snow our salt; and, when all the other uses of snow should be at last of no more avail, our coffins and graves were to be graves and coffins of snow.

Is this not more than enough of snow that suffices for admiration?

Narrative of a Second Voyage in Search of a North West Passage, 1835.

Ross's image of an igloo settlement on Boothia resembles a human anthill. Never a man to follow the letter of scientific law, he attracted much abuse after his first voyage for having described the Etah Eskimos as 'Arctic Highlanders'. He did not care. In 1830 he named this particular village 'North Hendon' after a London suburb.

JOHN STEPHENS 1805–52

The lost cities of Central America

LAWYER AND ARCHAEOLOGIST, *Stephens travelled widely throughout the Middle East, Poland and Russia before being appointed Special Ambassador to Central America in 1839. Here he became enthralled by the ruins of Mayan civilization and made several trips into the relatively unexplored region of Yucatán. The overgrown structures he discovered were almost as impenetrable as the forests surrounding them. Of Copán, for example, he wrote, 'The city was desolate...It lay before us like a shattered bark in the midst of the ocean, her masts gone, her name effaced, her crew perished, and none to tell whence she came, to whom she belonged, how long on her voyage, or what caused her destruction; her lost people to be traced only by some fancied resemblance in the construction of the vessel, and, perhaps, never to be known at all...All was mystery, dark, impenetrable mystery, and every circumstance increased it.' Descriptions such as these turned his journals into best-sellers – as did the illustrations supplied by his companion Frederick Catherwood. Stephens later bought Copán from a local landowner for fifty dollars, but died in Panama before (as rumoured) he could realize his ambition of transplanting it to Central Park.*

STEPHENS WAS INTRIGUED BY A CAVE AT MAXCANU, KNOWN TO THE LOCALS AS EL LAVERINTO, 'THE LABYRINTH'.

I had heard before so much of caves, and had been so often disappointed, that I did not expect much from this; but the first view satisfied me in regard to the main point, viz., that it was not a natural cave, and that, as had been represented to me, it was hecha a mano, or made by hand...

Notwithstanding its wonderful reputation, and a name which alone, in any other country, would induce a thorough exploration, it is a singular fact, and exhibits more strikingly than anything I can mention the indifference of the people of all classes to the antiquities of the country, that up to the time of my arrival at the door, this Laberinto had never been examined...Several people had penetrated to some distance with a string held outside, but had turned back, and the universal belief was, that it contained passages without number and without end.

Under these circumstances, I certainly felt some degree of excitement as I stood in the doorway. The very name called up those stupendous works in Crete and on the shores of the Moeritic Lake which are now almost discredited as fabulous.

My retinue consisted of eight men, who considered themselves in my employ, besides three or four supernumeraries, and all together formed a crowd round the door. Except the mayoral of Uxmal, I had never seen one of them before, and as I considered it important to have a reliable man outside, I stationed him at the door with a ball of twine. I tied one end round my left wrist, and told one of the men to light a torch and follow me, but he refused absolutely, and all the rest, one after the other, did the same. They were all ready enough to hold the string; and I was curious to know, and had a conference with them on the interesting point, whether they expected any pay for their services in standing out of doors. One expected pay for showing me the place, others for carrying water, another for taking care of the horses, and so on, but I terminated the matter abruptly by

F. Catherwood   S H Gimber

F. Catherwood

S.H.Gimber.

declaring that I should not pay one of them a medio; and ordering them all away from the door, which they were smothering,...I entered with a candle in one hand and a pistol in the other...

I was not entirely free from the apprehension of starting some wild animal, and moved very slowly and very cautiously. In the mean time, in turning the corners, my twine would be entangled, and the Indians, moved by the probability of getting no pay, entered to clear it, and by degrees all came up with me in a body.. I got a glimpse of their torches behind me just as I was turning into a new passage, and at the moment I was startled by a noise which sent me back rather quickly, and completely routed them. It proceeded from a rushing of bats, and, having a sort of horror of these beastly birds, this was an ugly place to meet them in, for the passage was so low, and there was so little room for a flight over head, that in walking upright there was great danger of their striking the face. It was necessary to move with the head bent down, and protecting the lights from the flapping of their wings. Nevertheless, every step was exciting, and called up recollections of the Pyramids and tombs of Egypt, and I could not but believe that these dark and intricate passages would introduce me to some large saloon, or perhaps some royal sepulchre...all at once I found the passage choked up and effectually stopped. The ceiling had fallen in, crushed by a great mass of superincumbent earth, and farther progress was utterly impossible...

In a spirit of utter disappointment, I pointed out to the Indians the mass of earth that, as it were, maliciously cut off all my hopes, and told them to put an end to their lying stories about the Laberinto and its having no end; and in my disappointment I began to feel most sensibly the excessive heat and closeness of the place, which I had hardly perceived before, and which now became almost insufferable from the smoke of the torches and the Indians choking the narrow passage.

All that I could do, and that was very unsatisfactory, was to find out the plan of this subterranean structure. I had with me a pocket compass, and, notwithstanding the heat and smoke, and the little help that the Indians afforded me, under all annoyances, and with the sweat dropping on my memorandum book, I measured back to the door...

Having heard the place spoken of as a subterraneous construction, and seeing, when I reached the ground, a half-buried door with a mass of overgrown earth above it, it had not occurred to me to think otherwise; but on examining outside, I found that what I had taken for an irregular natural formation, like a hill-side, was a pyramidal mound...Heretofore it had been our impression that these mounds were solid and compact masses of stone and earth, without any chambers or structures of any kind, and the discovery of this gave rise to the exciting idea that all the great mounds scattered over the country contained secret, unknown, and hidden chambers, presenting an immense field for exploration and discovery, and, ruined as the buildings on their summits were, perhaps the only source left for acquiring knowledge of the people by whom the cities were constructed.

I was really at a loss to know what to do. I was almost tempted to abandon everything else, send word to my companions, and not leave the spot till I had pulled down the whole mound, and discovered every secret it contained; but it was not a work to be undertaken in a hurry, and I determined to leave it for a future occasion. I never had an opportunity of returning to this mound. It remains with all its mystery around it, worthy the enterprise of some future explorer, and I cannot but indulge the hope that the time is not dar distant when its mystery will be removed and all that is hidden brought to light.

J. Stephens, *Incidents of Travel in Yucatan, Vol I, 1843.*

A precarious wooden stairway gives access to a cave near Bolonchén. This was the start of an underground system that led via tunnels and further caves to a subterranean well. 'Our Indians began the descent', Stephens wrote, 'but the foremost had hardly got his head below the surface, before one of the rounds broke, and he only saved himself by clinging to another. We attempted a descent with some little misgivings; but by keeping each hand and foot on a different round, with an occasional crash and slide, we all reached the foot of the ladder.'

CHARLES DARWIN 1808–82

The voyage of the Beagle

DARWIN WAS PONDERING *a career as a cleric when a friend recommended him for the post of naturalist on a survey ship bound for South America. With nothing much on his hands, Darwin accepted. From this almost accidental chain of events sprang one of the most momentous journeys in the history of exploration. The 1831-36 voyage of the* Beagle *took it not just to South America but to the South Pacific and South Africa on a full circumnavigation of the globe. While discovering no new territory it gave Darwin remarkable insights into the nature of the planet. Six years later he published his first set of findings in a book describing the formation of coral reefs. It was not until 1859, however, that he produced* The Origin of Species *in which he used observations made on the Galapagos Islands to elaborate the theory of evolution. Contemplating his experiences, he wrote with mild understatement: 'It appears to me that nothing can be more improving to a young naturalist than a journey in distant countries.'*

IN THE GALAPAGOS ISLANDS, SEPTEMBER 1835.

17th...The Bay swarmed with animals; Fish, Shark & Turtles were popping their heads up in all parts. Fishing lines were soon put overboard & great numbers of fine fish 2 & even 3 feet long were caught. This sport makes all hands very merry; loud laughter & the heavy flapping of fish are heard on every side. – After dinner a party went on shore to try to catch Tortoises, but were unsuccessful. – These islands appear paradises for the whole family of Reptiles. Besides three kinds of Turtles, the Tortoise is so abundant that [a] single Ship's company here caught from 500-800 in a short time. – The black Lava rocks on the beach are frequented by large (2-3 ft.) most disgusting, clumsy Lizards. They are as black as the porous rocks over which they crawl & seek their prey from the Sea. – Somebody calls them 'imps of darkness'. – They assuredly well become the land they inhabit. – When on shore I proceeded to botanize & obtained 10 different flowers; but such insignificant, ugly little flowers, as would better become an Arctic, than a Tropical country. – The little birds are Strangers to Man & think him as innocent as their countrymen the huge Tortoises. Little birds within 3 & four feet, quietly hopped about the bushes & were not frightened by stones being thrown at them. Mr. King killed one with his hat & I pushed off a branch with the end of my gun a large Hawk.

21st. My servant & self were landed a few miles to the NE in order that I might examine the district mentioned...as resembling chimney. The comparison would have been more exact if I had said the iron furnaces near Wolverhampton. – From one point of view I counted 60 of these truncated hillocks, which are only from 50 to 100 ft above the plain of Lava. – The age of the various streams is distinctly marked by the presence & absence of Vegetation; in the latter & more modern nothing can be imagined more rough & horrid. – Such a surface has been aptly compared to a sea in its most boisterous moments. No sea however presents such irregular indentations, – nor such deep & long chasms. The craters are all entirely inert; consisting indeed of of nothing more than a ring of cinders. – There are large circular pits, from 30 to 80 ft deep; which might be mistaken for Craters, but are in reality formed by the subsidence of the roofs of great caverns, which probably were produced by a volume of gaz at the time when the Lava was liquid. – The scene was

This South American rhea was painted by John Gould, a leading ornithologist whom Darwin recruited to analyze the specimens he brought home. Gould's study of the finches found on the Galapagos Islands helped Darwin formulate his theory of evolution. Of the thirteen new species that Gould identified in 1837 only nine exist today.

Rhea Darwinii.

to me novel & full of interest; it is always delightful to behold anything which has been long familiar, but only by description. – In my walk I met two very large Tortoises (circumference of shell about 7 ft). One was eating a Cactus & then quietly walked away. The other gave a deep & loud hiss & then drew back his head. – They were so heavy, I could scarcely lift them off the ground. – Surrounded by the black Lava, the leafless shrubs & large Cacti, they appeared most old-fashioned antediluvian animals; or rather inhabitants of some other planet.

22nd. We slept on the sand-beach, & in the morning after having collected many new plants, birds, shells & insects, we returned in the evening on board. – This day was glowing hot, & was the first when our closeness to the Equator was very sensible...

25th...The inhabitants here lead a sort of Robinson Crusoe life; the houses are very simple, built of poles and thatched with grass. – Part of their time is employed in hunting the wild pigs & goats with which the woods abound; from the climate, agriculture requires but a small portion. – The main article however of animal food is the Terrapin or Tortoise: such numbers yet remain that it is calculated two days hunting will find food for the other five in the week. – Of course the numbers have been much reduced; not many years since the Ship's company of a Frigate brought down to the Beach more than 200, – where the settlement now is, around the Springs, they formerly swarmed. – Mr. Lawson thinks there is yet left sufficient for for 20 years; he has however sent a party to Jame's Island to salt (there is a Salt mine there) the meat. – Some of the animals are there so very large that, upwards of 200£b of meat have been procured from one. Mr. Lawson recollect having seen a Terrapin which 6 men could scarcely lift & two could not turn over on its back. These immense creatures must be very old, in the year 1830 one was caught (which required 6 men to lift it into the boat) which had various dates carved on its shells; one was 1786. – The only reason why it was not at that time carried away must have been, that it was too big for two men to manage. – The Whalers always send away their men in pairs to hunt.

26th and 27th. I industriously collected all the animals, plants, insects & reptiles from this Island. – It will be very interesting to find from future comparison to what district or 'centre of creation' the organized beings of this archipelago must be attached.

9th [October]...The tortoise when it can procure it, drinks great quantities of water: Hence these animals swarm in the neighbourhood of the Springs. – The average size of the full-grown ones is nearly a yard ling in its back shell: they are so strong as easily to carry me, & too heavy to lift from the ground. - In the pathway many are travelling to the water & others returning, having drunk their fill. - The effect is very comical in seeing these huge creatures with outstretched neck so deliberately pacing onwards. - I think they march at the rate 360 yards in an hour; perhaps four miles in the 24. - When they arrive at the Spring, they bury their heads above the eyes in the muddy water & greedily suck in great mouthfulls, quite regardless of lookers on. -

Wherever there is water...roads lead from all sides to it, these extend for distances of miles. -It is by this means that these watering places have been discovered by the fishermen. -In the low dry region there are but few Tortoises: they are replaced by infinite numbers of the large yellow herbiverous Lizard mentioned at Albemarle Isd. – The burrows of this animal are so very numerous; that we had difficulty in finding a spot to pitch the tents. – These lizards live entirely on vegetable productions; berrys, leaves, for which latter they frequently crawl up the trees, especially a Mimosa; never drinking water, they much like the succulent Cactus, & for a piece of it they will, like dogs, struggle [to] seize it from another. Their congeners the 'imps of darkness' in like manner live entirely on sea weed. – I suspect such habits are nearly unique in the Saurian race...

During our residence of two days at the Hovels, we lived on the meat of the Tortoise fried in the transparent Oil which is procured from the fat. – The Breast-plate with the meat attached to it is roasted as the Gauchos do 'Carne con cuero. It is then very good. – Young Tortoises make capital soup – otherwise the meat is but, to my taste, indifferent food.

Charles Darwin's Beagle Diary.

JULES-SÉBASTIEN-CÉSAR DUMONT D'URVILLE 1790–1842

The first landing on Antarctica

DUMONT D'URVILLE JOINED *the navy at the age of 17 and by the age of 40 he had learned seven languages (including Hebrew), had acquired the 'Venus de Milo' for France, had completed two circumnavigations of the globe, and had charted the South Pacific with such precision that he became the first to identify its three major island groups: Melanesia, Polynesia and Micronesia. Accused of falsifying his records and mistreating the crew, D'Urville spent almost ten years at a desk before being ordered on a third circumnavigation in 1837. This time he was to dip south like Cook before him and go 'as far as the ice permits' in search of Antarctica. He took two ships, L'Astrolabe and La Zelée, carrying 183 officers and crew, with the reward of 100 gold coins for reaching the 75th parallel, an extra 20 for each degree beyond that and 'whatever you choose to ask' for attaining the Pole. The Pole was beyond their grasp, but they did become the first to land on the main Antarctic continent, at a spot that D'Urville named Adelie Land after his wife. The return journey was plagued by desertions and scurvy, and when they returned to France in November 1840 D'Urville's command had shrunk to 130 men. Nevertheless, the voyage had broken all records for Antarctic exploration.*

THE EXPEDITION APPROACHES ANTARCTICA.

In the silence of the night, the huge masses of ice about us looked majestic, but also forbidding. The whole crew watched as the sun sank beneath the horizon, trailing after it a long curtain of light. At midnight it was still dusk and we could easily read on the bridge. We judged that there was no more than half an hour of proper night. I took advantage of it to go below for a rest, emerging the following day to confirm the existence of any land that might lie ahead.

At four in the morning, I counted sixty bergs in the vicinity. I knew that we had not changed position during the night, yet of the enormous blocks that had surrounded us the day before, each of which looked very similar but had an individual shape, I did not recognise a single one. The sun had been up now for a while...we could feel its heat; as could the bergs, which underwent an abrupt decomposition. My attention was drawn to one in particular, which was not far off. Countless streams of water poured from its summit, running in deep furrows down its sides before plunging as waterfalls onto the sea. The weather was magnificent, but alas there was no wind. Before us, continually, we could see land, could follow its undulations: it had no obvious features, was smothered with snow, stretched from west to east, and seemed to slope gently towards the sea. But we could not make out a single peak nor find a dark spot to relieve its grey blandness. Therefore we had reason enough to doubt its existence. However, at midday all uncertainty vanished. A boat from the Zelée came alongside, and announced that they had seen land yesterday. Less distrustful than myself, every officer aboard the Zelée was already convinced of the discovery. Calm weather, unfortunately, prevented a positive confirmation. Still, there was general rejoicing. Henceforth the success of our enterprise was assured; because the expedition could report, whatever else, the finding of a new country...The two boats that were sent to find land did not return until half past ten, loaded with rock specimens that they had collected from the shore.

Here is an excerpt from the journal of M. Dubouzet [naturalist aboard the *Zelée*] recounting this interesting excursion. 'Throughout the whole day our eyes were fixed on the coast, trying to find a spot where we could see something other than snow and ice. We were near despair when, having passed a mass of large ice bergs that completely hid the shore, we finally sighted a number of small islands whose flanks bore the darker shades of earth that we so keenly sought. A few moments later, we saw the Astrolabe's boat heading for the coast carrying an officer and two naturalists. Immediately, I requested Captain Jacquinot to put me in the skiff that he was lowering into the sea. The Astrolabe's boat had already gained a lead on us; but we strained at the oars and after two and a half hours we reached the nearest island. Our men were so fired with ardour that they hardly noticed that their exertions had brought them, in so short a space of time, a distance of more than seven miles. Along the way, we passed beneath gigantic ice bergs, whose perpendicular sides, gnawed below by the sea, were wreathed above with long needles of greenish ice, formed as a result of thawing. No sight could have been more dramatic. They appeared to form a mighty wall, to the east of the islands for which we were headed, which made me think that they were grounded in perhaps eighty to a hundred fathoms. Their height seemed to indicate roughly this draught. The sea was covered with fragments of ice, which forced us to make frequent detours. On the floes we saw a crowd of penguins that stared stupidly as we glided past.

It was almost nine o'clock when, to our inexpressible delight, we landed on the western promontory of the highest and farthest east of the islands. The Astrolabe's boat had arrived a moment before us, and its crew were already climbing the rocky cliffs, hurling down the penguins, who were astonished to find themselves so brutally dispossessed of a realm of which they had considered themselves to be the sole inhabitants. We leaped ashore, armed with pick axes and hammers. The surf made this operation very

difficult and I was forced to leave several men to hold the boat in position. Immediately thereafter I sent one of the sailors to raise a tricouleur on this land which no human being before us had ever seen or trodden. Following the ancient custom, which the English have jealously maintained, we took possession in the name of France, claiming too the nearby coast which we had been unable to reach on account of the ice. Our enthusiasm and our joy were increased by the fact that a new addition had been made to France's territories by dint of peaceful conquest. If the abuse that one heaps on these rites of possession makes one often regard them as ridiculous and worthless, in this case at least, we felt justified in preserving the ancient custom to our country's benefit: we had dispossesed nobody, and our title was incontestable.

We considered ourselves thereafter as being on French soil, and did so in the comfort that we had not involved our nation in war.

The ceremony ended, as it should, with a toast. We consumed, to the glory of France, a bottle of its most noble wine which one of our companions had had the presence of mind to bring with him. Never was the wine of Bordeaux called upon to play a more worthy role; never was a bottle emptied so fittingly. Surrounded on all sides by eternal snow and ice, the cold was brisk, and this generous spirit was an excellent consolation against the temperature. All this took less time than it does to write it down. We then set to work, to see what this desolate land might yield of interest to natural history...

We did not leave the islands until half past nine, enraptured by the riches we carried. Before raising our sails, and to say a last farewell, we saluted our discovery with a general hurrah. The echoes from these silent regions, troubled for the first time by human voices, returned our cries, then resumed their habitual silence, so sombre and imposing. Driven by a gentle breeze from the east, we headed for our ships, which by now were well out to sea and when tacking were often obscured by massive ice bergs. We did not reach them until eleven o'clock in the evening. The cold was bitter. The thermometer showed 5 degrees below zero. The outsides of our boats were covered with layers of ice. We were glad to be once again aboard the corvettes, grateful to have been able to complete our discoveries without mishap because, in this frigid and capricious climate, it is best not to leave a ship for very long.

J. DUMONT D'URVILLE, *Voyage au Pole Sud et dans L'Oceanie, Vol VIII, 1844.*

D'Urville's men wrestle to free the Astrolabe *from the pack ice. 'Seeing our two ships', he wrote, 'one thought of two crayfish stranded by the tide on a beach full of stones...and struggling to regain the open sea.' Most of the crew and all three surgeons suffered from frostbite during the rescue operation.*

ELISHA KENT KANE 1820–57

Stranded in search of the Pole

IN 1853, KANE TOOK the tiny Advance *up the west coast of Greenland with the avowed aim of finding Sir John Franklin – in fact, his real agenda was to reach the North Pole. He achieved neither goal, instead surviving two winters in the ice, a mutiny, the loss of his ship, scurvy, the death of several men and a perilous boat journey to safety. His account was the most readable of its kind to date and sold in prodigious quantities. When he died at the age of 37, it took three days for the mourners to file past his grave.*

HAVING RESCUED A STRICKEN SLEDGE PARTY.

I began to feel certain of reaching our half-way station of the day before, where we had left our tent. But we were still nine miles from it, when, almost without premonition, we all became aware of an alarming failure of our energies.

I was, of course, familiar with the benumbed and almost lethargic sensation of extreme cold; and once, when exposed for some hours in the midwinter of Baffin's Bay, I had experienced symptoms which I compared to the diffused paralysis of the electro-galvanic shock. But I had treated the sleepy comfort of freezing as something like the embellishment of romance. I had evidence now to the contrary.

Bonsall and Morton, two of our stoutest men, came to me begging permission to sleep: 'they were not cold: the wind did not enter them now: a little sleep was all they wanted.' Presently Hans was found nearly stiff under a drift; and Thomas, bolt upright, had his eyes closed, and could hardly articulate. At last, John Blake threw himself on the snow, and refused to rise. They did not complain of feeling cold; but it was in vain that I wrestled, boxed, ran, argued, jeered, or reprimanded: an immediate halt could not be avoided...

[Pressing ahead with one other companion] I cannot tell how long it took for us to make the nine miles; for we were in a strange sort of stupor, and had little apprehension of time. It was probably about four hours...I recall those hours as among the most wretched I have ever gone through: we were neither of us in our right senses, and retained a very confused recollection of what preceded our arrival at the tent. We both of us, however, remember a bear, who walked leisurely before us and tore up as he went a jumper that Mr. McGary had improvidently thrown off the day before. He tore it into shreds and rolled it into a ball, but never offered to interfere with our progress..We were so drunken with cold that we strode on steadily, and, for aught I know, without quickening our pace...

[When the others had caught up] Our halts multiplied, and we fell half-sleeping on the snow. I could not prevent it. Strange to say, it refreshed us. I ventured on the experiment myself, making Riley wake me at the end of three minutes; and I felt so much benefited by it that I timed the men in the same way. They sat on the runners of the sledge, fell asleep instantly, and were forced to wakefulness when their three minutes were out...We now took a longer rest, and a last but stouter dram, and reached the brig at 1 p.m., we believe without a halt.

I say we believe; and here perhaps is the most decided proof of our sufferings: we were quite delirious, and had ceased to entertain a sane apprehension of the circumstances

A remarkable Greenland rock feature, Kane named 'Tennyson's Monument' after Britain's poet laureate. Like many explorers, he found writing his journal a chore. 'This book, poor as it is, has been my coffin', he told his father. Sure enough he died in 1857, the year in which its second and final volume was published.

about us. We moved on like men in a dream. Our footprints seen afterward showed that we had steered a bee-line for the brig. It must have been by a sort of instinct, for it left no impress on the memory...I thought myself the soundest of all, for I went through all the formula of sanity, and can recall the muttering delirium of my comrades when we got back into the cabin of our brig. Yet I have been told since of some speeches and some orders too of mine, which I should have remembered for their absurdity if my mind had retained its balance...

Dr. Hayes...reported none of our brain-symptoms as serious, referring them properly to the class of those indications of exhausted power which yield to generous diet and rest. Mr. Ohlsen suffered some time from strabismus and blindness: two others underwent amputation of parts of the foot, without unpleasant consequences; and two died in spite of all our efforts. The rescue party had been out for seventy-two hours. We had halted in all eight hours, half our number sleeping at a time. We travelled between eighty and ninety miles, most of the way dragging a heavy sledge. The mean temperature of the whole time, including the warmest hours of three days, was at minus 41°.2. We had no water except at our two halts, and were at no time able to intermit vigorous exercise without freezing.

E.KANE, *Arctic Explorations, Vol I, 1856.*

IN 1854, THE CREW OF THE ADVANCE MUTINIED.

August 18, Friday. – Reduced our allowance of wood to six pounds a meal. This, among eighteen mouths, is one-third of a pound of fuel for each. It allows us coffee twice a day, and soup once. Our fare besides this is cold pork boiled in quantity and eaten as required. This sort of thing works badly; but I must save coal for other emergencies. I see 'darkness ahead'.

I inspected the ice again to-day. Bad! bad! – I must look another winter in the face.

I do not shrink from the thought; but, while we have the chance ahead, it is my first duty to have all things in readiness to meet it. It is horrible – yes, that is the word – to look forward to another year of disease and darkness to be met without fresh food and without fuel. I should meet it with a more tempered sadness if I had no comrades to think for and protect...

August 21, Monday. – The question of detaching a party was in my mind some time ago; but the more I thought it over, the more I was convinced that it would be neither right in itself nor practically safe. For myself personally, it is a simple duty of honor to remain by the brig... – Come what may, I share her fortunes.

But it is a different question with my associates. I cannot expect them to adopt my impulses; and I am by no means sure that I ought to hold them bound to my conclusions. Have I the moral right? For, as to nautical rules, they do not fit the circumstances: among the whalers, when a ship is hopelessly beset, the master's authority gives way, and the crew take counsel for themselves whether to go or stay by her...

But what presses upon me is of another character. I cannot disguise it from myself that we are wretchedly prepared for another winter on board. We are a set of scurvy-riddled, broken-down men; our provisions are sorely reduced in quantity, and are altogether unsuited to our condition. My only hope of maintaining or restoring such a degree of health among us as is indispensable to our escape in the spring has been and must be in a wholesome elastic tone of feeling among the men: a reluctant, brooding, disheartened spirit would sweep our decks like a pestilence. I fear the bane of depressing example...

August 23, Wednesday.– The brig cannot escape. I got an eligible position with my sledge to review the floes, and returned this morning at two o'clock. There is no possibility of our release, unless by some extreme intervention of the coming tides...I am very doubtful, indeed, whether our brig can get away at all. It would be inexpedient to attempt leaving her now in boats; the water-streams closing, the pack nearly fast again, and the young ice almost impenetrable.

I shall call the officers and crew together, and make known to them very fully how things look, and what hazards must attend such an effort as has been proposed among them. They shall have my views unequivocally expressed...

August 24, Thursday. – At noon to-day I had all hands called, and explained to them frankly the conditions which have determined me to remain where we are. I endeavoured to show them that an escape to open water could not succeed, and that the effort must be exceedingly hazardous: I alluded to our duties to the ship: in a word, I advised them strenuously to forego the project. I then told them...that I should require them to place themselves under the command of the officers selected by them before setting out, and to renounce in writing all claims upon myself and the rest who were resolved to stay by the vessel. Having done this, I directed the roll to be called, and each man to answer for himself.

In the result, eight out of seventeen survivors of my party resolved to stand by the brig.

E. KANE, *Arctic Explorations, Vol I, 1856.*

An illustration from Kane's journal shows the rigours his sledge parties endured. The ice was so rugged that one crewman said that it would be easier to cross Manhattan by going from top to top of the buildings.

RICHARD BURTON 1821–1890
In Africa and the Orient

BURTON WAS THE ENFANT TERRIBLE of 19th-century exploration. Highly intelligent, the master of 27 languages, a resolute traveller, an indefatigable anthropologist and so fiercely moustached that he prided himself on looking like the devil, he declared that the only place in which he did not feel comfortable was home. His peregrinations took him to India, Africa and the Middle East – he had himself circumcised before undertaking a trip to Mecca – and provided material for several contentious books. He became famous for a squabble with John Hanning Speke as to who had found the source of the Nile but achieved lasting notoriety for his descriptions of sexual practices in the Orient. His wife Isabel burned his last manuscripts in order to preserve Western civilization from their contents.

ON THE PERILS OF PILGRIMAGE TO MECCA.

As the ceremony of 'Ramy,' or Lapidation, must be performed on the first day by all pilgrims between sunrise and sunset, and as the fiend was malicious enough to appear in a rugged Pass, the crowd makes the place dangerous. On one side of the road, which is not forty feet broad, stood a row of shops belonging principally to barbers. On the other side is the rugged wall against which the pillar stands, with a chevaux de frise of Badawin [Bedouin] and naked boys. The narrow space was crowded with pilgrims, all struggling like drowning men to approach as near as possible to the Devil; it would have been easy to run over the heads of the mass. Amongst them were horsemen with rearing chargers. Badawin on wild camels, and grandees on mules and asses, with out-runners, were breaking a way by assault and battery. I had read Ali Bey's self-felicitations upon escaping this place with 'only two wounds in the left leg,' and I had duly provided myself with a hidden dagger. The precaution was not useless. Scarcely had my donkey entered the crowd than he was overthrown by a dromedary, and I found myself under the stamping and roaring beast's stomach. Avoiding being trampled upon by a judicious use of the knife, I lost no time in escaping from a place so ignobly dangerous. Some Moslem travellers assert, in proof of the sanctity of the spot, that no Moslem is ever killed here: Meccans assured me that accidents are by no means rare.

Presently the boy Mohammed fought his way out of the crowd with a bleeding nose. We both sat down upon a bench in front of a barber's booth, and, schooled by adversity, waited with patience an opportunity. Finding an opening, we approached within about five cubits of the place, and holding each stone between the thumb and forefinger* of the right hand, we cast it at the pillar...

Some hold the pebble as a schoolboy does a marble, others between the thumb and forefinger extended, others shoot them from the thumb knuckle, and most men consult their own convenience...

The amount of risk which a stranger must encounter at the pilgrimage rites is still considerable. A learned Orientalist and divine intimated his intention, in a work published but a few years ago, of visiting Meccah without disguise. He was assured that the Turkish governor would now offer no obstacle to a European traveller. I would strongly dissuade a friend from making the attempt. It is true that the Frank is no longer...insulted when he

ventures out of the Meccan Gate of Jeddah; and that our Vice-Consuls and travellers are allowed, on condition that their glance do not pollute the shrine, to visit Taif and the regions lying Eastward of the Holy City...But the first Badawi who caught sight of a Frank's hat would not deem himself a man if he did not drive a bullet through the wearer's head. At the pilgrimage season disguise is easy on account of the vast and varied multitudes which visit Meccah exposing the traveller only to 'stand the buffet with knaves who smell of sweat.' But woe to the unfortunate who happens to be recognised in public as an Infidel – unless at least he could throw himself at once upon the protection of the government. Amidst, however, a crowd of pilgrims, whose fanaticism is worked up to the highest pitch, detection would probably ensure his dismissal at once al numero de' piu. Those who find danger the salt of pleasure may visit Meccah; but if asked whether the results justify the risk, I should reply in the negative. And the Vice-Consul at Jeddah would only do his duty in peremptorily forbidding European travellers to attempt Meccah without disguise, until the day comes when such steps can be taken in the certainty of not causing a mishap; and accident would not redound to our reputation, as we could not in justice revenge it.

R. Burton, *Personal Narrative of a Pilgrimage to Al-Madinah & Meccah, (Vol II), 1873.*

Isabel Burton accompanied her husband on several journeys and published a journal of the time they spent together in Syria, as well as a memoir of their wider travels. At times eminently practical, she could also be unbearably priggish. When her husband died she burned his manuscripts as being too rude for publication. The following extracts show both sides of her character.

ISABEL BURTON'S ACCOUNT OF AN UPRISING IN SYRIA.

When I had parted from Richard in the plain, I climbed up to my eagle's nest at Bludan, the view from which commanded the country, and I felt that as long as our ammunition lasted we could defend ourselves, unless overpowered by numbers. Night was coming on, and of course I had not the slightest idea of what would happen, but feared the worst. I knew what had happened at the previous massacre of Christians at Damascus; and flying, excited stragglers dropped in, and from what they said one would have supposed that Damascus was already being deluged in blood, and that eventually crowds of Moslems would surge up to Bludan and exterminate us also. I fully expected an attack, so I collected every available weapon and all the ammunition. I had five men in the house; to each one I gave a gun, a revolver, and a bowi knife. I put one on the roof with a pair of elephant guns carrying four-ounce balls, and a man to each of the four sides of the house, and I commanded the terrace myself. I planted the Union Jack on the flagstaff at the top of my house, and I turned my bull terriers into the garden to give notice of any approach. I locked up a little Syrian girl whom I had taken into my service, and who was terribly frightened, in the safest room; but my English maid, who was as brave as any man, I told off to supply us with provisions and make herself generally useful. I then rode down the hill to the American Mission and begged them to come up and take shelter with me, and then into the village of Bludan to tell the Christians to come up to me on the slightest sign of danger...

During the three days we were in suspense a monster vulture kept hovering over our house. The people said it was a bad omen, and so I fetched my little gun, though I rather begrudged the cartridge just then; and when it was out of what they call reach, I had the good luck to bring it down. This gave them great comfort, and we hung the vulture on the top of the tallest tree.

At last at midnight on the third day a mounted messenger rode up with a letter from Richard, saying that all was well at Damascus, but that he would not be back for a week.'

I.BURTON & W. WILKINS, *The Romance of Isabel Lady Burton, Vol II, 1897*

WITH BURTON TO GOA.

About five o'clock, as the captain told me overnight not to hurry myself, I got up leisurely. Presently a black steward came down, and said:

'Please, ma'am, the agent's here with your boat to convey you ashore. The captain desired me to say that he's going to steam on directly.'

I was just at the stage of my toilet which rendered it impossible for me to open the door or come out, so I called through the keyhole:

'Please go with my compliments to the captain, and beg him to give me ten minutes or a quarter of an hour, and tell my husband what is the matter.'

Lady Isabel Burton lounges in oriental style. A stalwart participant in her husbands travels, she wrote the following lines to her mother shortly before her marriage: 'I wish I were a man. If I were, I would be Richard Burton, but being only a woman, I would be Richard Burton's wife. I long to rush round the world in an express: I feel I shall go mad if I remain at home.'

Burton encountered this
grandee's litter during
his travels through
Arabia. Like himself,
the occupants were
bound for Mecca – but
in far grander style.
When necessary they
left their comfortable
cocoon by means of the
ladder carried by the
rear camel.

'I will go, ma'am,' he answered; 'but I am afraid the captain can't wait. It is his duty to go on.'

'Go!' I shouted; and he went.

In two minutes down came the negro again.

'Captain says it's impossible; in fact the ship's moving now.'

Well, as we were tied to time and many other things, and could not afford to miss our landing, I threw on a shawl and a petticoat, as one might in a shipwreck, and rushed out with my hair down, crying to the steward:

'Bundle all the things into the boat as well you can; and if anything is left, take it back to the hotel at Bombay.'

I hurried on deck, and to my surprise found that the steamer was not moving at all. Richard and the captain were quietly chatting together, and when they saw me all excited and dishevelled they asked me the cause of my undress and agitation. When I told them, the captain said:

'I never sent any message of the kind. I told you last night I should steam on at seven, and it is now only five.'

I was intensely angry at the idea of a negro servant playing such a practical joke. I was paying £10 for a thirty-six hours' passage; and as I always treated everybody courteously, it was quite uncalled for and unprovoked. I thought it exceedingly impertinent, and told the captain so. Nevertheless, he did not trouble to inquire into the matter. The Bishop of Ascalon, Vicar-Apostolic at Bombay, was on board, and I told him about it, and he said that he had been treated just in the same way a year before on the same spot. The idea that such things should be allowed is a little too outrageous. Suppose that I had been a delicate and nervous passenger with heart complaint, it might have done me a great deal of harm.

The Romance of Isabel Lady Burton, Vol II.

CHARLES STURT 1795–1869
Mapping Australia

Sturt's men take bearings in the featureless desert that would later be named after their leader. 'There was a peculiar hue over the scene from the colour of the sand; and it almost appeared as if we were the last of the human race left to witness the destruction of our Planet. Fancy never coloured such a place; imagination could form no idea of its chilling and repulsive aspect', Sturt wrote. A few hundred miles farther north the expedition was halted by six months of drought. When their thermometers burst under the extremes of temperature, they decided it was time to turn back.

IN 1843, A MINOR COLONIAL official named Charles Sturt found himself in financial 'confusion' (as he put it). He sought, therefore to make some money from exploration. He had already helped map Australia's south-eastern river system, but now he proposed to open the unknown heart of the continent. 'Let any man lay the map of Australia before him, and regard the blank upon its surface', he declaimed, 'and then let me ask him if it would not be an honourable achievement to be the first to place a foot in its centre.' His party left Adelaide in 1844 and returned the following year, having reached neither the centre nor the inland sea that many geographers thought might be there, finding instead only an uncompromising desert. Sturt's party departed in a drought year and suffered accordingly. They were stricken by scurvy, hunger, thirst and temperatures so high that their thermometers burst; one man died of an aneurysm and Sturt very nearly went blind. But they did go further than any European to date and laid the ground for subsequent, more successful expeditions. Sturt recorded his progress in weekly letters to his wife Charlotte. Intended to comfort her during his absence, their never-ending catalogue of disaster, disease and disappointment can only have had the opposite effect. Sturt died in typically dispiriting fashion in 1869 having broken his leg while crossing a road.

FOR FOUR MONTHS STURT AND HIS MEN TRIED TO FORGE A PATH THROUGH THE DESERT. THEIR EFFORTS, HOWEVER, WERE FRUITLESS.

Sunday August 31st 1845...The scene was awfully frightful, dear Charlotte. A kind of dread (and I am not subject to such feelings) came over me as I gazed upon it. It looked like the entrance into Hell. Mr. Browne stood horrified. 'Did man', he exclaimed, 'ever see such a place?'...In truth, Dearest, I saw that Mr. Browne was not in a fit condition to expose himself to hardship. I expected every morning to hear that the fatal blackness had shewn itself on his legs...I determined therefore to turn back to the creek and try some other quarter...

Sunday September 14th 1845...The valley below us was dark with samphire bushes, and white with salt that blew into our faces and eyes like snow drifts before the heavy breeze that was blowing, and to the westward there were a succession of sand hills gradually increasing in height as far as the eye could reach. My heart sank within me at so hopeless a prospect. This was the journey on which we hoped to pass the desert, to make the centre, but all was apparently blighted. I continued onwards however for about 8 miles when I ascended the loftiest hill we had seen for some time from which too I had the same forbidding scene before...Gigantic red sand hills running parallel to each other for miles upon miles, dark and gloomy valleys, and a region overgrown with spinifex and membrysanthemum. Nevertheless I pushed on, until at length I observed that Mr. Browne was suffering very accutely. A sudden thought struck me on which I determined immediately to act. I gave up the attempt to push on and told Mr. Browne that I had resolved on returning to the Depot. That night our horses had nothing to eat or drink. We fastened them to acacia bushes and there they stood all night.

Sunday September 28th 1845...On Friday, Dearest, we made the first creek, and yesterday, instead of going to the creek at which we before stopped, we passed it knowing

that we should not find any water, and made for a clump of trees to which I had sent Mr. Browne as we came out and at which we found an abundance both of feed and water. As we were riding along some natives called to us, and on going up to them, they told us that they came from the north and were going to water, that all the water to the north was gone, and that they had been a long time without any. Their lips were parched and cracked and swollen, and they appeared reduced to the last extremity, and at length started off at a rapid trot. When I told them I had been to the north-west they shook their heads, and said there was no water there either. I really do not know what these poor creatures will do if the drought continues, as every water hole we have seen must shortly be dry. It is a most dreadful region.

Today, Dearest, we reached the first creek and are now only 76 miles from the Depot. All my men are knocked up, my horses are very weak and Mr. Browne exceedingly unwell. However we shall reach the camp in three days, I hope, when they will have temporary rest...

Sunday October 5th 1845. I am writing to you, my Dearest Charlotte, from the Depot Camp...We...dismounted after an absence of seven weeks of as excessive exposure as any to which man was ever subjected. We had ridden from first to last a distance of 963 miles, and had generally been on horse-back from the earliest dawn to 3 or 4 often to 6 o'clock, having no shelter of any kind from the tremendous heat of the fiery deserts in which we had been wandering, subsisting on an insufficient supply of food, and drinking water that your pigs would have refused. How I have stood it so well I know not....

Thus, my Dearest Charlotte, terminated an excursion that was to decide the success or failure of the expedition. A second time we had been forced back from the interior...and I had the painful reflection before me that whatever my exertions had been, I had made no discovery to entitle me to credit or reward, and that therefore I should fail in the only object for which I sought and undertook this tremendous and anxious task. Providence had denied that success to me with which it had been pleased to crown my former efforts, and I felt that instead of benefitting those for whose happiness and welfare I had made such sacrifices, I should only have inflicted an injury upon them. In vain had I prayed to the Almighty for success on this to me all important occasion. In vain had I implored for a blessing on you and on my children, if not on myself. But my prayer had been rejected, my petition refused, and so far from any ray of hope having ever crossed my path I felt that I had been contending against the very powers of Heaven, in the desperate show I had made against the seasons, and I now stood blighted and a blasted man over whose head the darkest destiny had settled. God knows Charlotte...difficulties and disappointments have overwhelmed me from first to last...

Sunday October 26th 1845 – Last Sunday my Dear and Beloved Charlotte we were in no enviable situation...That adamantine, that iron shod plain, stretched before me in all its gloominess and monotony. At 11 miles I reached the hills, and here fresh disappointment awaited me. Instead of finding them like ordinary hills or as at all indicative of a change of country, I found them to be no more than sand hills of a greater height than any we had seen...Gaining the crest of one of these hills I looked around me, and never saw such a view in my life. It was all – dark, dark, dark. Before me the same kind of hills as that on which I stood rose one after the other as far as I could see, and in no direction could I see a glimmering of hope.

I dismounted and sat down to consider whether I should go on or return. I felt quite convinced that if I went on and that we did not find water that night the whole party would perish. My horses had already been 34 hours without water, and they could not bear privation in their exhausted state. They were fast wearing their hoofs down to a level with their quicks being unshod, and their hoofs were so dry that splinters flew from them at every step. Men and animals could not indeed have been in a more fearful position for we were nearly 50 miles from any known water...Yet an almost irresistible desire to push on took possession of me, but, an unknown and a secret influence prevailed and at length determined me to turn back. I slowly and sullenly led my horse down the hill, and when at the bottom could not but contemplate with amazement the force of the element that must have produced the effects around me. There was a plain as extensive as the sea covered over with the shivered fragments of former mountains. There were hills over which the floods must have swept clad if I may say so with the same imperishable materials. The heat from the stones was overpowering and a steady blush was parching our lips and skins...

Sunday November 23rd 1845 – You will no doubt, Dearest, be anxious to know the events of the past week. There is nothing I am sorry to say cheering in them...Last Monday fortnight...at 9 a hot wind set in from the north-east that I thought would have burnt us up. I was seated under the shade of a gum tree at noon, and taking the thermometer out of a zinc case in my box found the mercury up to 125°, the instrument being only graduated to 127°. Thinking that it had been unduly affected I put it in the fork of the tree, a very large one five feet from the ground, and on going to look at it at 2, I found that it had risen as high as it would go, and the expansion of the mercury had burst the bulb, a fact that I believe no traveller ever before had it in his power to record, and one that will give you some idea of the terrific heat to which we were almost daily exposed...

I thought, Dearest, that I should never get to my journey's end, but we reached the Depot at 11 on Wednesday and found it silent and deserted [the men having left because of dysentery]. Mr. Stuart...observed a crow scratching in one of the garden beds, from which he pulled a large piece of bacon and flew away. This induced Mr. Stuart to examine the spot when he rooted up another piece of bacon and two pieces of suet which the dogs had buried there...These Morgan cleaned, and, bringing me a small piece of the bacon certainly not larger than a five shilling piece, told me that it was perfectly clean and good, that he had cut it out of the centre, and that he had brought it to me as I had had nothing for so long a time. I took it malgre moi I wanted it not, relished it not, my appetite was sunk below that but I took it because I felt that I wanted nourishment and I did not dream of so small a piece of meat doing me any harm. The very next day, however, I was seized with shooting pains in my legs, that increased towards the evening and were worse the next morning...

I dismounted, Dearest, having ridden 917 miles in five weeks and three days. When I got off my horse I felt as if the old dog had put his head between my legs as is his wont on welcoming any one and was pushing me forward. I turned round therefore to chide him but no dog was there. It was the jerking of the muscles of my thighs, and was the forerunner of something worse. My two journeys combined made up 1878 miles that I had travelled since the 14th of August...I had tired and worn out every man in the party and started on my last journey with entirely new hands. I had been exposed from sunrise to sunset to a scorching sun and at night had slept under the canopy of heaven alone. No wonder then that I was at length reduced, but the object I had in view made me reckless alike of exposure and privation. The day after I arrived in the camp, I lost the use of my left leg, the main muscles contracted and I lost all power of straightening my limb. Gradually my right leg became affected until at length I am stretched on my mattress a helpless and prostrate being. However, Dearest, I complain not...

Sunday December 21st. – Last Sunday, Dearest, we were on the north side of the ranges; today we have gained the south side and are established on the banks of the Darling river...My little journal is therefore drawing to a close...On Friday we started at 6 in the morning and travelled until 2 in the afternoon when I had halted for the men to have their dinners. We pushed on again at 4 and got to the edge of the plains at 3 am on Saturday, and then I halted for an hour. At 4 we again started and reached Cawndilla at 7 in the evening, that being 9 miles from the Darling but the bullocks were so tired that I was forced to stop and this morning pushed on to join Mr. Piesse's party who had been doing all he could to ascertain our fate, and had stuck letters against every tree informing me that he had seen you and that you was well.

Thankful indeed, Dearest, was I for the news, and having read one or two of your letters I have determined on sending in to Adelaide express by natives to relieve your anxiety. I will therefore close this for other business, only regretting that the hurry in which it has occasionally been written will scarcely render it intelligible to you. Yet if it affords you gratification I shall have attained my end.

God bless you

Amen

C. STURT, *Journal of the Central Australian Expedition 1844-45.*

JOHN HANNING SPEKE 1827–64

The source of the Nile

ARMY OFFICER AND INDEFATIGABLE *game hunter, Speke accompanied Richard Burton on an expedition to discover the source of the Nile. Between 1856 and 1858 they traipsed through East Africa, trying to find a river that Burton hoped would link Lake Tanganyika to the Nile. No such river existed, but while Burton was recovering from an attack of fever, Speke made an excursion to the north, during which he discovered a lake 'so broad you could not see across it, and so long that nobody knew its length'. He called it Victoria Nyanza. On a second expedition in 1862, accompanied by James Grant, he found its outflow. 'The expedition had now performed its functions', he wrote. 'Old Father Nile without any doubt rises in the Victoria Nyanza.' Burton disputed his claim – with good reason, because Speke's calculations were so imperfect that he had the Nile flowing uphill for 144 kilometres – and arranged a public debate at the Royal Geographical Society. Speke did not appear. He had emptied a shotgun into his chest that afternoon. Circumstance suggested it was an accident: rumour held that he had killed himself rather than appear onstage with Burton.*

ON 8 MARCH 1858, WHILE EXPLORING LAKE TANGANYIKA, SPEKE WAS PLAGUED BY BEETLES.
This day passed in rest and idleness, recruiting from our late exertions. At night a violent storm of rain and wind beat on my tent with such fury that its nether parts were torn away from the pegs, and the tent itself was only kept upright by sheer force. On the wind's abating, a candle was lighted to rearrange the kit, and in a moment, as though by magic, the whole interior became covered with a host of small black beetles, evidently attracted by the glimmer of the candle. They were so annoyingly determined in their choice of place for peregrinating, that it seemed hopeless my trying to brush them off the clothes or bedding, for as one was knocked aside another came on, and then another; till at last, worn out, I extinguished the candle, and with difficulty - trying to overcome the tickling annoyance occasioned by these intruders crawling up my sleeves and into my hair, or down my back and legs - fell off to sleep.

ON FINDING AN INSECT HAD CRAWLED INTO HIS EAR.
He went his course, struggling up the narrow channel, until he got arrested for want of passage-room. This impediment evidently enraged him, for he began with exceeding vigour, like a rabbit at a hole, to dig violently away at my typanum. The queer sensation this amusing measure excited in me is past description. I felt inclined to act as our donkeys once did, when beset by a swarm of bees, who buzzed about their ears and stung their heads and eyes until they were so irritated and confused that they galloped about in the most distracted order, trying to knock them off by treading on their heads, or by rushing under bushes, into houses, or through any jungle they could find. Indeed I do not know which was worst off. The bees killed some of them, and this beetle nearly did for me. What to do I knew not. Neither tobacco, oil, nor salt could be found: I therefore tried melted butter; that failing, I applied the point of a penknife to his back, which did more harm than good; for though a few thrusts quieted him, the point also wounded my ear so badly, that inflammation set in, severe suppuration took place, and all the facial glands

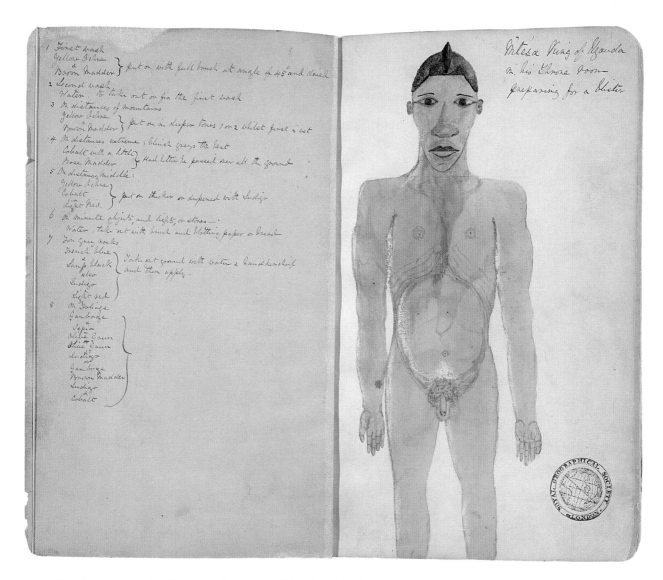

extending from that point down to the point of the shoulder became contorted and drawn aside, and a string of boils decorated the whole length of that region. It was the most painful thing I ever remember to have endured; but, more annoying still, I could not masticate for several days, and had to feed on broth alone. For many months the tumour made me almost deaf, and ate a hole between the ear and the nose, so that when I blew it, my ear whistled so audibly that those who heard it laughed. Six or seven months after this accident happened, bits of the beetle – a leg, a wing, or parts of its body – came away in the wax.

J. SPEKE, *What Led to the Discovery of the Source of the Nile, 1864.*

EN ROUTE TO LAKE VICTORIA, AT THE COURT OF KING KAMRASI.

18 Sept, 1862 – The present was then opened, and everything in turn placed upon the red blanket. The goggles created some mirth; so did the scissors, as Bombay, to show their use, clipped his beard, and the lucifers were considered a wonder; but the king scarcely moved or uttered any remarks till all was over, when, at the instigation of the courtiers, my chronometer was asked for and shown. This wonderful instrument, said the officers (mistaking it for my compass), was the magic horn by which the white men found their way everywhere. Kamrasi said he must have it, for, besides it, the gun was the only thing

WHITE RHINOCEROS. *R. simus*

R. simus

S. Africa

AFRICAN RHINOCEROS.
*Shot male & female in Ugogo
no other sort seen*

*R. bicornis
of S. Africa
like this is
R. cucullatus
of N. Africa*

new to him. The chronometer, however, I said, was the only one left, and could not possibly be parted with; though if Kamrasi liked to send men to Gani, a new one could be obtained for him.

Then changing the subject, much to my relief, Kamrasi asked Bombay, 'Who governs England?' 'A woman.' 'Has she any children?' 'Yes,' said Bombay, with ready impudence; 'these are two of them' (pointing to Grant and myself). That settled, Kamrasi wished to know if we had any speckeled cows, or cows of any peculiar colour, and if we would like to change four large cows for four small ones, as he coveted some of ours. This was a staggerer. We had totally failed, then, in conveying...the impression that we were not mere traders, ready to bargain with him...

19th...Kamrasi, in the metaphorical language of a black man, said, 'It would be unbecoming of me to keep secrets from you, and therefore I will tell you at once; I am sadly afflicted with a disorder that you alone can cure.' 'What is it, your majesty? I can see nothing in your face; it may perhaps require a private inspection.' 'My heart,' he said, 'is troubled, because you will not give me your magic horn – the thing, I mean, in your pocket, which you pulled out one day when Budja and Vittagura were discussing the way; and you no sooner looked at it than you said, 'That is the way to the palace.''

So! the sly fellow has been angling for the chronometer all this time, and I can get nothing out of him until he has go it – the road to the lake, the road to Gani, everything seemed risked on his getting my watch – a chronometer worth £50, which would be spoilt in his hands in one day. To undeceive him, and tell him it was the compass which I looked at and not the watch, I knew would end in my losing that instrument as well; so I told him it was not my guide, but a time-keeper, made for the purpose of knowing what time to eat my dinner by. It was the only chronometer I had with me; and I begged he would have patience until Bombay returned from Gani with another, when he would have the option of taking this or the new one. 'No. I must have the one in your pocket; pull it out and show it.' This was done, and I placed it on the ground, saying, 'The instrument is yours, but I must keep it until another one comes.' 'No; I must have it now, and will send it to you three times every day to look at.'

The watch went, gold chain and all, without any blessings following it; and the horrid king asked if I could make up another magic horn, for he hoped he had deprived us of the power of travelling, and plumed himself in the notion that the glory of opening the road would devolve upon himself. When I told him that to purchase another would cost five hundred cows, the whole party were more confirmed than ever as to its magical powers; for who in his senses would give five hundred cows for the mere gratification of seeing at what time his dinner should be eaten?...In the evening four pots of pombe and a pack of flour were brought, together with the chronometer, which was sent to be wound up – damaged of course – the seconds hand had been dislodged.

J. SPEKE, *Journal of the Discovery of The Source of the Nile, 1863.*

A brace of rhino adorn a page from Speke's journal. His enthusiasm for exploration took second place to an even greater passion for big-game hunting. His discovery of Lake Victoria Nyanza came about almost by accident: he had really been looking for something new to shoot.

SAM BAKER 1821–1893
A Victorian in Africa

A FANATICAL BIG-GAME HUNTER, Baker travelled the world in search of exotic locations and new things to kill in them. Among his many expeditions was one to the source of the Nile. When he arrived on the scene in 1863 he learned that John Hanning Speke had already found it. Undeterred, he went in search of a mysterious lake, Luta Nzige, rumoured to be part of the river system. Armed with a variety of rifles, a ceremonial Highland uniform, an unassailable sense of righteousness and a heavy pair of fists – plus an ever-diminishing entourage of porters and servants – Baker thundered his way across Africa until he found Luta Nzige. Then, renaming it Albert Nyanza, he thundered back. Before his death in 1873 he took his guns to Egypt, Cyprus, Syria, India, Japan and America.

RETURNING FROM ALBERT NYANZA, A SHORT BATTLE QUICKENED BAKER'S SPIRITS.
One day, during the heat of noon, after a long march in the burning sun through a tree-less desert, we descried a solitary tree in the distance, to which we hurried as to a friend. Upon arrival we found its shade occupied by a number of Hadendowda Arabs. Dismounting from our camels, we requested them to move and give place for our party – as a tree upon the desert is like a well of water, to be shared by every traveller. Far from giving the desired place, they most insolently refused to allow us to share the tree. Upon Richarn attempting to take possession, he was rudely pushed on one side, and an Arab drew his knife...Out flashed the broadswords from their sheaths! and the headman of the party aimed a well-directed cut at my head. Parrying the cut with my sun-umbrella, I returned with a quick thrust directly in the mouth, the point of the peaceful weapon penetrating his throat with such force that he fell upon his back. Almost at the same moment I had to parry another cut from one of the crowd that smashed my umbrella completely, and left me with my remaining weapons, a stout Turkish pipe-stick about four feet long, and my fist. Parrying with the stick, thrusting in return at the face, and hitting sharp with the left hand, I managed to keep three or four of the party on and off upon their backs, receiving a slight cut with a sword upon my left arm in countering a blow which just grazed me as I knocked down the owner, and disarmed him. My wife picked up the sword, as I had no time to stoop, and she stood well at bay with her newly-acquired weapon that a disarmed Arab wished to wrest from her, but dared not close with the naked blade. I had had the fight all my own way, as, being beneath the tree (the boughs of which were very near the ground), the Arabs, who do not understand the use of the point, were unable to use their swords, as their intended cuts were intercepted by the branches. Vigorous thrusting and straight hitting cleared the tree, and the party were scattered right and left...One of the Arabs, armed with a lance, rushed up to attack Richarn from behind; but Zeneb was of the warlike Dinka tribe, and having armed herself with the hard wood handle of the axe, she went into the row [and] gave the Arab such a whack upon his head that she knocked him down on the spot, and seizing his lance she disarmed him. Thus armed, she rushed into the thickest of the fray.

'Bravo Zeneb!' I could not help shouting. Seizing a thick stick that had been dropped by one of the Arabs, I called Richarn and our little party together, and attacking the few Arabs who offered resistance, they were immediately knocked down and disarmed.

Food running short, Sam and Florence Baker await the butchering of their pet monkey. In a mood of despondency Sam Baker wrote: 'I shall be truly thankful to quit this abominable land...Altogether I am thoroughly sick of this expedition, but I shall plod onwards with dogged obstinacy; God only knows the end. I should be grateful should the day ever arrive once more to see Old England.'

The leader of the party, who had been the first to draw his sword and had received a mouthful of umbrella, had not moved from the spot where he fell, but amused himself with coughing and spitting. I now ordered him to be bound, and threatened to tie him to my camel's tail and lead him a prisoner to the Governor of Souakim, unless he called all those of his party who had run away. They were now standing at a distance in the desert, and I insisted upon the delivery of their weapons. Being thoroughly beaten and cowed, he conferred with those whom we had taken prisoners, and the affair ended by all the arms being delivered up. We counted six swords, eleven lances, and a heap of knives, the number of which I forget.

S. Baker, *Great Basin of the Nile, The Albert Nynza, Vol 2, 1867.*

Baker's wife was a Hungarian named Florence, whom he had purchased at a slave market in the Balkans. A woman of remarkable tenacity, she accompanied her husband in all his schemes.

BAKER ON FLORENCE:

The river was about eighty yards wide, and I had scarcely completed a fourth of the distance and looked back to see if my wife followed close to me, when I was horrified to see her standing in one spot, and sinking gradually through the weeds, while her face was distorted and perfectly purple. Almost as soon as I perceived her, she fell, as though shot dead. In an instant I was by her side; and with the assistance of eight or ten of my men, who were fortunately close to me, I dragged her like a corpse through the yielding vegetation...I laid her under a tree, and bathed her head and face with water, as for the moment I thought she had fainted; but she lay perfectly insensible, as though dead, with teeth and hands firmly clenched, and her eyes open but fixed...It was in vain that I rubbed her heart, and the black women rubbed her feet, to endeavour to restore animation. At length the litter came, and after changing her clothes, she was carried mournfully forward as a corpse. Constantly we had to halt and support her head, as a painful rattling in the throat betokened suffocation. At length we reached a village, and halted for the night...

I was watching the first red streak that heralded the rising sun, when I was startled by the words, 'Thank God,' faintly uttered behind me. Suddenly she had awoke from her torpor, and with a heart overflowing I went to her bedside. Her eyes were full of madness! She spoke; but the brain was gone!...

I will not inflict a description of the terrible trial of seven days of brain fever, with its attendant horrors...For seven nights I had not slept, and although as weak as a reed, I had marched by the side of her litter...We reached a village one evening; she had been in violent convulsions successively – it was all but over. I laid her down on a litter within the hut; covered her with a Scotch plaid; and I fell upon my mat insensible, worn out with sorrow and fatigue. My men put a new handle to the pickaxe that evening, and sought for a dry spot to dig her grave.

The sun had risen when I woke...She lay flat upon her bed, pale as marble...but as I gazed upon her in fear, her chest gently heaved, not with the convulsoive throbs of fever, but naturally...She was saved! When not a ray of hope remained, God alone knows what helped us. The gratitude of that moment I will not attempt to describe.

The Albert Nyanza, 1867.

Between 1871 and 1873 Florence accompanied her husband on a second expedition to the Nile. In a letter to her step-daughter she described the difficulties they encountered.

Africa White Nile, Gondokoro May 19, 1871

My own darling Edith,

At last we arrived here – after a fearful struggle and weary journey in dragging a flotilla of 59 vessels including a steamer of thirty two horse power over high grass and marshes...It would be quite impossible by any description to give you an idea of the obstacles to navigation through which we have toiled with the fleet, but you can imagine the trouble when you hear that we were thirty two days with 1,500 men in accomplishing a distance of only 2 miles...

Our vessels drew four feet of water but in many places the depth of the river was only two feet. These terrible shallows extended over about twenty miles with intervals of deep water.

The whole force wearied with the hard work of cutting canals through the floating marshes. We were broken-hearted on arrival at the shallows and the men made up their minds that we must turn back. The river was falling rapidly, thus it was a race against time as it might be perfectly dry by the time we should have overcome a present obstruction. It appeared that the expedition must be utterly ruined.

Thank goodness dear Papa had forseen and provided for the difficulties by having a large supply of good tools – such as spades, hoes, billhook, etc., and he always went many many miles ahead in a small rowing boat to sound the depth of the water and to explore the miserable and frightful country generally. There was no dry land – neither was there depth, nothing but horrible marsh and mosquitoes. Many of our men died.

At length, after deepening the channel in many places with spades, we, by degrees, after some months heavy labour dragged our fleet with ropes to the limit where the water ceased altogether and the fleet was hard and fast aground in a long but narrow lake from which the water had escaped before we could cut a canal in advance...

Thank God dear Papa with all the responsibility and hard work and anxiety of the expedition never lost his health – this was most fortunate or we should have been entirely ruined. On the day when all appeared hopeless he spent five hours in dragging a small boat over high grass and marsh with about fifteen men and he happily discovered a large lake of deep water the overflow of which formed the difficult channel through which we have been ploughing our way during three months.

On the following day he explored the whole lake in the little boat and after rowing and sailing for sixteen miles, to the delight of all he returned at night with the good news that he had discovered the true White Nile junction – he had even drunk water out of the great river...

The difficulty was 'how to reach the lake'? The fleet was fast aground and [with] no navigable channel before us we now determined to cut a channel to the lake and then to make a large dam across the river behind the fleet, so that not a drop of water should escape, and the rise in the level would then float the vessels and allow them to pass up the shallow channel...The effect was magical. The water rose nearly three feet in a few hours...Once in the lake the great difficulties passed away, and we shortly entered the great White Nile...We arrived at Gondokoro on 14 April and it appeared really quite like heaven to us...

My dear Edith, I will trouble you now with a mission. Will you be good enough to send me out by the first opportunity addressed to dear Papa, His Excellency Samuel Baker Pasha, to the care of the British Consulate, Cairo, to be forwarded immediately:-

6 pairs of the best brown gauntlet gloves
6 pairs of different colour gloves
1 pair of best rather short French stays with 6 pairs of silk long stay laces.
2 pair of yellow gloves for Papa, I think they are number 7 but they must be the best you can get.
2 dozen lead pencils.
I hope my darling that it will not really give you too much trouble in sending me out all those things. Mind you keep the account of these little things.
6 pairs of best steels for stays.
Give my very warmest and affectionate love to dear Robert and darling Agnes, and give plenty of kisses to my dear own grandchildren.

Ever my own Edith
Your very loving
Florence Baker.

The stays to be 23 inches.
My darling Edith, I forgot to beg you also to send me out 12 good fine handkerchiefs 6 for dear Papa. We are getting very short of handkerchiefs – in fact we are getting short of everything.

A. Baker, *Morning Star: Florence Baker's Diary of the Expedition to put down the Slave Trade on the Nile, 1870–73.*

EDWARD WHYMPER 1840–1911
The conquest of the Matterhorn

A reluctant mountaineer is assisted forcefully over a bergschrund on the Col de Pilate. Whymper found the occasion highly amusing. However, even he confessed to a degree of nervousness: 'Had anyone then said to me, "You are a great fool for coming here", I should have answered with humility, "It is too true." And had my monitor gone on to say, "Swear that you will never ascend another mountain if you get down safely," I am inclined to think I should have taken the oath.'

A WOOD-ENGRAVER BY TRADE, *Whymper first visited Switzerland in 1860 to illustrate a travel book. He did not enjoy the trip. 'The scenery is very commonplace', he wrote of the St Bernard Pass, 'and the people on the whole very stupid and somewhat uncivil.' But if he didn't appreciate the region's aesthetic allure he did like the thought of climbing its peaks. By 1865 he had become Europe's most redoubtable alpinist, with scores of summits to his credit. One year, in the course of just eighteen days, he climbed 30,500 metres of mountainside. As one contemporary remarked, 'To Mr. Whymper belongs the credit of having had no weak spot at all.' In 1865, however, he lost four of the seven-strong team with whom he had just made the first ascent of the Matterhorn in a tragedy that became one of the most notorious episodes in Victorian exploration. It spelled an end to Whymper's Alpine career and marked, too, the climax of what has since been called the Golden Age of Mountaineering. The journal that he wrote of his exploits, complete with his own illustrations, remains the Bible of early alpinism.*

DESCENDING THE MATTERHORN.

Michel Croz had laid aside his axe, and in order to give Mr. Hadow greater security, was absolutely taking hold of his legs, and putting his feet, one by one, into their proper positions. As far as I know, no one was actually descending. I cannot speak with certainty, because the two leading men were partially hidden from my sight by an intervening mass of rock, but it is my belief, from the movements of their shoulders, that Croz, having done as I have said, was in the act of turning round to go down a step or two himself; at this moment Mr. Hadow slipped, fell against him, and knocked him over. I heard one startled exclamation from Croz, then saw him and Mr. Hadow flying downwards; in another moment Hudson was dragged from his steps, and Lord. F. Douglas immediately after him. All this was a work of a moment. Immediately we heard Croz's exclamation, old Peter and I planted ourselves as firmly as the rocks would permit: the rope was taut between us, and the jerk came on us both as one man. We held; but the rope broke midway between Taugwalder and Lord Francis Douglas. For a few seconds we saw our unfortunate companions sliding downwards on their backs, and spreading out their hands, endeavouring to save themselves. They passed from our sight uninjured, disappeared one by one, and fell from the precipice on to the Matterhorngletscher below, a distance of nearly 4000 feet in height. From the moment the rope broke it was impossible to save them.

So perished our comrades! For the space of half-an-hour we remained on the spot without moving a single step. The two men, paralysed by terror, cried like infants, and trembled in such a manner as to threaten us with the fate of the others...Fixed between the two, I could neither move up nor down. I begged Young Peter to descend, but he dared not. Unless he did, we could not advance...At last old Peter summoned up his courage, and changed his position to a rock to which he could fix the rope; the young man then descended, and we all stood together...

For more than two hours afterwards I thought almost every moment that the next would be my last; for the Taugwalders, utterly unnerved, were not only incapable of giving assistance, but were in such a state that a slip might have been expected from them

at any moment. After a time, we were able to do that which should have been done at first, and fixed ropes to firm rocks, in addition to being tied together. These ropes were cut from time to time, and were left behind. Even with their assurance the men were afraid to proceed, and several times old Peter turned with ashy face and faltering limbs, and said, with terrible emphasis, 'I cannot.'

At about 6 p.m. we arrived at the snow upon the ridge descending towards Zermatt, and all peril was over. We frequently looked, but in vain, for traces of our unfortunate companions...Convinced at last that they were neither within sight nor hearing, we ceased from our useless efforts; and, too cast down for speech, silently gathered up our things...preparatory to continuing the descent. When, lo! A mighty, arch appeared, rising above the Lyskamm, high into the sky. Pale, colourless, and noiseless, but perfectly sharp and defined, except where it was lost in the clouds, this unearthly apparition seemed like a vision from another world; and, almost appalled, we arched with amazement the gradual development of two vast crosses, one on either side. If the Taugwalders had not been the first to perceive it, I should have doubted my senses. They thought it might have some connection with the accident, and I, after a while, that it might bear some relation to ourselves. But our movements had no effect on it. It was a fearful and wonderful sight; unique in my experience, and impressive beyond description, coming at such a moment...

I tore down the cliff, madly and recklessly, in a way that caused them, more than once, to inquire if I wished to kill them. Night fell; and for an hour the descent was continued in the darkness. At half-past 9 a resting-place was found, and upon a wretched slab, barely large enough to hold the three of us, we passed six miserable hours. At daybreak the descent was resumed, and from the Hornli ridge we ran down to the chalets of Buhl, and on to Zermatt. Seiler [the hotel keeper] met me at his door, and followed in silence to my room. 'What is the matter?' 'The Taugwalders and I have returned.' He did not need more, and burst into tears; but lost no time in useless lamentations, and set to work to arouse the village. Ere long a score of men had started to ascend the Hohlicht heights, above Kalbermatt and Z'Mutt...They returned after six hours, and reported that they had seen the bodies lying motionless in the snow. This was on Saturday; and they proposed that we should leave on Sunday evening, so as to arrive upon the plateau at daybreak on Monday.

We started at 2 a.m. on Sunday 16th, and followed the route that we had taken on the previous Thursday as far as the Hornli. From thence we went down to the right of the ridge, and mounted through the seracs of the Matterhorngletscher. By 8.30 we had got to the plateau at the top of the glacier, and within sight of the corner in which we knew my companions must be. As we saw one weather-beaten man after another raise the telescope, turn deadly pale, and pass it on without a word to the next, we knew that all hope was gone. We approached. They had fallen below as they had fallen above - Croz a little in advance, Hadow near him, and Hudson some distance behind; but of Lord F. Douglas we could see nothing. We left them where they fell; buried in the snow at the base of the grandest cliff of the most majestic mountain of the Alps...

So the traditional inaccessibility of the Matterhorn was vanquished, and was replaced by legends of a more real character. Others will essay to scale its proud cliffs, but to none will it be the mountain that it was to its early explorers. It proved to be a stubborn foe; it resisted long, and gave many a hard blow; it was defeated at last with an ease that none could have anticipated, but, like a relentless enemy – conquered but not crushed – it took terrible vengeance.

E. WHYMPER, *Scrambles Among the Alps, 1871.*

Following the Matterhorn tragedy, Whymper and his two surviving companions saw crosses materialise in the sky. A rare example of a fog-bow, it seemed at the time to have supernatural significance. Reflecting on his Alpine career, Whymper wrote: 'There have been joys too great to be described in words, and there have been griefs upon which I have not dared to dwell; and with these in mind I say, Climb if you will, but remember that a momentary negligence may destroy the happiness of a lifetime. Do nothing in haste; look well to each step; and from the beginning think what may be the end.'

CARL KOLDEWEY 1837–1908
PAUL HEGEMANN c.1835–1902
Marooned off Greenland

Entering Franz Josef Fjord on Greenland's eastern coast, the crew of the Germania *were faced by a massive rock formation that they christened the Devil's Castle. Patriotically proud of his achievements, Koldewey wrote: 'For the first time a German expedition, under the auspices of the black, white and red flag, had visited...the least known region of the globe.'*

IN 1869, THE GERMANIA *and the* Hansa *left Bremerhaven on Germany's first serious Arctic expedition. Their destination was the east coast of Greenland where it was hoped they might find a sea route to the North Pole. Before they even reached land the* Hansa *sank in the ice, leaving Hegemann and his crew stranded on a floe. They built a miniature chalet (complete with dormer windows) from salvaged coal bricks, decorated its walls with gilt mirrors and barometers from Hegemann's cabin, installed a stove and waited to see where the current took them. After 965 kilometres, with the floe disintegrating beneath them, they escaped in boats to a missionary settlement on the southern tip of Greenland. 'We cannot flatter ourselves that we have greatly increased the knowledge of Greenland', Hegemann wrote with wry understatement, 'but we have shown what man's strength and perseverance can accomplish.' Koldewey, commanding the* Germania, *was more successful. Landing on the east coast he sent sledge parties as far north as 77°. Among them was the official artist, an Austrian named Julius von Payer, who would later become famous for discovering the Franz Josef Land archipelago north of Siberia. Payer also contributed to Koldewey's journal, which reads at times as if it had been written by the Brothers Grimm.*

A POLAR BEAR ATTACKS ONE OF THE GERMANIA'S CREW.

On the morning of the 13th, Theodor Klenzer, during the time the men were busied without, climbed the Germaniaberg to view the landscape in the increasing mid-day light. Reaching the top, he seated himself on a rock, and sang a song in the still air. As he looked behind him, however, he saw, not many steps off, a huge bear, which, with great gravity was watching the stranger. Now to our 'Theodor,' who was as quiet and decided a man as he was powerful, this would, under other circumstances, have been nothing; for the bear stood wonderfully well for a shot, and could not easily be missed, but Klentzer was totally unarmed, not having even a knife! Incredible! Is it not? But as Lieut. Payer writes, 'the bears always come when one has forgotten all about them.'

Thus Klentzer saw himself unarmed and all alone, far from his companions, and close to the bear. Flight is the only, though a doubtful, chance of safety, and the audacious thought struck him of plunging down the steep side of the glacier; but he chose the softer side-slope, and began to hurry down the mountain. Upon looking back, after a time, he perceived the great bear trotting behind him at a little distance, like a great dog. Thus they descended the mountain for some time. If Klentzer halted, so did the bear; when he went on, the bear followed slowly; if he began to run, the bear did the same. Thus the two had gone some distance, and Klentzer thought seriously of saving himself, as the bear, finding the chase somewhat wearisome, might press close upon his heels. He therefore uttered a loud shout, but the bear, only disconcerted for a moment, seemed to get more angry and approached quicker, so that he seemed to feel the hot breath of the monster. At this dreadful moment – and it was most likely his preservation – he remembered the stories he had heard, and, while running, pulled off his jacket, throwing it behind him. And see! the trick answers: the bear stops and begins to examine the jacket. Klentzer gains courage,

rushes on down the mountain, sending out a shout for help, which resounds through the silent region. But soon the bear is again at his heels, and he must throw away cap and waistcoat, by which means he gains a little. Now Klentzer sees help approaching – several friends hurrying over the ice. Collecting his last strength, he shouts and runs on. But help seems in vain, for the pursuer hurries too, and he is obliged to take the last thing he has, his shawl, which he throws exactly over the monster's snout, who, more excited still by renewed shouting, throws it back again contemptuously with a toss of his head, and presses forward upon the defenceless man, who feels the cold black snout touch his hand. Klenzer now gave himself up for lost; he could do no more; but the wonderful thought struck him of fastening up the bear's throat with the leathern belt which he wore round his body. Fixedly he stared into the merciless eyes of the beast – one short moment of doubt – the bear was startled, his attention seemed drawn aside, and the next moment he was off at a gallop. The shouts of the many hurrying to the rescue had evidently frightened him. Klenzer was saved by a miracle...From the effects of this day several suffered slightly from pains in the chest, and Mr. Sengstacke and P. Iverson had large frost-blisters on their feet. No wonder, when they had run about in stockinged feet for a whole hour and a half!

C. KOLDEWEY, *The German Arctic Expedition of 1869-70, 1874.*

DAVID LIVINGSTONE 1813–73
Through the African interior

AVOWEDLY A MISSIONARY *whose sole job was to bring Christianity to the unenlightened, Livingstone was in fact one of the 19th century's most dogged missionary-explorers. Between 1852 and 1873 he travelled through sub-Saharan Africa, discovering en route the Victoria Falls, Lake Ngami and Lake Nyasa, and providing valuable information as to the region's religious and commercial potential. His tireless efforts to expose the activities of Portuguese slave traders endeared him to Victorian Britain, as did his hugely popular journals about life in the 'Dark Continent'. Determined to discover new territory, he eventually abandoned missionary work in favour of purely geographical conquest. He died in 1873 while attempting to prove his theory that the River Lualaba was linked to the Nile. (Actually, it was a tributary of the Congo.) His European companions considered him too fanatical for comfort. It was not unknown on a Livingstone expedition for most of the members to die or be dismissed, while the doctor pressed on regardless. Such was his single-mindedness that even when his wife died in 1862, during a foray to the Zambezi, Livingstone only abandoned the quest when ordered to do so by London. However, his African servants thought so highly of him that, after his death, they embalmed his body and carried it to the coast, from where it was transported to England for burial in Westminster Abbey.*

IN HIS ATTITUDE TO SLAVERY LIVINGSTONE DISPLAYED WHAT WAS FOR THE TIME A TYPICAL – AND CONTRADICTORY – MIX OF COMPASSION, PRAGMATISM AND BIGOTRY. The Portuguese of Tette have many slaves, with all the usual vices of their class, as theft, lying, and impurity. As a general rule the real Portuguese are tolerably humane masters and rarely treat a slave cruelly; this may be due as much to kindness of heart as to a fear of losing the slaves by their running away. When they purchase an adult slave they buy at the same time, if possible, all his relations along with him. They thus contrive to secure him to his new home by domestic ties. Running away then would be to forsake all who hold a place in his heart, for the mere chance of acquiring a freedom, which would probably be forfeited on his entrance into the first native village, for the Chief might, without compunction, again sell him into slavery.

A rather singular case of voluntary slavery came to our knowledge: a free black, an intelligent active young fellow, called Chibanti, who had been our pilot on the river, told us that he had sold himself into slavery. On asking why he had done this, he replied that he was all alone in the world, had neither father nor mother, nor any one else to give him water when sick, or food when hungry; so he sold himself to Major Sicard, a notoriously kind master, whose slaves had little to do, and plenty to eat. 'And how much did you get for yourself?' We asked. 'Three thirty-yard pieces of cotton cloth,' he replied; 'and I forthwith bought a man, a woman, and a child, who cost me two of the pieces, and I had one piece left.' This, at all events, showed a cool and calculating spirit; he afterwards bought more slaves, and in two years owned a sufficient number to man one of the large canoes. His master subsequently employed him in carrying ivory to Quillimane, and gave him cloth to hire mariners for the voyage; he took his own slaves, of course, and thus drove a thriving business; and was fully convinced that he had made a good speculation by the

A herd of buffalo teeters on the brink of Victoria Falls. It was almost certainly not what Livingstone saw when he first encountered Africa's most majestic natural feature. Defensively, Baines claimed that although his paintings were true to life an occasional flourish lent his pictures artistic credence.

sale of himself, for had he been sick his master must have supported him. Occcasionally some of the free blacks become slaves voluntarily by going through the simple but significant ceremony of breaking a spear in the presence of their future master. A Portuguese officer, since dead, persuaded one of the Makololo to remain in Tette, instead of returning him to his own country, and tried also to induce him to break a spear before him, and thus ackowledge himself his slave, but the man was too shrewd for this; he was a great elephant doctor, who accompanied the hunters, told them when to attack the huge beast, and gave them medicine to ensure success. Unlike the real Portuguese, many of the half-castes are merciless slaveholders; their brutal treatment of the wretched slaves is notorious. What a human native of Portugal once said of them is appropriate of not true: 'God made white men, and God made black men, but the devil made half-castes.'

The officers and merchants send parties of slaves under faithful headmen to hunt elephants and to trade...requiring so much ivory in return. These slaves think they have made a good thing of it, when they kill an elephant near a village, as the natives give them beer and meal in exchange for some of the elephant's meat, and over every tusk that is bought there is expended a vast amount of time, talk, and beer. Most of the Africans are natural-born traders, they love trade more for the sake of trading than for what they make by it. An intelligent gentleman of Tette told us that native traders often come to him with with a tusk for sale, consider the price he offers, demand more, talk, consider, get puzzled and go off as on the previous day, and continue this course daily until they have perhaps seen every merchant in the village, and then at last end by selling the precious tusk to some one for even less than the first merchant had offered.

D. LIVINGSTONE, *Narrative of an Expedition to the Zambezi and its Tributaries. 1865.*

At times Livingstone was more comfortable describing Africa's wildlife than he was its human inhabitants.

Our camp on the Sinjere stood under a wide-spreading wild fig-tree. The soil teemed with white ants, whose clay tunnels, formed to screen them from the birds, thread over the ground, up the trunks of trees and along the branches, from which the little architects clear away all the rotten or dead wood. Very often the exact shape of the branches is left in tunnels on the ground and not a bit of the wood inside. The first night we passed here these destructive insects ate through our grass-beds, and attacked our blankets, and certain large red-headed ones even bit our flesh.

A strong marauding party of large black ants attacked a nest of white ones near the camp: as the contest took place beneath the surface, we could not see the order of the battle; but it soon became apparent that the blacks had gained the day, and sacked the white town, for they returned in triumph, bearing off the eggs, and the choice bits of the bodies of the vanquished. A gift, analogous to that of language, has not been withheld from ants: if part of their building is destroyed, an official is seen coming out to inspect the damage; and after a careful survey of the ruins, he chirrups a few clear and distinct notes, and a crowd of workers begins at once to repair the breach. When the work is completed, another order is given, and the workmen retire, as will appear on removing the soft freshly-built portion. We tried to sleep one rainy night in a native hut, but could not because of attacks by the fighting battalions of a very small species of formica, not more than one-sixteenth of an inch in length. It soon became obvious that they were under regular discipline, and even attempting to carry out the skilful plans and stratagems of some eminent leader. Our hands and necks were the first objects of attack. Large bodies of these little pests were massed in silence round the point to be assaulted. We could hear the sharp shrill word of command two or three times repeated, though, until then, we had not believed in the vocal power of an ant; the instant after we felt the storming hosts range over head and neck, biting the tender skin, clinging with a death-grip to the hair, and parting with their jaws, rather than quit their hold. On our lying down again in the hope of their having been driven off, no sooner was the light out, and all still, than the manoeuvre was repeated. Clear and audible orders were issued, and the assault renewed. It was as hard to sleep in that hut...The white ant...devours articles of vegetable origin only, and leather, which, by tanning, is imbued with a vegetable flavour...

The reddish ant, in the west called drivers, crossed our path daily, in solid columns an inch wide, and never did the pugnacity of either man or beast exceed theirs. It is a sufficient cause of war if you only approach them, even by accident. Some turn out of the ranks and stand with open mandibles, or, charging with extended jaws, bite with savage ferocity. When hunting, we lighted among them too often; while we were intent on the game, and without a thought of ants, they quietly covered us from head to foot, then all began to bite at the same instant; seizing a piece of skin with their powerful pincers, they twisted themselves round with it, as if determined to tear it out. Their bites are so terribly sharp that the bravest must run, and then strip to pick off those that still cling with their hooked jaws, as with steel forceps. This kind abounds in damp places, and is usually met with on the banks of streams. We have not heard of their actually killing any animal except the Python, and that only when gorged and quite lethargic, but they soon clear away any dead animal matter; this appears to be their principal food, and their use in the economy of nature is clearly in the scavenger line.

Narrative of an Expedition to the Zambezi.

Sketchbook in hand, Baines stands before the Zambezi's Kebrabrasa Gorge. On a rock below, Livingstone's brother Charles fumbles with his camera. 'Some who aspire to more exactitude of detail than an artist can hope for in a hasty sketch may wish to practise photography,' Baines explained, 'but unless the traveller possesses...chemical knowledge enough to enable him to contend successfully against the various contingencies of changing climate, impurity or scarcity of water, and innumerable other new and unexpected difficulties, we are inclined to think that the pencil, guided by what artistic skill the individual may be able to command, will afford, if not the best, at least the most certainly available results.'

GEORGE NARES 1831–1915

Britain's attempt at the North Pole

IN 1875, NARES WAS *sailing happily through the south pacific whappily through the south pacifichen, to his surprise, the Admiralty ordered him to the North Pole. Commanding the* Discovery *and the* Alert, *he steamed through the ice to Ellesmere Island, attaining a point farther north than any ship to date. From here he despatched man-hauled sledge parties into the unknown: one west over Ellesmere Island; another east across Greenland; and a third north to the Pole. The sledgers and both ships' companies succumbed to scurvy, forcing Nares to return in 1876, a year before schedule. He summed up his ordeal in a terse cable:* NORTH POLE IMPRACTICABLE. *He was roundly castigated for his failure – even though one of his lieutenants, Albert Markham, had reached a northernmost record of 83° 20°. After almost one hundred years of involvement, this was the British government's last official expedition to the Arctic.*

NARES'S SLEDGE EXPEDITIONS WERE ALL HARROWING BUT THAT ACROSS GREENLAND UNDER LT LEWIS BEAUMONT, WAS POSSIBLY THE WORST.

The travelling [became] worse and worse, the snow varied from two-and-a half to four-and-a-half feet in thickness, and was no longer crisp and dry, but of the consistency of moist sugar; walking was most exhausting, one literally had to climb out of the holes made by each foot in succession, the hard crust on the top, which would only just not bear you, as well as the depth of the snow preventing you from pushing forward through it, each leg sank to about three inches above the knee, and the effort of lifting them so high to extricate them from their tight-fitting holes, soon began to tell upon the men. William Jenkins, Peter Craig, and Charles Paul complained of stiffness in the hamstrings, and all of us were very tired...Our next march was made under a hot sun, through snow never less than three feet thick; we were parched with thirst, and obliged to halt every fifty yards to recover breath

The shore for which we were making did not seem more than two miles off, so I went ahead to see if the travelling was better under the cliffs. I got about a mile and-a-half ahead of the sledge in three hours, and then gave it up. I was nearly done...In the meantime the men had been struggling on as best they could, sometimes dragging the sledge on their hands and knees to relieve their aching legs, or hauling her ahead with a long rope and standing pulls. When we encamped we had hardly done two miles, and Jones was added to the list of the stiff-legged ones.

The next march, May 19th, they could hardly bend their legs. We tried every kind of expedient...[but] at last went back to the usual way, and tugged and gasped on, resting at every ten or twelve yards. In my journal I find this entry for the day: 'Nobody will ever believe what hard work this becomes on the fourth day; but this may give them some idea of it. When halted for lunch, two of the men crawled for 200 yards on their hands and knees, rather than walk unneccessarily through this awful snow; but although tired, stiff, and sore, there is not a word of complaint; they are cheerful, hopeful, and determined. Since twelve o'clock it has been my bithday; but I can safely say I never spent one so before, and I don't want to be wished any happy returns of it.' That march we did not make much over a mile. Everyone was very tired with the unusual exertions of the last few

days, and the work was pain and grief to those with stiff legs. Matters did not look promising at all...We went on for two days, until going back seemed as hard work as going
on...We could not do two miles a-day, and the men were falling sick. I did not encourage
inspection of legs, and tried to make them think as little of the stiffness as possible, for
I knew the unpleasant truth would soon enough be forced upon us...

　　We started again on the evening of the 19th, and worked away as before; but our
progress was ridiculously small...[On the 21st] I now saw to my great disappointment
that...it would be useless to advance any farther...two men, J. Craig and Wm. Jenkins
[were] unmistakably scurvy-stricken...I therefore decided to wait where we were, if necessary, for two days, in hopes of being able to ascend a high peak just over the glacier...
It seemed too cruel to have to turn back after such hard work, without reaching the land
or seeing anything, and I was pleased and encouraged by the anxiety the men showed to
make the end of our expedition more successful. But it was not to be. May 21st –
it snowed hard all day; May 22nd – the same; and a strict survey of the provisions warned
us that we must start homewards...We once more started, making for Cape Fulford; the
gloomy and unfavourable weather had a depressing influence on the men's spirits, who,
poor fellows, were already rather desponding, for out of seven only Gray and myself were
perfectly free from scorbutic symptoms...

　　Quite a foot of snow had fallen...and it was rotting the old crust underneath, which
gave way under the weight of sledge and men, and made the sledge seem a ton in

Four lantern slides offer a glimpse of life in the Arctic. Top left: a scene from the weekly 'Arctic Theatre', one of the many entertainments that Nares devised to prevent the Alert's *crew from succumbing to depression during the sunless winter. Top right: a sledge party struggles with the weight of a frostbitten and scorbutic casualty. Bottom left: sledgers in harness navigate a labyrinth of ice hummocks. Bottom right: the rugged land-scape of what Nares dubbed Palaeocrystic Ice, a field of ridges so unyielding that he could only surmise it had been formed in prehistoric times.*

weight...We gradually retraced our steps until the mornng of the 3rd of June. Up to this time the weather had been one continuous snow-fall with thick fogs; the sun once or twice came out for an hour or so and then the snow fell again. The sick were getting worse steadily...neither Paul nor Jenkins could keep up with the sledge, but crawled along after it...Craig was very bad...Dobing and Jones were getting stiffer and stiffer...Gray and myself were the only sound ones left. The sick scarcely ate anything; they could not sleep or lie still...

We started again in the evening, and had not gone ten yards before Paul fell down quite powerless, and from that time until the end he was like one paralysed, his legs were so completely useless to him. Jenkins still crawled along, but his time was drawing near, and on the 7th he took his place alongside Paul on the sledge...[On the 11th] Dobing broke down altogether, and Jones felt so bad he did not think he could walk much longer. Poor fellows!...This was our darkest day. We were forty miles off Polaris Bay at the very least, and only Gray and myself to drag the sledges and the sick – the thing did not seem possible. However, it was clear that we must take all the provisions, and then push on as long and as far as we could...

Craig now could barely walk, but his courage did not fail. Dobing became rapidly worse, but fortunately Jones revived, and there were still three on the drag-ropes. We toiled painfully through McCormick Pass, a very hard road, all rocks and water, but very little snow. The work towards the end became excessively severe on account of the narrowness and steepness of the passes. The sledge had to be unloaded and the sick lowered down separately in the sail...We were travelling very slowly now, for Craig, who had held out so long, could scarcely stand, and he and Dobing had to be waited for constantly.

On the 21st. of June...we managed to pitch the tent after an hour's hard work. We put the sick in, and tried to make them comfortable; but the tent was badly pitched, and the squalls from the cliffs, more like whirlwinds, sometimes made the two sides meet in the middle. We were all huddled up in a heap, wet through, and nobody could sleep...[On the 22nd] for the first time I felt the scurvy pains in my legs. Craig and Dobing almost dragged themselves along, their breath failing entirely at every ten yards...it was painful to watch them. We were a long way from Polaris Bay still, and I did not see how we were to reach it under the circumstances. On the 23rd of June it became necessary to carry both Dobing and Craig, to enable us to advance at all...

On the evening of the 24th...finding that Jones and Gray were scarcely able to pull, I had determined to reach the shore at the plain, pitch the tent, and walk over by myself to Polaris Bay to see if there was anyone there to help us; if not, come back...remain with the sick and get them on as best I could. But I thank God it did not come to this, for as we were plodding along the now water-sodden floe towards the shore, I saw what turned out to be a dog-sledge and three men, and soon after had the pleasure of shaking hands with Lieutenant Rawson and Dr. Coppinger. Words cannot express the pleasure, relief, and gratitude we all felt at this timely meeting.

G. NARES, *A Voyage to the Polar Sea, Vol II, 1878.*

HENRY MORTON STANLEY 1841–1904
Congo journey

To HENRY MORTON STANLEY, *one of his top correspondents, James Gordon Bennett, millionaire proprietor of the New York* Herald, *said in 1869: 'I will tell you what you will do. Draw a thousand pounds now and when you have gone through that, draw another thousand, and when that is spent, draw another, and when you have finished that, draw another thousand and so on – BUT FIND LIVINGSTONE.' Stanley did as he was instructed, and in 1871 duly 'found' the missing explorer – who, far from needing assistance, gave him the first decent meal he had had in months – then briefly joined him in the exploration of Lake Tanganyika. Stanley was so impressed by Livingstone's example that he, too, became an African explorer. He treated it almost as a crusade: when Livingstone died he exhorted fellow Britons not to lose heart. 'Close up, boys! Close up!' he cried. 'Death must find us everywhere!' He led a series of expeditions across Africa, during one of which he not only circumnavigated Lake Victoria Nyanza but traced the Congo to its mouth. Later, he helped create King Leopold I of Belgium's notoriously vicious Congo Free State. Stanley's journeys were infamous for their belligerence – hundreds of Africans were killed on his Congo expedition – and for their arduous nature. He took pride in the fact that his native porters nicknamed him Bula Matari, 'Breaker of Stones'. (According to one historian, 'Breaker of Balls' would have been an even more apt description.) Undoubtedly an effective explorer, Stanley was at the same time one of the more brutal ambassadors of European imperialism.*

BY THE END OF HIS TRANS-CONTINENTAL EXPEDITION TO THE MOUTH OF THE CONGO, JOINTLY FUNDED BY THE NEW YORK HERALD AND BRITAIN'S DAILY TELEGRAPH, STANLEY HAD LOST ALL HIS WHITE COMPANIONS AND MORE THAN TWO-THIRDS OF THE 347 AFRICANS WITH WHOM HE HAD SET OUT. APPROACHING HIS DESTINATION, HE WROTE THE FOLLOWING LETTER.

Village of Nsanda, August 4, 1877,
To any Gentleman who speaks English at Embomma.

Dear Sir,

I have arrived at this place from Zanzibar with 115 souls, men, women, and children. We are now in a state of imminent starvation. We can buy nothing from the natives, for they laugh at our kinds of cloth, beads, and wire. There are no provisions in the country that may be purchased, except on market days, and starving people cannot afford to wait for these markets. I, therefore, have made bold to despatch three of my young men, natives of Zanzibar, with a boy named Robert Feruzi, of the English Mission at Zanzibar, with this letter, craving relief from you. I do not know you; but I am told there is an Englishman at Embomma, and as you are a Christian and a gentleman, I beg you not to disregard my request. The boy Robert will be better able to describe our lone condition than I can tell you in this letter. We are in a state of the greatest distress; but if your supplies arrive in time, I may be able to reach Embomma within four days. I want three hundred cloths, each four yards long, of such quality as you trade with, which is very different from what we have; but better

A portrait of Stanley before he left for Central Africa. When a similar photograph was taken on his return it showed a drawn and emaciated figure with a head of prematurely white hair. Although a successful explorer, Stanley was a complex and solitary character disliked by most. In his retirement a resentful sponsor sent a journalist to enquire whether he still beat his wife.

than all that would be ten or fifteen man-loads of rice or grain to fill their pinched bellies immediately, as even with the cloths it would require time to purchase food and starving people cannot wait. The supplies must arrive within two days, or I may have a fearful time of it among the dying. Of course I hold myself responsible for any expense you may incur in this business. What is wanted is immediate relief; and I pray you to use your utmost energies to forward it at once. For myself, if you have such little luxuries as tea, coffee, sugar, and biscuits by you, such as one man can easily carry, I beg you on my own behalf that you will send a small supply, and add to the great debt of gratitude due to you upon the timely arrival of supplies for my people. Until that time I beg you to believe me,

Yours sincerely.
H. M. Stanley, Commanding Anglo-American Expedition for Exploration of Africa.

P.S. You may not know me by name; I therefore add, I am the person who discovered Livingstone in 1871 – H. M. S.

H.M.STANLEY, *Through the Dark Continent, Vol. II, 1878.*

ISABELLA BIRD 1831–1904

An Englishwoman abroad

A SICKLY WOMAN, Bird was bedevilled by back trouble, insomnia and depression until, at the age of 40, she went to Australia and Hawaii. Her health improved miraculously. Thereafter she never looked back, travelling through America, Japan, Tibet, Korea, China, Persia and Afghanistan. Her exploits included climbing the world's largest volcano and crossing the Rockies alone in winter on horseback. She did not break new ground but covered the recently broken so redoubtably that, as one reviewer remarked, 'There was never anybody who had adventures as well as Miss Bird.' Her journals, which often took the form of letters to her sister, gave an intimate description of her experiences.

APPROACHING THE ROCKIES, BIRD DESCRIBES HOW SHE WAS STRUCK BY THE HARDSHIPS OF PIONEERING LIFE.

Great Platte Canyon, October 23. My letters on this tour will, I fear, be very dull, for after riding all day, looking after my pony, getting supper, hearing about various routes, and the pastoral, agricultural, mining and hunting gossip of the neighbourhood, I am so sleepy and wholesomely tired that I can hardly write...It is a dreary ride of thirty miles over the low brown plains to Denver, very little settled, and with trails going in all directions. My sailing orders were 'steer south, and keep to the best-beaten track,' and it seemed like embarking on the ocean without a compass. The rolling brown waves on which you see a horse a mile and a half off impress one strangely, and at noon the sky darkened up for another storm, the mountains swept down in blackness to the Plains, and the higher peaks took on a ghastly grimness horrible to behold. It was first very cold, then very hot, and finally settled down to a fierce east-windly cold, difficult to endure. It was free and breezy, however, and my horse was companionable. Sometimes herds of cattle were browsing on the sun-cured grass, then herds of horses. Occasionally, I met a horseman with a rifle lying across his saddle, or a waggon of the ordinary sort, but oftener I saw a waggon with a white tilt, of the kind known as a 'Prairie Schooner,' labouring across the grass, or a train of them, accompanied by herds, mules, and horsemen, bearing emigrants and their household goods in dreary exodus from the Western States to the much-vaunted prairies of Colorado. The host and hostess of one of these waggons invited me to join their mid-day meal, I providing tea (which they had not tasted for four weeks) and they hominy. They had been three months on the journey from Illinois, and their oxen were so lean and weak that they expected to be another month in reaching Wet Mountain Valley. They had buried a child en route, had lost several oxen, and were rather out of heart. Owing to their long isolation and the monotony of the march they had lost count of events, and seemed like people of another planet. They wanted me to join them, but their rate of travel was too slow, so we parted with mutual expressions of goodwill, and as their white tilt went 'hull down' in the distance on the lonely prairie sea, I felt sadder than I often feel on taking leave of old acquaintances. That night they must have been nearly frozen, camping out in the deep snow in the fierce wind. I met afterwards 2000 lean Texan cattle, herded by three wild-looking men on horseback, followed by two waggons containing women, children, and rifles. They had travelled 1000 miles. Then I saw two prairie wolves, like jackals, with gray fur, cowardly creatures, which fled from me with long leaps.

The windy cold became intense, and for the next eleven miles I rode a pace with the coming storm. At the top of every prairie roll I expected to see Denver, but it was not until five that from a considerable height I looked down upon the great 'City of the Plains,' the 'Metropolis of the Territories.' There the great braggart city lay spread out, brown and treeless, upon the brown and treeless plain, which seemed to nourish nothing but wormwood and the Spanish bayonet. The shallow Platte, shrivelled into a narrow stream with a shingly bed six times too large for it, and fringed by shrivelled cottonwood, wound along by Denver, and two miles up its course I saw a great sandstorm, which in a few minutes covered the city, blotting it out with a dense brown cloud. Then, with gusts of wind the snowstorm began...

    I. Bird, *A Lady's Life in the Rocky Mountains, 1879.*

FRIDTJOF NANSEN 1861–1930

Farthest North

Nansen reads a deep-sea thermometer from the Arctic Ocean. Although his goal of reaching the North Pole was not reached, the Fram's drift was of immeasurable benefit to science, providing information not only about the depth and shape of the Arctic floor but of currents and weather patterns in a zone that nobody had ever visited before.

IN 1888, NANSEN ABANDONED *his career as a neuroscientist in favour of polar exploration. That year he became the first man to traverse Greenland by ski; and between 1893 and 1896 he made a record-breaking journey across the Arctic pack. Hitherto, the great fear of all polar navigators had been that their ships would be crushed by the ice. Nansen therefore commissioned the* Fram, *an egg-shaped vessel that would bob to the surface when caught between floes. He put it into the pack off Siberia and let the currents carry it towards the Pole. The revolutionary design worked perfectly, allowing the* Fram *to slip from every nip the ice sent its way. At what he judged a suitable moment, Nansen left with a stoker named Hjalmar Johanssen for a dash by ski to the top of the world. They reached 86° 10°N before turning back for Franz Josef Land where, having eaten their dogs, they spent the winter in a stone hut that they named 'The Hole'. They had planned to paddle by kayak to Norway but were instead rescued by a British explorer, Frederick Jackson, who by pure chance happened to be in the region. 'I can positively state that not a million to one chance of Nansen reaching Europe existed', Jackson wrote, 'and, but for our finding him on the ice, as we did, the world would never have heard of him again.' The* Fram, *meanwhile, continued its drift through the pack until it reached Spitsbergen. The crew fell ashore and let the pebbles spill through their hands. They had not seen a stone for four years. Carefully planned, daringly executed, of enormous scientific benefit and (unusually) involving no loss of life, the expedition was a text-book example of its kind. A man of many parts, Nansen was later awarded the Nobel Peace Prize for repatriating refugees after World War One.*

ABOARD THE FRAM.

Tuesday, November 28th [1893]...I went on deck this evening in rather a gloomy frame of mind, but was nailed to the spot the moment I got outside. There is the supernatural for you – the northern lights flashing in matchless power and beauty over the sky in all the colours of the rainbow! Seldom or never have I seen the colours so brilliant. The prevailing one at first was yellow, but that gradually flickered over into green, and then a sparkling ruby-red began to show at the bottom of the rays on the under side of the arch, soon spreading over the whole arch. And now from the far-away western horizon a fiery serpent writhing itself up over the sky, shining brighter and brighter as it came. It split into three, all brilliantly glittering. Then the colours changed. The serpent to the south turned almost ruby-red with spots of yellow; the one in the middle, yellow; and the one to the north, greenish-white. Sheafs of rays swept along the sides of the serpents, driven through the ether-like waves before a storm-wind. They sway backwards and forwards, now strong, now fainter again. The serpents reached and passed the zenith. Though I was thinly dressed and shivering with cold, I could not tear myself away till the spectacle was over, and only a faintly-glowing fiery serpent near the western horizon showed where it had begun. When I came on deck later the masses of light had passed northwards, and spread themselves in incomplete arches over the northern sky. If one wants to read mystic meanings into the phenomena of nature, here, surely, is the opportunity...

Thursday, November 30th [1893]...The lead showed a depth of exactly 93 fathoms

(170m.) to-day, and it seemed by the line as if we were drifting north-west. We are almost certainly further north now; hopes are rising, and life is looking brighter again. My spirits are like a pendulum...giving all sorts of irregular swings backwards and forwards. It is no good trying to take the thing philosophically; I cannot deny that the question whether we are to return successful or unsuccessful affects me very deeply. It is quite easy to convince myself with the most incontrovertible reasoning that what really matters is to carry through the expedition, whether successful or not, and get safe home again. I could not but undertake it; for my plan was one that I felt must succeed, and therefore it was my duty to try it. Well, if it does not succeed, is that my affair? I have done my duty, done all that could be done, and can return home with an easy conscience to the quiet happiness I have left behind. What can it matter whether chance, or whatever name you like to give it, does or does not allow the plan to succeed and make our names immortal? The worth of the plan is the same whether chance smiles or frowns upon it. And as to immortality, happiness is all we want, and that is not to be had here.

Supremely self-absorbed in the summer of 1894, Nansen smokes his pipe and contemplates the ice during the long drift across the Arctic pack. A man of action he rapidly became bored. 'Can't something happen?' he complained. 'Could not a hurricane come and tear up this ice and set it rolling in high waves like the open sea?' The laundry line of dog and bear pelts suggests that nothing had happened for a long while. At the outset, however, the prospect of danger had appealed. 'We are like tiny dwarfs in a struggle with Titans', he wrote, 'one must save oneself with cunning and ingenuity if one is to escape from this giant fist that rarely lets go what it has seized.'

Johanssen takes the strain on an ice ridge. On their last lap he and Nansen had only one dog apiece – the rest had been eaten. 'It was undeniable cruelty to the poor animals from start to finish', he wrote, 'and one must often look back on it with horror. When I think of all those splendid animals, toiling for us without a murmur, as long as they could strain a muscle, never getting any thanks or even so much as a kind word, daily writhing under the lash until the time came when they could do no more and death freed them from their pains, I have moments of bitter self-reproach.'

I can say all this to myself a thousand times; I can bring myself to believe honestly that it is all a matter of indifference to me; but none the less my spirits change like the clouds of heaven according as the wind blows from this direction or from that, or the soundings show the depth to be increasing or not, or the observations show a northerly or southerly drift. When I think of the many that trust us, think of Norway, think of all the friends that gave us their time, their faith, and their money, the wish comes that they may not be disappointed, and I grow sombre when our progress is not what we expected it to be. And she [his wife] that gave most - does she deserve that her sacrifice should have been made in vain? Ah, yes, we must and will succeed!

F. NANSEN, *Farthest North, Vol II, 1897.*

IN 'THE HOLE'.

Wednesday, January 1st, 1896 [in the 'Hut'] – 41.5°C (42.2° below zero Fahr.). So a new year has come, the year of joy and home-coming. In bright moonlight 1895 departed, and in bright moonlight 1896 begins; but it is bitterly cold, the coldest days we have yet known here. I felt it, too yesterday, when all my finger-tips were frost-bitten. I thought I had done with all that last spring...

Wednesday, January 8th. Last night the wind blew the sledge to which our thermometer was hanging over the slope. Stormy weather outside – furious weather, almost taking away your breath if you put your head out. We lie here trying to sleep – sleep the time away. But we cannot always do it. Oh, those long sleepless nights when you turn from side to side, kick your feet to put a little warmth into them, and wish for only one

thing in the world – sleep! The thoughts are constantly busy with everything at home, but the long, heavy body lies here trying in vain to find an endurable position among the rough stones. However, time crawls on, and now little Liv's birthday has come. She is three years old to-day, and must be a big girl now. Poor little thing! You don't miss your father now; and next birthday I shall be with you, I hope. What good friends we shall be! You shall ride-a-cock-horse, and I will tell you stories from the north about bears, foxes, walruses, and all the strange animals up there in the ice. No, I can't bear to think of it.

Sunday, February 1st. Here I am down with rheumatism. Outside it is gradually growing lighter day by day, the sky above the glaciers in the south grows redder, until at last one day the sun will rise above the crest, and our last winter night will be past. Spring is coming! I have often thought spring sad. Was it because it vanished so quickly, because it carried promises that summer never fulfilled? But there is no sadness in this spring; its promises will be kept; it would be too cruel if they were not.

Farthest North, Vol II, 1897.

OF THE SAME PERIOD IN 'THE HOLE' NANSEN LATER WROTE:

How we longed for a change in the uniformity of our diet. If only we could have had a little sugar and farinaceous food, in addition to all the excellent meat we had, we could have lived like princes...But better even than food would be clean clothes we could put on. And then books – only to think of books! Ugh, the clothes we lived in were horrible! and when we wanted to enjoy a really delightful hour we would set to work imagining a great, bright, clean shop, where the walls were hung with nothing but new, clean, soft, wollen

Otto Sverdrup aboard the Fram. *Following Nansen's departure, Sverdrup took command of the ship – a duty that he fulfilled admirably, commanding the respect of all his men. 'Your duty...is to bring home in the safest possible way the human beings hereby confined to your care, and not to expose them to any unnecessary danger, either for the sake of the ship and its contents, or the outcome of the expedition', Nansen instructed. Having brought the* Fram *safely home Sverdrup took it in 1898 to Greenland on an expedition that mapped 673,400 square kilometres of unexplored territory.*

clothes, from which we could pick out everything we wanted. Only to think of shirts, vests, drawers, soft and warm woollen trousers, deliciously comfortable jerseys, and then clean woollen stockings and warm felt slippers – could anything more delightful be imagined? And then a Turkish bath! We would sit up side by side in our sleeping bag for hours at a time, and talk of all these things. They seemed almost unimaginable. Fancy being able to throw away all the heavy, oily rags we had to live in, glued as they were to our bodies. Our legs suffered most; for there our trousers stuck fast to our knees, so that when we moved they abraded and tore the skin inside our thighs till it was all raw and bleeding. I had the greatest difficulty in keeping these sores from becoming altogether too ingrained with fat and dirt, and had to be perpetually washing them with moss, or a rag from one of the bandages in our medicine-bag, and a little water, which I warmed in a cup over the lamp. I have never before understood what a magnificent invention soap really is. We made all sorts of attempts to wash the worst of the dirt away; but they were all equally unsuccessful. Water had no effect upon all this grease; it was better to scour oneself with moss and sand. We could find plenty of sand in the walls of the hut, when we hacked the ice off them. The best method, however, was to get our hands thoroughly lubricated with warm bears' blood and train-oil, and then scrub it off again with moss. They thus became as white and soft as the hands of the most delicate lady, and we could scarcely believe that they belonged to our own bodies. When there was none of this toilet preparation to be had, we found the next best plan was to scrape our skin with a knife.

If it was difficult to get our own bodies clean, it was a sheer impossibility as regards our clothes. We tried all possible ways; we washed them both in Eskimo fashion and in our own; but neither was of much avail. We boiled our shirts in the pot hour after hour, but took them out only to find them just as full of grease as when we put them in. Then we took to wringing the train-oil out of them. This was a little better; but the only thing that produced any real effect was to boil them, and then scrape them with a knife while they were still warm. By holding them in our teeth and our left hand and stretching them out, while we scraped them all over with the right hand, we managed to get amazing quantities of fat out of them; and we could almost have believed they were quite clean when we put them on again after they were dry. The fat which we scraped off was, of course, a welcome addition to our fuel.

Farthest North, Vol II, 1897.

Equipped with an accordion and dark glasses the crew of the Fram *look like a group of blind beggars. In reality they were well provisioned – there was even a library of six hundred books on board – and all energy needs were supplied by a windmill. The crew's main problems were feelings of* boredom, isolation and shifting moods, often dictated by the drift. 'You cannot conceive how fed up we are with each other', Scott Hansen commented on the third winter onboard. 'It has got to the point where we can hardly stand the sight of each other.' When they reached Spitsbergen in June 1896 one observer remarked, 'It was like a dream to see these men, who have spent 3 long years on this ship...It is strange, moving, magnificent. [The ship] seems almost sacred', wrote one observer. All discord forgotten, the crew played with the stones on the beach in child-like joy at being back on land.

FRANCIS YOUNGHUSBAND 1863–1942
Tales from Tibet

YOUNGHUSBAND WAS AN EXOTIC *mix of soldier, spy mountaineer and mystic. Stationed on the northern border of India, he made several journeys into Afghanistan before venturing across the Himalayas to the Gobi and lands beyond. Militarily, his most notorious hour came in 1903 when he led a British force on a bloody conquest of Tibet. In the field of discovery, however, he is best remembered for his persistent exploration of Central Asia and for making one of the first attempts to conquer Mount Everest. Deeply moved by his experiences, he retired from active service in 1910 to pursue a more spiritual life, and in 1936 founded the World Congress of Faiths to promote greater accord between the major religions.*

CROSSING THE HIMALAYAS IN 1887 – AN EXPERIENCE THAT YOUNGHUSBAND LATER DESCRIBED AS HIS 'BAPTISM OF FEAR'.

At the first dawn of day on the following morning we were astir. The small stream was frozen, and the air bitingly cold; so we hurried about loading up, had a good breakfast, and, as the sun rose, started off straight at the mountain wall - a regular battlement of rocky peaks covered with snow, where it was possible, but for the most part too steep for snow to lie. After travelling for three or four miles, a valley suddenly opened up to the left. The guide immediately remembered it, and said that up it was an easy pass which would completely outflank the mountain barrier. The going was good. I left the ponies, and in my eagerness hurried on rapidly in front of them, straining to see the top of the pass, and the 'other side' - that will-o'-the-wisp which ever attracts explorers and never satisfies them, for there is ever another side beyond. The height was beginning to tell, and the pass seemed to recede the nearer I approached it. One rise after another I surmounted, thinking it would prove the summit, but there was always another beyond...At length, I reached a small lake, about a quarter of a mile in length, and a small rise above it at the further end was the summit of the pass. I rushed up it, and there before me lay the 'other side,' and surely no view which man has ever seen can excel that. To describe the scene in words would be impossible. There are no words with which to do so, and to attempt it with those that are at our disposal would but stain its simple grandeur and magnificence.

Before me rose tier after tier of stately mountains, among the highest in the world - peaks of untainted snow, whose summits reached to heights of twenty-five thousand, twenty-six thousand, and, in one supreme case, twenty-eight thousand feet above sea-level. There was this wonderful array of mountain majesty set out before me across a deep rock-bound valley, and away in the distance, filling up the head of this, could be seen a vast glacier, the outpourings of the mountain masses which gave it birth. It was a scene which, as I viewed it, and realized that this seemingly impregnable array must be passed and overcome, seemed to put the iron into my soul and stiffen all my energies for the task before me.

Buried in the stirring feelings to which such a scene gives rise, I sat there for more than an hour, till the caravan arrived, and then we slowly descended from the pass into the valley bottom at our feet. The way was rough and steep, but we reached the banks of the river without any serious difficulty. Here, however, we were brought to a standstill, for

there was a sheer cliff of a couple of hundred feet or so in height running far away on either side along the river's edge. This at first seemed a serious obstacle, but I had noticed on the way down some tracks of kyang (wild asses), and as there was no water above, I knew that these animals must get down to the river to drink some way or other, and that where they could go we could go also. I therefore went back to these tracks, carefully followed them up, and was relieved to find they led down a practicable 'shoot' in the cliff. It was very steep and rocky, but by unloading the ponies, and putting one man on to lead each in front and two others to hold on to the tail behind, we managed to let the ponies down one by one, and after a good deal of labour found ourselves, bag and baggage, on the edge of a river...On either bank the mountains rose very steeply out of the valley, and were quite barren, except for a small growth of the hardy wormwood. There were no trees, and shrubs or bushes were only to be found in small patches along the river-bed.

Next day we continued down the valley of the Oprang (Shaksgam) River till we came to another, which my Baltis called the Sarpo Laggo, flowing down from the main range and joining it on the left bank. This we ascended till we reached a patch of jungle called Suget Jangal. Just before arriving there I chanced to look up rather suddenly, and a sight met my eyes which fairly staggered me. We had just turned a corner which brought into view, on the left hand, a peak of appalling height, which could be none other than K.2, 28,278 feet in height, second only to Mount Everest. Viewed from this direction, it appeared to rise in an almost perfect cone, but to an inconceivable height. We were quite close under it – perhaps not a dozen miles from its summit – and here on the northern

A pair of dishevelled
yak drivers shiver
cheerfully on the high
Tibetan plateau. Unlike
many explorers,
Younghusband had a
great affection and
respect for the locals
who assisted him in
his travels. "Evil is the
superficial, goodness
the fundamental
characteristic of the
world; affection and not
animosity the root
disposition of men
towards one another,'
ran his dictum. 'Men
are inherently good not
inherently wicked.'

side, where it is literally clothed in glacier, there must have been from fourteen to sixteen thousand feet of solid ice. It was one of those sights which impress a man for ever, and produce a permanent effect upon the mind – a lasting sense of the greatness and grandeur of Nature's works - which he can never lose or forget...

ON THE PERILOUS, 6000-METRE MUSTAGH PASS.

The ascent was easy enough, leading over smooth snow, but we went very slowly on account of the difficulty of breathing. On reaching the summit we looked about for a way down, but there was nothing but a sheer precipice, and blocks of ice broken and tumbled about in such a way as to be quite impracticable.

I freely confess that I myself could never have attempted the descent, and that I – an Englishman – was afraid to go first...Luckily my guides were better plucked than myself, and, tying a rope around the leading man's waist, the rest of us hung on while he hewed steps down to the precipice.

Step by step we advanced across it, all the time facing the precipice, and knowing that if we slipped (and the ice was very slippery) we should all roll down the icy slope and over the precipice into eternity. Halfway across, my Ladaki servant, whom Colonel Bell had sent back to me as a man thoroughly acquainted with Himalayan travel, turned back saying he was trembling all over and could not face the precipice. It rather upset me seeing a hill-man so affected; but I pretended not to care a bit, and laughed it off, pour encourager les autres, as the thing had to be done.

After a time, and a very nasty time it was, we reached terra firma in the shape of a large projecting shelf of rock, and from there began the descent of the precipice. The icy slope was a perfect joke to this. We let ourselves down very gradually from any little ledge or projecting piece of rock. On getting halfway down, I heard my Ladaki servant appealing to me from above. He had mustered up courage to cross the icy slope, and had descended the precipice for a few steps, and was now squatting on a rock salaaming profusely to me with both hands, and saying he dare not move another step, and that he would go back and take my ponies by Ladak. So I sent him back.

For six hours we descended the precipice, partly rock and partly icy slope, and when I reached the bottom and looked back, it seemed utterly impossible that any man could have come down such a place.

For several hours after we trudged on in the moonlight over the snow, with crevasses every fifty yards or so. Often we fell in, but had no accident; and at last, late at night, we reached a dry spot, and I spread out my rugs behind a rock while one of my men made a small fire of some dry grass and a couple of alpenstocks broken up to cook tea by. After eating some biscuits with the tea, I rolled myself up in my sheepskin and slept as soundly as ever I did.

F. YOUNGHUSBAND, *The Heart of a Continent, 1896.*

SVEN HEDIN 1865–1952
Adventures in Central Asia

BY THE DAWN *of the 20th century, Hedin had established himself as a ruthlessly competent explorer of Central Asia. He seemed to take pride in exposing himself and his companions to dreadful hardships – indeed, to enlist in some Hedin projects was an almost certain guarantee of death. Reviled for his support of Germany in both the First and Second World Wars, he nevertheless won praise from even his harshest critics – as, for example, when in 1927, aged 62, he led an expedition to Inner Mongolia. 'For six years this amazing man beyond middle age directed the work of an international team of specialists in the field', wrote one man. 'Not content with this, he carried out for the Nanking Government a survey of the ancient Silk Road...Then he went home and spent the next twelve years, in spite of increasing blindness, writing up and editing the results in three large quarto volumes.' By the time of his death he was regarded with awe and distaste in equal measure.*

IN 1908 HEDIN MADE AN EXPEDITION TO CROSS THE UNEXPLORED SECTIONS OF TIBET. On January 24 the whole country was covered with dazzling snow and the sun shone, but a stormy blast drove the fine snow particles in streaks over the land, and a roaring sound was heard. Antelopes careered lightly over the ground, dark against the white snow. A mule died on the way; not even Tibetan mules can bear this climate. I was benumbed and half-dead with cold before I reached the camp.

After a temperature of −21.3° the neighbourhood was enveloped in semi-darkness by heavy clouds. The jagged mountains to the south reminded me of a squadron of armoured vessels at gunnery practice in rainy weather. Their grey outlines peeped out from the low clouds. The valley was about 6 miles broad. Towards the east the snow lay less thickly, and finally only the footprints of wild animals were filled with snow, like a string of pearls in the dark ground.

As I turn over the leaves of my diary of this terrible journey how often I come across the remark that this was the hardest day we had hitherto experienced. And yet days were always coming when we suffered still more. So it was on January 26. The sky was covered with such compact clouds that we might fancy we were riding under a prison vault. The storm raged with undiminished violence, and a quarter of an hour after I had mounted my horse I was benumbed and powerless. My hands ached, and I tried to thaw my right hand by breathing on it whenever I had to take a note, but after reading the compass for two seconds my hands lost all feeling. My feet troubled me less, for I had no feeling at all in them. I only hoped I should reach the camp before the blood froze in my veins...

[Jan. 27] It snowed thickly all day. It was warm and comfortable under cover, and we pitied the poor animals which were out grazing in the cold...A sheep was slaughtered.

At night the cold was more severe again, and the thermometer sank to −30.3°. The sick mule sought shelter behind the men's tent, lay down at once and gave vent to a piteous sound. I went out to look at it, and caused it to be put out of its misery.

On the morning of the 28th we found two horses dead on the grass...We now had only twenty-three animals left, and my small white Ladaki was the last of the veterans. Little I thought, as he carried me over the Chang-lung-yogma, that he would survive a hundred

and fifty comrades. Every morning two long icicles hung down from his nostrils. He was taken great care of, and I always saved a piece bread from my breakfast for him. I had a particular affection for him and for Brown Puppy. They had been with me so long and had passed through so many adventures.

A loss of three animals in one day was serious for such a caravan as ours. How would it all end? We had still an immense distance before us. We struggled for three hours with halting steps up this terrible pass which had a height of 18,281 feet. We encamped in the shelter of a rock and killed the last worn-out sheep, and then had no live store of meat.

The temperature fell to −24.5°, and the first sound I heard on the morning of the 29th was the everlasting howl of the storm. We marched south-eastwards through snow a foot deep. 'One of our worst days,' it is styled in my diary. We cared about nothing except to get to our camp alive. I had a scarf wound several times over my face, but it was quickly turned into a sheet of ice, which cracked when I turned my head. I tried to smoke a cigarette, but it froze on my lips. Two horses died on the way…

Abdul Kerim came into my tent very cast down and asked if we should fall in with nomads within ten days, for otherwise he considered our condition desperate. In truth, I could give him no consolation, but could only tell him that we must go on as long as there was a single mule left, and then try to drag ourselves along with the nomads with as much food as we could carry. Now we thought no longer of pursuers behind, or of dangers before us, but only wished to preserve our lives and come to country where we could find means of substinence. Behind us the white snow obliterated our tracks and the future awaited us with its impenetrable secrets.

The storm howled round us all night long, and our thin tent canvas fluttered in the blast...This day, January 30, we had to keep together, for the driving snow obliterated the tracks immediately...A brown horse which carried no burden lay down and died in the snow. We could see the snow making ready its grave before it was cold. It vanished behind us in the dreadful solitude.

We move forwards at a very slow pace through the snowdrifts. The fury of the storm carries away the warning shouts from the lips of the guides and they do not reach our ears; we simply follow the trail. Lobsang goes first, and he often disappears in the dry loose snow and has to seek another direction. In the hollows the snow lies 3 feet deep, and we can only take one step at a time after the spades have cut us a ditch through the snow. One or other of the animals is always falling, and the removal of his load and readjusting it causes a block, for all must follow in the same furrow. All, men and animals, are half-dead with fatigue and labour for breath. The snow sweeps round in suffocating wreaths; we turn our backs to the wind and lean forwards. Only the nearest mules are plainly visible, the fifth is indistinct amidst the universal whiteness. I cannot catch a glimpse of the guides. Thus the troop passes on a few steps till it comes to the next block, and when the mule immediately in front of me moves on again it is only to plunge into a hollow filled with snow, where two men wait to keep up its load. The direction is now east and the ground rises. A few such days and the caravan will be lost.

S. HEDIN, *Trans-Himalaya: Discoveries and Adventures in Tibet, 1909.*

A mountain camp in Tibet, 1899-1902. 'The whole of Asia was open before me', he wrote at the start of his career. 'I felt I had been called to make discoveries without limits – they just waited for me in the middle of the deserts and the mountain peaks.'

DUKE OF ABRUZZI 1873–1933

A voyage in the Arctic Sea

An ice shelter at the northermost tip of Franz Josef Land from where Abruzzi's men kept look-out in case Cagni needed help on his way back from the Pole. In fact, the wind and currents drove Cagni so far to the west that he almost missed Franz Josef Land altogether. 'In seven days of severe toil we have not advanced three feet to the east', he wrote in a moment of despair. 'What will become of us?' When, by a combination of luck and perseverance Cagni eventually worked his way back to the Stella Polare from the south, Abruzzi was shocked by the sight: 'The sledges that remained had been mended with pieces of other sledges. All that was left of their cooking equipment was the outer covering of the stove...The Primus lamp had been replaced by a lamp in which dog's grease had been burned for the last few weeks. The sleeping bags had been thrown away, and only the thick canvas lining kept. Their clothes were in rags.'

THE DUKE OF ABRUZZI, *cousin to the king of italy, was the 19th century's outstanding (if not only) royal explorer. He travelled to Alaska, Africa and Asia but his most famous exploit was a record-breaking attempt at the North Pole in 1899. Inspired by Nansen's journey, he took the* Stella Polare *to Franz Josef Land from where he hoped to make a dash by dog sled across the Arctic pack. Unfortunately, frostbite forced him to cede command of the polar group to an old mountaineering friend, Captain Umberto Cagni. Accompanied by support teams, who hauled food and fuel to prearranged distances before turning back, Cagni reached a farthest north of 86° 32°. On the return journey, however, the drifting pack carried him off course and it was only by superhuman effort that he and his three companions regained Franz Josef Land. One of his support parties, meanwhile, did not return at all, having fallen through the ice.*

CAGNI ESTABLISHES A NEW FARTHEST NORTH.

Saturday, April 21st. – Our dreams and hopes, which two days ago were still very uncertain, rise again full of life and brilliancy, and fill us with a joy never before experienced in these regions of suffering and desolation!...We are at 85° 29°...the fact excites enthusiasm in all of us, but especially in Fenoillet, who is usually very undemonstrative...As we advance, the snow becomes harder; the dogs never went so well as they are going to-day; and we proceed rapidly, at the double, without any incident, until six. We perspire, although we have had our anorakers off since morning...

Very naturally, the idea of returning does not enter my mind, but it is only just that I should mention it to my companions, whose life, closely connected with mine, is in my hands. After dinner I lay before them our present situation and my projects...

'We have still provisions for thirty days, which, by reducing the rations, may suffice for forty-four – that is to say, until the end of May. Now, with six or seven days' marching like yesterday and the day before yesterday, we might obtain, if not complete success, at least a very satisfactory result. On the other hand, a prolongation of our march forward may expose us to great privations while returning, and perhaps even to serious danger if we were unfortunately overtaken by a snowstorm. The thirty miles which we have done in two days might not perhaps be travelled again in four, and if our return were slow, we should not only want provisions, but might be surprised by a thaw, an event which might prove fatal.

Having thus shown the arguments for and against making a final effort, I asked the men for their opinion. They cried out unanimously, 'Forward! Let us go on till we reach at least the 87th degree of latitude!'

Will God abandon us just at this moment? I am full of hope, and these three men, for whom I feel a sincere admiration, are as well.

Sunday, April 22nd. – We rose this morning at five, feeling a slight heaviness, as often happens after coming to an important decision. I reflected much last night, and [have decided] that I shall return as soon as I reach 86° 30°, even if I were to get there in a very few days. I have hardly come to that decision when I am assailed by a doubt; shall we reach even 86° 30°?...

We only stop at half-past seven; we must have done fully the thirteen miles which separated us from the 86th degree...We feel very nervous, in spite of our fatigue, and have reason to be; we speak of reaching 86° 16° to-morrow if the ice will allow us, and Nansen more than ever is the subject of conversation this evening...

Monday, April 23rd. – ...We resumed our march. I had never felt so weary. I could hardly stand; the dogs refused to go on and we had to beat them every minute. At half-past two we found a channel which we crossed [then] we sought for some shelter...and made our luncheon with coffee. The meridian altitude gave us 86° 4°. We still wanted ten miles to reach Nansen's farthest latitude, and in four hours at most we ought to be able to cover them. We resolved at all costs to attempt to reach 86°16° that evening...

The dogs seemed to have felt great relief from the short rest, and pulled willingly without stopping. I, too, was completely freed from the strange and sudden fatigue of this morning...Petigax and Fenoillet walked singly, about a hundred steps ahead of the convoy, which went on in silence, leaving behind it two furrows, which faded away in the distance. Every now and then I looked at the time; in spite of the rapidity of our march, we advance for more than an hour, or an hour and a half, without the briefest halt, the, after five minutes' rest, on again. Seven o'clock passed, eight o'clock passed, and still we went on...

[Having passed Nansen's farthest] We were astounded at our success. [Petigax and I] had not exchanged a word for several hours; I held out my hand to him and we clasped each other's warmly. I thanked him for all he had done to help me; I wished to tell him that the hand he clasped was that of a grateful friend, but I do not know what I said to him, nor do I know if he heard me. He replied, stammering, that he had only done his duty, but his voice, like mine, was choked by emotion and, as in mine, tears shone in his eyes.

'The flag!' I said to him...We searched hastily in the kayak for our little flag; tied it to a bamboo pole and I waved it to the cry of 'Long live Italy! Long live the King! Long live the Duke of the Abruzzi!' And to each of my cries the others answered with a shout which expressed all the exultation of their souls.

Resound on, sacred words, resound throughout these regions of pure and eternal ice, this sparkling gem! For never shall a conquest won by the sword, nor by the favours of fortune, adorn the Crown of the House of Savoy with one of greater lustre!

Tuesday, April 24th. – ... I decided yesterday evening that I would go on all day and to-morrow until noon; then take a meridian altitude, have our meal, and afterwards try by a single march to return to encamp in this place. I calculate that thus I shall certainly reach 86° 30°.

The men are pleased with my plan, though their eyes showed the desire they felt in their hearts of reaching the 87th degree. But I resist this general wish; I try to persuade all, including myself, that it is merely vanity to want to make up the round number...

[By 6.00 that evening, the ice had worsened considerably] We consider that we are in 86° 31° N. Lat., and if we did push forward on the ice, even for half a day, we would gain very few miles...The dogs are much tired, and we, too, feel the effects of yesterday's strain. I therefore consider that it is more prudent to definitively stop here...

We had a repetition of yesterday's feast, followed by a hearty toast to the Duke of the Abruzzi; while pronouncing it I feel agitated, and perceive that my emotion is strongly shared by my companions; after a short silence, our conversation begins again with an animation it never attained before under this poor, ragged tent. The idea which occurs most often, and amuses us most, is that of our arrival at the cabin – the surprise the Prince and our companions, who, after the details of our first march, must have lost all hope of our ever succeeding in doing anything, would feel. It is suggested that we should make a great placard, with a piece of the tent, and write upon it 86° 30°, so that they should see it from afar upon our arrival. We talk about our homes, and our return to our country. Oh, how the future smiles on us!

We go out into the open air. The thermometer indicates −35°; but,...we all remain outside for a long time, our minds enchanted by our great happiness. We have reached the end of all our fatigues; our return seems to us now like an excursion...The air is very clear...[far away] on the bright, horizon, in a chain from east to west, is a great azure wall, which from afar seems insurmountable. It is our 'Terrae ultima Thule'!...

Wednesday, April 25th. – I was not able to close my eyes last night, either on account of the cold or of my state of nervous excitement; and the men, also, slept little. We rose at seven; we ate only pemmican, and set to work to get the sledges ready...At eleven we have everything quite ready, and I take the meridian altitude...We are at 86° 32° N. Lat.

The convoy is ready to start; I photograph it, and give the signal of departure. Petigax goes forward, following the tracks made yesterday, and our hearts beat quickly as we take the first steps of our return to our country.

Abruzzi, L., *On the Polar Star in the Arctic Sea, Vol II, 1903.*

A member of Abruzzi's team paddles through the gloomy waters off Franz Josef Land. Abruzzi had hoped to alleviate the passage to the pole by attaching helium balloons to the sledges. In the end his plan came to nothing: the helium generator was required to pump the Stella Polare *dry after its hull had been punctured by ice. Instead, the polar party relied on trusted methods such as dogs and kayaks. Unlike other expeditions they did not use skis but ran alongside the sledges in finneskoes – felt boots from Lapland that were insulated with dried grass.*

ROBERT EDWIN PEARY 1856–1920

Nearest the Pole

HAVING LOST HIS FATHER *at the age of two, Peary developed an overpowering urge to prove himself. Aged thirty he wrote, 'Remember, mother, I must have fame, and I cannot reconcile myself to years of commonplace drudgery and a name late in life when I see an opportunity to gain it now and sip the delicious draught while I yet have youth and strength and capacity to enjoy it to its utmost...I want my fame now.' He turned his eye*

to the North Pole and, after several failed expeditions via Greenland and Ellesmere Island, reached it in 1909. 'The Pole at last!!!' he wrote. 'The prize of 3 centuries, my dream and ambition for 23 years. Mine at last.' Subsequent analyses have concluded that he falsified his readings and came, at best, within 96 kilometres of the Pole. Nevertheless, to have gone even that far, with the equipment available at the time, shows him to have been a remarkable man.

Peary's polar success depended upon the adoption of Eskimo survival techniques. He advocated the use of furs instead of woollens (the publicity picture of him, left, shows him in his travelling furs), dogs instead of man-hauling, the consumption of raw meat to keep scurvy at bay and the construction of igloos instead of tents. Indeed, it was only with the assistance of Eskimos that he made his great polar trip of 1909.

Like most Westerners of the time, Peary viewed the 'noble savage' through a prism of paternalism, laissez-faire capitalism and racism, to which he added a glint of home-grown eugenics. 'If colonisation is to be a success in the polar regions let white men take with them native wives', he wrote, 'then from this union may spring a race combining the hardiness of the mothers with the intelligence of the fathers. Such a race would surely reach the Pole if their fathers did not succeed in doing it.' In pursuit of this programme he fathered at least two mixed-race children.

ON 21 APRIL 1906 PEARY, HIS BLACK SERVANT MATTHEW HENSON, AND SIX ESKIMOS, REACHED A FARTHEST NORTH ON THE ARCTIC PACK OF 87°06°. THE RETURN WAS HAZARDOUS.

In the third march from Storm Camp we crossed the scar of the 'big lead'...where the edges of the 'big lead' had been driven together and had frozen fast. There was no mistaking it, and I foolishly allowed myself to be encouraged by the thought that this obstacle was at last behind us...I should have known better than to feel this way, for I certainly had sufficient Arctic experience to know that one should never feel encouraged at anything nor ever expect anything in these regions except the worst. On the second march south of the scar we came upon a region of huge pressure ridges running in every direction...and I was not surprised a few hours later when an Eskimo whom I had sent in advance to reconnoitre a trail for the sledges, signalled to me from the summit of a pinnacle 'open water.'...there was our friend the 'big lead,' a broad band of black water, perhaps half a mile in width...reaching east and west farther than I could see...

The next day we continued eastward and found a mixture of half-congealed rubble-ice, barely sufficient to support us, spanning the lead. The sledge were hurried on to this

and we were within a few yards of firm ice on the south side, when our bridge failed us, and the ice under us began to go apart. It was a rapid and uncertain but finally successful scramble to get back. We camped on a piece of big floe [where] we remained, drifting steadily eastward, warching the lead slowly widen...

Each day the number of my dogs dwindled and sledges were broken up to cook those of the animals that we ate ourselves. But here let me say that personally I have no objection whatever to dog, if only there is enough of it. Serious Arctic work quickly brings a man to consider quantity only in connection with the food question. One day leads formed entirely around the ice on which we were, making it an island of two or three miles' diameter.

Later, two Eskimo scouts...came hurrying back breathless, with the report that a few miles from camp there was a film of young ice extending clear across the lead - now something over two miles wide - which they thought might support us on snowshoes...It was evident to us all that now was our chance or never, and I gave the word to put on snowshoes and make the attempt. I tied mine on more carefully than I had ever done before. I think every man did the same, for we felt a slip or stumble would be fatal...

When we started it was with...the party abreast in widely extended skirmish line, fifty to sixty feet between each two men, some distance behind the sledge. We crossed in silence, each man busy with his thoughts and intent upon his snowshoes. Frankly I do not care for more similar experiences. Once started, we could not stop, we could not lift our snowshoes. It was a matter of constantly and smoothly gliding one past the other with utmost care and evenness of pressure, and from every man as he slid a snowshoe forward, undulations went out in every direction through the thin film incrusting the black water. The sledge was preceded and followed by a broad swell. It was the first and only time in all my Arctic work that I felt doubtful as to the outcome, but when near the middle of the lead the toe of my rear kamik as I slid forward from it broke through twice in succession, I thought to myself 'this is the finish,' and when a little later there was a cry from someone in the line, the words sprang from me of themselves: 'God help him, which one is it?' But I dared not take my eyes from the steady, even gliding of my snowshoes, and the fascination of the glassy swell at the toes of them.

When we stepped upon the firm ice of the southern side of the lead, the sighs of the two men nearest me in the line on either side were distinctly audible. I was more than glad myself...When we stood up from unfastening our snowshoes, and looked back for a moment before turning our faces southward, a narrow black ribbon cut the frail bridge on which we had crossed, in two. The lead was widening again and we had just made it.

The ice on the southern side of the lead was an awful mess...a hell of shattered ice as I had never seen before and hope never to see again, a conglomeration of fragments from the size of paving stones to literally and without exaggeration the dome of the Capitol, all rounded by the terrific grinding they had received between the jaws of the 'big lead' when its edges were together and shearing past each other. It did not seem as if anything not possessing wings could negotiate it...

During this march and the next and part of the next, we stumbled desperately southward through this frozen Hades, constantly falling and receiving numerous uncomfortable bruises. My uncushioned stumps seemed to catch it especially, and it is no exaggeration to say that at our first camp my jaws were actually aching from the viciousness with which I had repeatedly ground my teeth together during the march...

The land (when at last we saw it) seemed bewitched and appeared every night to move away from us as far as we had advanced the day before. Slowly, however, its detail sharp-

Peary had a predeliction for Eskimo studies – often nude, and often women. He titled this portrait 'Study in Bronze'. It has been suggested that the subject was probably of mixed Scandinavian and Eskimo parentage, the Danes having put Peary's eugenic theories to the test long before he ever came to Greenland.

ened, and I headed directly for the rolling bit of shore at Cape Neumeyer, where I was positive we would find a few hare and hoped that we might find musk-oxen round in Mascart Inlet.

Finally we dragged ourselves on to the ice-foot at Cape Neumeyer and inside of an hour had four hare, and very delicious they were, even though unassisted by such frills as salt or fire.

R. PEARY, *Nearest the Pole*, 1907.

Peary's wife Josephine accompanied him to Greenland in 1891, 1893 and 1900. She was unpopular with the men, who found her as dictatorial as Peary himself. 'I will never go home in the same ship as that man and that woman', wrote a participant in the 1891 expedition. (He did not have to: while crossing a glacier he vanished into a crevasse.) Their opinions did not deter her in the slightest: she was far more worried by the unhygienic conditions of camp life.

ROBERT PEARY ON JOSEPHINE PEARY.

She has been where no white woman has ever been, and where many a man has hesitated to go...I rarely, if ever, take up the thread of our Arctic experiences without reverting to two pictures: one is the first night we spent on the Greenland shore after the departure of the Kite, when in a little tent on the rocks – a tent which the furious wind threatened at every moment to carry away bodily, – she watched by my side as I lay a helpless cripple with a broken leg, our small party the only human beings upon that shore...Long afterward she told me that every unwonted sound set her heart beating with the thoughts of some hungry bear roaming along the shore...Yet she never gave a sign at the time of her fears, lest it disturb me.

The other picture is that of a scene perhaps a month or two later, when – myself still a cripple, but not entirely helpless – this same woman sat beside me in the stern of a boat, calmly reloading our empty firearms while a herd of infuriated walrus about us thrust their savage heads with gleaming tusks and bloodshot eyes out of the water close to the muzzles of our rifles, so that she could have touched them with her hand...I may perhaps be pardoned for saying that I never think of these two experiences without a thrill of pride and admiration for her pluck.

J. PEARY, *My Arctic Journal*, 1893.

JOSEPHINE PEARY ON LIVING CONDITIONS

Monday, December 21. The dark night is just half over; to-day is the shortest day. So far the time has not seemed very long, but I am afraid before we have had many more dark days we shall all think it long enough. I have done nothing yet toward celebrating Christmas, but I want to make some little thing for Mr. Peary. As far as the boys are concerned, I think an exceptionally good dinner will please them more than anything else I could give them. M'gipsu has made a pair of deerskin trousers for one of the boys, and has also completed a deerskin coat. She is now at work on a deerskin sleeping-bag, which is to be fastened about the neck of the occupant, over a fur hood with a shoulder cape, which I am endeavouring to fashion.

She is sitting on the floor in my room (an unusual honor), and her husband, Annowkah, comes in as often as he can find an excuse for doing so. He frequently rubs his face against hers, and they sniffle at each other; this takes the place of kissing. I should think they could smell each other without doing this, but they are probably so accustomed to the (to me) terrible odor that they fail to notice it.

Josephine Peary poses with an Eskimo family in 1891. Two years later, while in Greenland, she gave birth to a daughter, Marie Anhighito – at the time the northernmost born white child in history. The Eskimos came from miles around to marvel at the girl they called 'Snow Baby'. In 1900, however, Josephine had to endure a winter in the ice with Peary's pregnant Eskimo mistress. 'You will have been surprised, perhaps annoyed, to hear I came up on a ship', she wrote, 'but believe me had I known how things were with you I should not have come.'

I dislike very much to have the natives in my room, on account of their dirty condition, and especially as they are alive with parasites, of which I am in deadly fear, much to the amusement of our party. But it is impossible for the women to sew in the other room, where the boys are at work on their sledges and ski, so I allow two at a time to come into my room, taking good care that they do not get near the bed. At the end of their day's work, I take my little broom, which is an ordinary whisk attached to a hoe-handle, and sweep the room carefully. The boys have made brooms out of the wings of ducks and gulls, which are very satisfactory, there being only the bare floor to sweep; but I have a carpet on my floor, and the feather brooms make no impression on it, so I am compelled to use my litle whisk. It answers the purpose admirably, but it takes me twice as long as it would otherwise have done. After the room has been thoroughly swept, I sprinkle it with a solution of corrosive sublimate, given to me by the doctor, and in this way manage to keep entirely free from the pests. Both Mr. Peary and myself rub down with alcohol every night before retiring as a further protection against these horrible 'koomakshuey,' and we are amply repaid for our trouble.

My Arctic Journal.

FREDERIC COOK 1865–1940

The great Arctic fraud

By 1900, DR DOOK was a polar explorer of fame. He had accompanied Peary to the Arctic, had made independent voyages to Greenland, and had served on the 1898 Belgica expedition to the Antarctic – the first to winter in the southern ice – during which his ministrations prevented the entire crew dying of scurvy. No less an authority than Roald Amundsen described him as 'a man of unfaltering courage, unfailing hope, endless cheerfulness, and unwearied kindness...his ingenuity and enterprise were boundless.' Indeed, Amundsen declared that the Belgica's survival was due, 'first and foremost to the skill, energy and persistence of Dr Cook'. Then something went wrong. In 1906 Cook led an expedition to Mt McKinley, North America's highest mountain, and announced himself the first man to stand on its 6193-metre summit. Two years later he returned from a winter in the Arctic and said that he had been to the North Pole. Both claims were supported by photographic evidence – and in both cases, the photographs were shown to be fake. He had not been to either place. What is puzzling about Cook's deceptions is that he was genuinely capable. If he had not been to the Pole in 1908 he had definitely spent the winter somewhere in the Arctic and had done so without outside assistance, living solely off the land; and he had subsequently traversed the western coast of Greenland – a feat considered impossible even by the Eskimos.

He remained unrepentant to the last: 'I have been humiliated and seriously hurt. But that doesn't matter any more. I'm getting old, and what does matter to me is that I want you to believe that I told you the truth. I state emphatically that I, Frederick A. Cook, discovered the North Pole.' Many people still believe that he did.

COOK'S OVERBLOWN DESCRIPTION TELLS OF THE POLE HE NEVER REACHED.

As we lifted the midnight's sun to the plane of the midday sun, the shifting Polar desert became floored with a sparkling sheen of millions of diamonds, through which we fought a way to ulterior and greater glory.

Our leg cramps eased and our languid feet lifted buoyantly from the steady drag as the soul arose to effervescence. Fields of rich purple, lined with running liquid gold, burning with flashes of iridescent colors, gave a sense of gladness long absent from our weary life. The ice was much better. We still forced a way over large fields, small pressure areas and narrow leads. But, when success is in sight, most troubles seem lighter. We were thin, with faces burned, withered, frozen and torn in fissures, with clothes ugly from overwear. Yet men never felt more proud than we did, as we militantly strode off the last steps to the world's very top.

Camp was pitched early in the morning of April 20. The sun was northeast, the pack glowed in tones of lilac, the normal westerly air brushed our frosty faces. Our surprising bust of enthusiasm had been nursed to its limits. Under it a long march had been made on average ice, with the usual result of overpowering fatigue. Too tired and sleepy to wait for a cup of tea, we poured melted snow into our stomach and pounded the pemmican with an axe to ease the jaws. Our eyes closed before the meal was finished, and the world was lost to us for eight hours...

Late at night, after another long rest, we hitched the dogs and loaded the sleds. When action began, the feeling came that no time must be lost. Feverish impatience seized me.

Cook's summit picture of Mt McKinley was, in fact, not the summit at all but a far lower peak with a similar shape. Numerous members of the climbing party objected to the deception. Ironically, Peary was among those who at first refused to believe the rumours. 'Oh no, I don't think he would do that', he remarked. Later, however, he did not hesitate to label Cook an impostor when he claimed to have beaten him to the Pole. 'He has not been to the Pole on April 21st 1908, or at any other time', he said in a press statement. 'He has simply handed the public a gold brick.'

Cracking our whips, we bounded ahead. The boys sang. The dogs howled. Midnight of April 21 had just passed.

Over the sparkling snows the post-midnight sun glowed like at noon. I seemed to be walking in some splendid golden realms of dreamland. As we bounded onward the ice swam about me in circling rivers of gold.

E-tuk-i-shook and Ah-we-lah, though thin and ragged, had the dignity of heroes of a battle which had been fought through to success.

We all were lifted to the paradise of winners as we stepped over the snows of a destiny for which we had risked life and willingly suffered the tortures of an icy hell. The ice under us, the goal for centuries of brave, heroic men, to reach which many had suffered terribly and terribly died, seemed almost sacred. Constantly and carefully I watched my instruments in recording this final reach. Nearer and nearer they recorded our final approach. Step by step, my heart filled with a strange rapture of conquest.

At last we step over colored fields of sparkle, climbing walls of purple and gold - finally, under skies of crystal blue, with flaming clouds of glory, we touch the mark! The soul awakens to a definite triumph; there is sunrise within us, and all the world of night-darkened trouble fades. We are at the top of the world! The flag is flung to the frigid breezes of the North Pole!

F. Cook, *My Attainment of the Pole, 1911.*

HIRAM BINGHAM 1875–1956
The discovery of Machu Picchu

BORN IN HAWAII, *the son of a missionary, Bingham was fascinated by Humboldt's descriptions of South America. With large areas of the continent yet to be explored, he decided that this was a place in which he could make his reputation - or, as he put it, 'to work in claims not already staked out.' Having already been taught the basics of mountaineering by his father, he trained as an archaeologist, then engineered a position as curator of Harvard Library's 'South American Collection'. That the collection did not yet exist gave him the perfect excuse for creating it. In the course of several journeys to South America he became intrigued by rumours of Vilcabamba, the lost capital of the Incas, hidden so deep within the Peruvian Andes that the conquistadores had never been able to find it. Bingham, too, was unable to find it. But in 1911 he discovered something just as good: the remote, mountain-top city of Machu Picchu. It was the archaeological equivalent of El Dorado. Bingham continued to explore the Andes, but nothing could ever match Machu Picchu. He was still writing about it forty years later.*

THE DISCOVERY OF MACHU PICCHU.

Without the slightest expectation of finding anything more interesting than the ruins of two or three stone houses such as we had encountered at various places on the road between Ollantaytambo and Torontoy, I finally left the cool shade of the pleasant little hut and climbed further up the ridge and round a slight promontory. Melchor Arteaga had 'been there once before', so he decided to rest and gossip with Richarte and Alvarez. They sent a small boy with me as a 'guide'. The sergeant was in duty bound to follow, but I think he may have been a little curious to see what there was to see.

Hardly had we left the hut and rounded the promontory than we were confronted with

an unexpected sight, a great flight of beautifully constructed stone-faced terraces, perhaps a hundred of them, each hundreds of feet long and 10 feet high. They had been recently rescued from the jungle by the Indians. A veritable forest of large trees which had been growing on them for centuries had been chopped down and partly burned to make a clearing for agricultural purposes. The task was too great for the two Indians so the tree trunks had been allowed to lie as they fell and only the smaller branches removed. But the ancient soil, carefully put in place by the Incas, was still capable of producing rich crops of maize and potatoes.

However, there was nothing to be excited about. Similar flights of well-made terraces are to be seen in the upper Urubamba Valley at Pisac and Ollantaytambo, as well as opposite Torontoy. So we patiently followed the little guide along one of the widest terraces, where there had once been a small conduit, and made our way into an untouched forest beyond. Suddenly I found myself confronted with the walls of ruined houses built of the finest quality of Inca stonework. It was hard to see them for they were partly covered with trees and moss, the growth of centuries, but in the dense shadow, hiding in bamboo thickets and tangled vines, appeared here and there walls of white granite ashlars carefully cut and exquisitely fitted together. We scrambled along through the dense undergrowth, climbing over terrace walls and in bamboo thickets, where our guide found it easier going than I did. Suddenly, without any warning, under a huge overhanging ledge the boy showed me a cave beautifully lined with the finest cut stone. It had evidently been a royal mausoleum. On top of this particular ledge was a semicircular building whose outer wall, gently sloping and slightly curved, bore a striking resemblance to the famous Temple of the Sun in Cuzco. This might also be a temple of the sun. It followed the natural curvature of the rock and was keyed to it by one of the finest examples of masonry I had ever seen. Furthermore it was tied into another beautiful wall, made of very carefully matched ashlars of pure white granite, especially selected for its fine grain. Clearly, it was the work of a master artist. The interior surface of the wall was broken by niches and square stone-

Overleaf
The mountain-top marvel of Macchu Pichu, photographed by Bingham, who declared: 'In the variety of its charms and the power of its spell, I know of no place in the world which can compare with it.' So powerfully did this photograph capture people's imagination that the National Geographic Society was swamped by several thousand new members following publication in its magazine.

pegs. The exterior surface was perfectly simple and unadorned. The lower courses, of particularly large ashlars, gave it a look of solidity. The upper courses, diminishing in size towards the top, lent grace and delicacy to the structure. The flowing lines, the symmetrical arrangement of the ashlars, and the gradual gradation of the courses, combined to produce a wonderful effect, softer and more pleasing than that of the marble temples of the Old World. Owing to the absence of mortar, there were no ugly spaces between the rocks. They might have grown together...On account of the beauty of the white granite this structure surpassed in attractiveness the best Inca walls in Cuzco, which had caused visitors to marvel for four centuries. It seemed like an unbelievable dream. Dinly, I began to realize that this wall and its adjoining semicircular temple over the cave were as fine as the finest stonework in the world.

It fairly took my breath away. What could this place be? Why had no one given us any idea of it? Even Melchor Artega was only modestly interested and had no appreciation of the importance of the ruins which Richarte and Alvarez had adopted for their little farm. Perhaps after all this was an isolated small place which had escaped notice because it was inaccessible.

Then the little boy urged us to climb up a steep hill over what seemed to be a flight of stone steps. Surprise followed surprise in bewildering succession. We came to a great stairway of large granite blocks. Then we walked along a path to a clearing where the Indians had planted a small vegetable garden. Suddenly we found ourselves standing in front of the ruins of two of the finest and most interesting structures in ancient America. Made of beautiful white granite, the walls contained blocks of Cyclopean size, higher than a man. The sight held me spellbound.

Each building had only three walls and was entirely open on one side. The principal temple had walls 12 feet high which were lined with exquisitely made niches, five feet up at each end, and seven on the back. There were seven courses of ashlars in the end walls. Under the seven rear niches was a rectangular block 14 feet long, possibly a sacrificial altar, but more probably a throne for the mummies of departed Incas, brought out to be worshipped. The building did not look as though it had ever had a roof. The top course of beautifully smooth ashlars was left uncovered so that the sun could be welcomed here by priests and mummies. I could scarcely believe my senses as I examined the larger blocks in the lower course and estimated that they must weigh from ten to fifteen tons each. Would anyone believe what I had found? Fortunately, in this land where accuracy in reporting what one has seen is not a prevailing characteristic of travellers, I had a good camera and the sun was shining.

H. Bingham, *Lost City of the Incas*, 1952.

Melchor Arteaga, the farmer who (for a consideration) showed Bingham where to find Macchu Pichu, negotiates a rickety bridge 'made of four tree trunks bound together with vines' over the Urubamba River. When Bingham returned a few weeks later all but one of the logs had been washed away in a storm. He wrote that he crossed the river on his hands and knees, fifteen centimetres at a time. His crew later rebuilt the bridge and excavated the site to reveal the true scale of the largest Inca city ever found in modern times.

ROALD AMUNDSEN 1872–1928

First to the South Pole

WHEN AMUNDSEN WAS A CHILD *he read the journals of Sir John Franklin. As he later wrote, '...they thrilled me as nothing I had ever read before. What appealed to me most was the sufferings that Sir John and his men had to endure. A strange ambition burned within me, to endure the same privations...I decided to be an explorer.' He pursued his dream with a single-mindedness that verged on mania. For Amundsen, exploration was not just an adventure: it was his career. Between 1903 and 1906 he took the tiny smack* Gjoa *through the North West Passage, thereby becoming the first person to navigate a seaway that had been sought for 500 years. In 1909 he turned his attention to the North Pole and would probably have reached it had not Peary beaten him to the mark. 'This was a blow indeed!' he wrote. 'If I was to maintain my prestige as an explorer I must quickly achieve a sensational success of some sort.' Accordingly he took his dog teams to the Antarctic and snatched the South Pole from Scott's luckless hands. In 1917 ('I had nothing else to do') he traversed the North East Passage from the Atlantic to the Pacific.*

By 1924, however, he was bankrupt. 'It seemed to me as if the future had closed solidly against me', he wrote, 'and that my career as an explorer had come to an inglorious end. Courage, will-power, indomitable faith – these qualities had carried me through many dangers and to many achievements. Now even their merits seemed of no avail.' An American millionaire, Lincoln Ellsworth, came to his aid. The following year both men were en route to the North Pole aboard a couple of Dornier flying boats. At 88°N engine failure forced them onto the ice. It took twenty-four days, working round the clock, before they cleared a runway on which they escaped in their one, serviceable plane. Undeterred by this near-disaster, Amundsen and Ellsworth returned to the Arctic in 1926 aboard an Italian Zeppelin piloted by Umberto Nobile. This time they were successful, becoming the not only the first people to have indisputably reached the North Pole but also the first to have crossed the Arctic pack.

THE POINT AT WHICH THE GJOA ENTERED UNCHARTED WATER ON ITS JOURNEY THROUGH THE NORTH WEST PASSAGE.

The needle of our compass, which had been gradually losing its capacity for self-adjustment, now absolutely declined to act. We were thus reduced to steering by the stars, like our forefathers the Vikings. This mode of navigation is of doubtful security even in ordinary waters, but it is worse here, where the sky, for two-thirds of the time, is veiled in impenetrable fog...Next day...I was walking up and down the deck in the afternoon, enjoying the sunshine whenever it broke through the fog. For the sake of my comrades, I maintained a calm demeanour as usual, but I was inwardly much agitated. We were fast approaching the De La Roquette Islands; they were already in sight. This was the point that Sir Allen Young reached with the 'Pandora' in 1875, but here he had encountered an invincible barrier of ice. Were we and the little 'Gjoa' to meet the same fate? Then, as I walked, I felt something like an irregular lurching motion, and I stopped in surprise. The sea all around was smooth and calm, and, annoyed at myself, I dismissed the nervousness from my mind. I continued my walk and there it was again! A sensation, as though, in stepping out, my foot touched the deck sooner than it should have done,

according to my calculation. I leaned over the rail and gazed at the surface of the sea, but it was as calm and smooth as ever. I continued my promenade, but had not gone many steps before the sensation came again, and this time so distinctly that I could not be mistaken; there was a slight irregular motion in the ship. I would not have sold this slight motion for any amount of money. It was a swell under the boat, a swell – a message from the open sea. The water to the south was open, the impenetrable wall of ice was not there.

I cast my eyes over the little 'Gjoa' from stem to stern, from the deck to the mast-top, and smiled. Would the 'Gjoa' victoriously carry us all, and the flag of our native land, in spite of scornful predictions, over waters which had been long ago abandoned as hopeless? Soon the swell became more perceptible, and high glee shone on all our faces.

When I awoke at 1.30 next morning - it still amazes me that I could go to my berth, and sleep like a top into the bargain, that night - the swell had become so heavy that I had to sit down to put my clothes on. I had never liked a swell; there is something very

Wisting toils over his sewing machine in a cave carved into the Ross Ice Shelf. When the temperature rose above freezing – as it did sporadically – he insulated the walls with blankets to prevent constant dripping. 'The sewing machine is a little sleepy first thing in the morning but later on works well', Amundsen wrote. 'He is sewing new, light groundsheets [in the tents]. By this means we save several kilos.'

uncomfortable about it, with its memories of nausea and headache, dating back to the earliest memories of my seafaring life. But this swell, at this place and time – it was not a delight, it was a rapture that filled me to the soul. When I came on deck it was rather dark, but on our beam, not far off, we could faintly discern the outlines of the De La Roquette Islands. And now we had reached the critical point, the 'Gjoa' was heading into virgin waters. Now, it seemed we had really commenced our task in earnest.

R. AMUNDSEN, *The North West Passage, 1908.*

AMUNDSEN'S DIARY OF THE JOURNEY TO THE SOUTH POLE.

30 November 1911 – The Devil's Glacier was worthy of its name. One has to move 2 miles to advance 1. Chasm after chasm, abyss after abyss has to be circumvented. Treacherous crevasses and much other unpleasantness make progress extremely hard. The dogs are struggling and the drivers not less...

1 December 1911 – How often have I discovered that a day one expects nothing of brings much. A south-easterly blizzard...overnight had half persuaded me to declare a rest

day for the dogs. But, during a little lull, we agreed to try and travel. It was cold to begin with. During the night the wind had swept large areas of the glacier bare and free of snow. The crevasses were horrible...But we managed inch by inch, foot by foot, sledge length by sledge length, sometimes east, sometimes west, sometimes north, sometimes south, round huge open crevasses and treacherous crevasses about to collapse...But we managed and, after a time [moving in] fog, gale and drift [we found] the chasms more and more filled with snow...until we reached the plateau, where they completely ceased....

4 December 1911 - [On the Devil's Ballroom] First we had to cross...mirror-smooth ice with filled crevasses here and there. This...was not difficult to cross...Naturally, there was no question of using ski. We all had to support the sledges

and help the dogs. The next terrain offered good going, and we congratulated ourselves on having overcome all difficulties. But no! We were not going to get off so lightly. (We encountered) a violent disturbance [in the ice]. Suddenly one of the runners of Wisting's sledge broke through to a bottomless crevasse...We were able to hoist it up again without damage...We got through safe and sound and climbed it on a rise. This again consisted of bare ice, but then we discovered it to be filled with hidden crevasses, where we could not set foot anywhere without breaking through. Luckily most of these crevasses were filled, but some were dangerous enough. It was hard work for the dogs. Bjaaland fell through, but managed to hold onto his sledge, otherwise he would have been irrevocably lost... We finally got over, and little by little [the terrain] changed to the real plateau, without any disturbance...No more chasms or crevasses...

8 December 1911 – One of our big days. This morning...the weather was thick, with poor visibility, as usual. But...the terrain and the skiing were of the best kind...We had not been travelling long, before it began to clear a little all round the horizon. [By midday] the sun appeared, not in all its glory, but...enough for a good observation...We had not had an observation since 86°47'S, and it was essential to establish our position...the result was almost exactly 88°16°. A splendid victory after...march in thick fog and snowdrift. Our observation and dead reckoning agreed to the minute...So now we are ready to take the Pole in any kind of weather...From the point where we took the observation to the Englishmen's (Shackleton's) world record only 7 miles remain. (88°23°.) I had given HH [Helmer Hanssen] our Pole flag, which he was to hoist on his sledge – the leading sledge – as soon as this was passed. I myself was forerunner at the time. The weather had

Amunden in his furs. Like Peary before him, he stressed the necessity of using native technology in polar travel. Transplanted from the Arctic to the Antarctic, Eskimo clothing, dogs and sledges were vital to his attainment of the South Pole. Similarly, Amundsen stressed the importance of eating fresh meat to keep scurvy at bay. Fortunately there was no lack: 'We are living in a never-never land. Seals come to the ship and allow themselves to be shot.'

A seal carcass attracts skuas in the Bay of Whales, the anchorage from which Amundsen left for the Pole. When Scott's Terra Nova *visited the Bay of Whales its officers were horrified to discover the Norwegians in place. They declared the* Fram *'very comfortable, very ugly outside', and noted that the occupants seemed 'very charming men, even the perfidious Amundsen' – his perfidy being that he dared attack the Pole when he knew that Scott was planning the same thing. On their departure they had 'heavy arguments ...about the rights and wrongs of Amundsen's party and the chances of being able to beat them. Their experience and number of dogs seem to leave us very little.'*

*At the South Pole
Amundsen shoots a
reading with his sextant
while Helmer Hanssen
bends over the artificial
horizon – a tray of
mercury from which, by
aligning the sun with its
reflection, polar
travellers were able to
determine their position.
Having always wanted
to conquer the North
Pole but now finding
himself, almost by
default, in possession of
the South, Amundsen
was a trifle disap-
pointed.' I cannot
say - though I know
it would sound more
effective – that the
object of my life was
attained', he wrote.
'I had better be honest
and admit straight out
that I have never known
any man to be placed in
such a diametrically
opposed position to the
goal of his desires than
I was at that moment.'*

improved and the sun had broken through properly. My snow goggles bothered me from time to time. A gentle breeze from the south made the mist over, so that it was difficult to see. Then I suddenly heard a stout, hearty cheer behind. I turned round. In the light breeze from the south, the brave, well-known colours [of the Norwegian flag] waved from the first sledge, we have passed and put behind us the Englishmen's record. It was a splendid sight. The sun had just broken through in all its glory...My goggles clouded over again, but this time it was not the south wind's fault.

9 December 1911 - We can prepare for the final onslaught. We laid a depot here to lighten the sledges...Bjaaland's dogs have lost so much weight recently and yesterday one of Wisting's dogs – 'The Major' - a sturdy old dog, disappeared.

14 December 1911 – So we arrived and planted our flag at the geographical South Pole. Thanks be to God!...The time was 3 p.m. when it happened. The weather was of the finest sort when we started this morning, but around 10 a.m. It became overcast. Fresh breeze from SE. The going has been partly good, partly bad. The plain – King Haakon VII's Plateau – has had the same appearance – quite flat and without what one can call sastrugi. The sun came out again during the afternoon, and we ought to get a midnight observation...We arrived here with three sledges and 17 dogs. Helmer Hanssen put one down immediately after arrival. 'Helgi' was worn out. Tomorrow we will go out in 3 directions to ring in the polar area. We have eaten our celebratory meal – a little piece of seal meat each...

16 December 1911 – [while confirming his position] It is quite interesting to see the sun wander round the heavens at so to speak the same altitude day and night. I think somehow we are the first to see this curious sight...[The dogs] are all lying stretched out in the heat of the sun, enjoying life, in spite of little food. They seem to be quite well. It has been so clear today, that we have all used our telescopes industriously to see if there is any sign of life in any direction – but in vain. We are the first here all right...

17 December 1911 - [The] Norwegian flag, with the Fram pennant underneath, are flying from the top of the tent pole. In the tent, I have placed various things: my sextant with a glass artificial horizon, a hypsometer, 3 reindeer fur boot warmers, some kamikks [fur boots], and mittens, and a few small things. In a folder, I left a letter for the King and some words to Scott who, I must assume, will be the first to visit the place after us... And so farewell, dear Pole. I don't think we'll meet again.

HUNTFORD, R (ED), *The Amundsen Photographs, 1987.*

ROBERT FALCON SCOTT 1868–1912

Tragedy in the Antarctic

ROBERT FALCON SCOTT *was an unremarkable torpedo officer in the Royal Navy until he came to the attention of Sir Clements Markham, President of the Royal Geographical Society. An old-style polar enthusiast, Markham admired the romance of humanity's struggle against the ice. Dogs and skis, in his view, were a form of cheating, best left to the foreigner. Instead, he envisaged squads of muscular British Christians trudging victoriously to the ends of the earth, dragging their sledges behind them. In Scott, he found a man of similar – though less extreme – opinions. He sent Scott on a number of forays to the South Pole, the last of which was in 1910. Although Scott reached the pole on in January 1912, he was beaten by his Norwegian rival Roald Amundsen – who used dogs and skis – and he and his entire party perished on the return journey. Amundsen was criticized (by the British) for being unhealthily competitive and Scott was elevated to the status of martyr. Condemned by many historians for his ineffciency, Scott was in fact an exceptionally tough and capable man who was defeated in part by agencies outside his control. The motorized sledges with which he had been equipped failed to work; and the ponies he took as back-up were not ready by the time he wanted to set out. As a result, he left in the knowledge that Amundsen would beat him to the Pole. His death from starvation, within just 18 kilometres of a depot, was caused, primarily, by a freak of Antarctic weather whose once-in-a-lifetime ferocity confined him and his men within their tent. His notebooks proved him to be one of the age's most memorable diarists.*

TOWARDS THE POLE.

Thursday, January 4. – In the afternoon the wind died away, and to-night it is flat calm; the sun so warm that in spite of the temperature we can stand about outside in the greatest comfort. It is amusing to stand thus and remember the constant horrors of our situation as they were painted for us: the sun is melting the snow on the ski, &c. The plateau is now very flat, but we are still ascending slowly. The sastrugi are getting more confused, predominant from the S.E. I wonder what is in store for us. At present everything seems to be going with extraordinary smoothness, and one can scarcely believe that obstacles will not present themselves to make our task more difficult. Perhaps the surface will be the element to trouble us...

Monday. January 8. – We lie so very comfortably, warmly clothed in our comfortable bags, within our double-walled tent. However, we do not want more than a day's delay at most, both on account of lost time and food and the slow accumulation of ice...

It is quite impossible to speak too highly of my companions. Each fulfills his office to the party; Wilson, first, as doctor, ever on the lookout to alleviate the small pains and troubles incidental to the work; now as cook, quick, careful and dextrous, ever thinking of some fresh expedient to help the camp life; tough as steel on the traces, never wavering from start to finish.

Evans, a giant worker with a really remarkable headpiece. It is only now I realise how much has been due to him. Our ski shoes and crampons have been absolutely indispensable, and if the original ideas were not his, the details of manufacture and design and good workmanship are his alone. He is responsible for every sledge, every sledge fitting,

tents, sleeping-bags, harness, and when one cannot recall a single expression of dissatisfaction with any one of these items, it shows what an invaluable assistant he has been. Now, besides superintending the putting up of the tent, he thinks out and arranges the packing of the sledge; it is extraordinary how neatly and handily everything is stowed, and how much study has been given to preserving the suppleness and good running qualities of the machine. On the Barrier, before the ponies were killed, he was ever roaming round, correcting faults of stowage.

Little Bowers remains a marvel – he is thoroughly enjoying himself. I leave all the provision arrangements in his hands, and at all times he knows exactly how we stand, or how each returning party should fare. It has been a complicated business to redistribute stores at various stages of re-organisation, but not one single mistake has been made. In addition to the stores, he keeps the most throrough and conscientious meterological record, and to this he now adds the duty of observer and photographer. Nothing comes amiss to him, and no work is too hard. It is a difficulty to get him into the tent; he seems quite oblivious of the cold, and he lies coiled in his bag writing and working out sights long after the others are asleep.

Of these three...each is sufficiently suited for his own work, but would not be capable of doing that of the others as well as it is done. Each is invaluable. Oates had his invaluable periods with the ponies; now he is a foot slogger and goes hard the whole time...and stands the hardship as well as any of us. I would not like to be without him either. So our five people are perhaps as happily selected as it is possible to imagine...

R.SCOTT, *Scott's Last Expedition, Vol I, 1913.*

RETURNING FROM THE POLE, EVANS DEAD AND OATES BADLY FROSTBITTEN.

Sunday, March 11. – Titus Oates is very near the end, one feels. What we or he will do, God only knows. We discussed the matter after breakfast; he is a brave fine fellow and understands the situation, but he practically asked for advice. Nothing could be said but to urge him to march along as he could. One satisfactory result to the discussion; I practically ordered Wilson to hand over the means of ending our troubles to us, so that any one of us may know how to do so. Wilson had no choice between doing so and our ransacking the medicine case. We have 30 opium tabloids apiece and he is left with a tube of morphine. So far the tragical side of our story...

Monday, March 12. – We did 6.9 miles yesterday, under our necessary average. Things are left much the same, Oates not pulling much, and now with hands as well as feet pretty well useless...We shall be 47 miles from the depot. I doubt if we can possibly do it. The surface remains awful, the cold intense, and out physical condition running down. God help us! Not a breath of favourable wind for more than a week, and apparently liable to head winds at any moment...We must go on, but now the making of every camp must be more difficult and dangerous. It must be near the end, but a pretty merciful end. Poor Oates got it again in the foot. I shudder to think what it will be like to-morrow. It is only with the greatest pains each of us keep off frostbites. No idea there could be temperatures like this at this time of year with such winds. Truly awful outside the tent. Must fight it out to the last biscuit, but can't reduce rations.

Friday, March 16 or Saturday 17. – Lost track of dates but think the last correct. Tragedy all along the line. At lunch, the day before yesterday, poor Titus Oates said he

Captain Oates tends to the expedition ponies. It was planned that the ponies would haul the expedition's supplies as far south as possible, leaving the final stretch to be covered by man-hauled sledges. The ponies performed surprisingly well but their obvious unsuitability for snow travel could not be ignored. They did, however, provide a source of fresh meat that was added to the food depots awaiting the polar party's return. While trying to reach these depots in the face of a blizzard a frost-bitten Oates voluntarily left the tent to give his companions a better chance of survival.

couldn't go on; he proposed we should leave him in his sleeping bag. That we could not do, and induced him to come on, on the afternoon march. In spite of its awful nature for him he struggled on and we made a few miles. At night he was worse and we knew the end had come.

Should this be found I want these facts recorded. Oates' last thoughts were of his Mother, but immediately before he took pride in thinking that his regiment would be pleased with the bold way in which he met his death. We can testify to his bravery. He has borne intense suffering for weeks without complaint, and to the very last was able and willing to discuss outside subjects. He did not – would not – give up hope to the very end. He was a brave soul.

This was the end. He slep through the night before last, hoping not to wake; but he woke in the morning – yesterday. It was blowing a blizzard. He said, 'I am just going outside and may be some time.' He went out into the blizzard and we have not seen him since.

I take this opportunity of saying that we have stuck to our sick companions to the last. In the case of Edgar Evans, when absolutely out of food and he lay insensible, the safety of the remainder seemed to demand his abandonment, but Providence mercifully removed him at this critical moment. He died a natural death, and we did not leave him till two hours after his death. We knew that poor Oates was walking to his death, but though we tried to dissuade him, we knew it was the act of a brave man and an English gentleman. We all hope to meet the end with a similar spirit, and assuredly the end is not far.

I can only write at lunch and then only occasionally. The cold is intense, −40° at midday. My companions are unendingly cheerful, but we are all on the verge of serious frostbites, and though we constantly talk of fetching through I don't think any one of us believes it in his heart...

Sunday, March 18. – To-day, lunch, we are 21 miles from the depot. Ill fortune presses, but better may come. We have had more wind and drift from ahead yesterday; had to stop marching; wind N.W., force 4, temp −35°. No human being could face it, and we are worn out nearly.

My right foot has gone, nearly all the toes – two days ago I was the proud possessor of best feet. These are the steps of my downfall. Like an ass I mixed a small spoonful of curry powder with my melted pemmican – it gave me violent indigestion. I lay awake and in pain all night; woke and felt done on the march; foot went and I didn't know it. A very small measure of neglect and have a foot which is not pleasant to contemplate. Bowers takes first place in condition, but there is not much to choose after all. The others are still confident of getting through – or pretend to be – I don't know! We have the last half fill of oil in our primus and a very small quantity of spirit - this alone between us and thirst...

Monday, March 19. - Lunch. We camped with difficulty last night and were dreadfully cold till after our supper of cold pemmican and biscuit and half a pannikin of cocoa cooked over the spirit. Then, contrary to expectation, we got warm and all slept well. To-day we started in the usual dragging manner. Sledge dreadfully heavy. We are 15 1/2 miles from the depot and ought to get there in three days. What progress! We have two days' food but barely a day's fuel. All our feet are getting worse – Wilson's best, my right foot worst, left all right. There is no chance to nurse one's feet till we can get hot food into us. Amputation is the least I can hope for now, but will the trouble spread? That is the serious question. The weather doesn't give us a chance – the wind from N. To N.W. and −40° temp.

Wednesday, March 21. – Got within 11 miles of depot Monday night; had to lay up

all yesterday in severe blizzard. To-day forlorn hope, Wilson and Bowers going to depot for fuel.

Thursday, March 22 and 23. – Blizzard bad as ever – Wilson and Bowers unable to start – to-morrow last chance – no fuel and only one or two of food left – must be near the end. Have decided it shall be natural – we shall march for the depot with or without our effects and die in our tracks.

Tuesday, March 29. – Since the 21st we have had a continuous gale from W.S.W. And S.W. We had fuel to make two cups of tea apiece and bare food for two days on the 20th. Every day we have been ready to start for our depot 11 miles away, but outside the door of the tent it remains a scene of whirling drift. I do not think we can hope for any better things now. We shall stick it out to the end, but we are getting weaker, of course, and the end cannot be far.

It seems a pity, but I do not think I can write more.

R. Scott

For God's sake look after our people.

Scott's Last Expedition, Vol I.

Captain Scott makes an entry in his journal. In a land devoid of indigenous culture, his diaries would later assume mythological status. They were to the untouched continent as Homer's Iliad and Odyssey *had been to ancient Europe – the first epics by which all other literary efforts would be judged. Reading them, it is hard not to imagine that Scott had such posterity in mind.*

DOUGLAS MAWSON 1882–1958

A solitary march in Antarctica

IN 1911, THE SAME YEAR *that scott embarked on his journey to the South Pole, Douglas Mawson led his own expedition to Antarctica. He had been invited to join Scott's polar party but chose the less glamorous – though, geographically, more profitable – task of surveying Adelie Land to the west of the Ross Ice Shelf. He very nearly suffered the same fate as Scott. Accompanied by two men, a British army officer Lt Belgrave Ninnis and a Swiss skiing champion Dr Xavier Mertz, he was several hundred kilometres from Base Camp when a crevasse swallowed Ninnis and most of their supplies. On the return journey Mertz also died, leaving Mawson with nothing but half a sledge and the stewed remnants of his dogs. He survived, and led subsequent expeditions to Antarctica – but he never recovered fully from that first ordeal.*

THE POWER OF THE WIND.

Whatever has been said relative to the wind-pressure exerted on inanimate objects, the same applied, with even more point, to our persons; so that progress in a hurricane became a fine art. The first difficulty to be encountered was a smooth, slippery surface offering no grip for the feet. Stepping out of the shelter of the Hut, one was apt to be hurled at full length down wind. No amount of exertion was of any avail unless a firm foothold had been secured. The strongest man, stepping on to ice or hard snow in plain leather or fur boots, would start sliding away with gradually increasing velocity; in the space of a few seconds, or earlier, exchanging the vertical for the horizontal position. He would then either stop suddenly against a jutting point of ice, or glide along for twenty or thirty yards till he reached a patch of rocks or some rough sastrugi.

Of course we soon learned never to go about without crampons on the feet...Shod with good spikes, in a steady wind, one had only to push hard to keep a sure footing. It would not be true to say 'to keep erect,' for equilibrium was maintained by leaning against the wind. In course of time, those whose duties habitually took them out of doors became thorough masters of the art of walking in hurricanes – an accomplishment comparable to skiing or skating. Ensconced in the lee of a substantial break-wind, one could leisurely observe the unnatural appearance of others walking about, apparently in imminent peril of falling on their faces.

Experiments were tried in the stready winds; firmly planting the feet on the ground, keeping the body rigid and leaning over on the invisible support. This 'lying on the wind,' at equilibrium, was a unique experience. As a rule the velocity remained uniform; when it fluctuated in a series of gusts, all our experience was likely to fail, for no sooner had the correct angle for the maximum velocity been assumed than a lull intervened – with the obvious result.

Before the art of 'hurricane-walking' was learnt, and in the primitive days of ice-nails and finnesko, progression in high winds degenerated into crawling on hands and knees. Many of the more conservative persisted in this method, and, as a compensation, became the first exponents of the popular art of 'board-sliding.' A small piece of board, a wide ice flat and a hurricane were the three essentials for this new sport.

Wind alone would not have been so bad; drift snow accompanied it in overwhelming

amount. In the autumn overcast weather with heavy falls of snow prevailed, with the result that the air for several months was seldom free from drift...Indeed, during that time, there were not many days when objects a hundred yards away could be seen distinctly. Whatever else happened, the wind never abated, and so, even when the snow had ceased falling and the sky was clear, the drift continued until all the loose accumulations on the hinterland, for hundreds of miles back, had been swept out to sea. Day after day deluges of drift streamed past the Hut, at times so dense as to obscure objects three feet away, until it seemed as if the atmosphere were almost solid snow.

Picture drift so dense that daylight comes through dully, though, maybe, the sun shines in a cloudless sky; the drift is hurled, screaming through space at a hundred miles an hour, and the temperature is below zero...

You have then the bare, rough facts concerning the worst blizzards of Adelie Land. The actual experience of them is another thing.

Shroud the infuriated elements in the darkness of a polar night, and the blizzard is presented in a severer aspect. A plunge into the writhing storm-whirl stamps upon the senses an indelible and awful impression seldom equalled in the whole gamut of natural experience. The world a void, grisly, fierce and appalling. We stumble and struggle through the Stygian gloom; the merciless blast – an incubus of vengeance – stabs, buffets

and freezes; the stinging drift blinds and chokes...It may well be imagined that none of us went out on these occasions for the pleasure of it.

D. MAWSON, *The Home of the Blizzard, Vol I, 1915.*

After Ninnis's death, and the loss of their provisions, Mawson and Mertz survived by eating their beloved dogs. Unfortunately, they ate too much of them. While it was known that the livers of polar bear contained toxic quantities of Vitamin A, it was not until the 1970s that scientists discovered husky livers were also rich in Vitamin A. An excess of Vitamin A causes nausea, dizziness, peeling of the skin, intestinal cramps, hair loss, fissures around the nose and eyes, the loss of smell and taste, delirium, convulsions, brain haemorrhage and, finally, death. Halfway home, Mertz succumbed to Vitamin A poisoning. Mawson, who was physically stronger, nevertheless lost most of his hair and the soles of both feet. On reaching Base Camp he fought the onset of brain damage for several months.

THE RETURN JOURNEY FOLLOWING NINNIS'S DEATH:
[14 December] The homeward track! A few days ago – only a few hours ago – our hearts had beat hopefully at the prospect and there was no hint of this, the overwhelming tragedy. Our fellow, comrade, chum, in a woeful instant, buried in the bowels of the awful glacier. We could not think of it; we strove to forget it in the necessity of work, but we

knew that the truth would assuredly enter our souls in the lonely days to come. It was to be a fight with Death and the great Providence would decide the issue...

[16 December] On that night ours was a mournful procession; the sky thickly clouded, snow falling, I with one eye bandaged and the dog Johnson broken down and strapped on top of the load on the sledge. There was scarcely a sound; only the rustle of the thick, soft snow as we pushed on, weary but full of hope. The dogs dumbly pressed forward in their harness, forlorn but eager to follow. Their weight now told little upon the sledge, the work falling mainly upon ourselves. Mertz was tempted to try hauling on skis, but came to the conclusion that it did not pay and thenceforth never again used them...At 2 a.m. on the 17th we had only covered eleven miles when we stopped to camp. Then Mertz shot and cut up Johnson while I prepared the supper. Johnson had always been a very faithful, hard-working and willing beast, with rather droll ways of his own, and we were sorry that his end should come so soon. He could never be accused of being a handsome dog, in fact he was generally disreputable and filthy.

All the dogs were miserable and thin when they reached the stage of extreme exhaustion. Their meat was tough, stringy and without a vestige of fat. For a change we sometimes chopped it up finely, mixed it with a little pemmican, and brought all to the boil in a large pot of water. We were exceedingly hungry, but there was nothing to satisfy our appetites. Only a few ounces were used of the stock of ordinary food, to which was added a portion of the dog's meat, for each animal yielded so very little, and the major part was fed to the surviving dogs. They crunched the bones and ate the skin, until nothing remained...

[24 December] Pavlova was killed and we made a very acceptable soup from her bones. In view of the dark oulook, our ration of food had to be still further cut down. We had no proper sleep, hunger gnawing at us all the time, and the question of food was for ever in our thoughts. Dozing in the fur bags, we dreamed of gorgeous 'spreads' and dinner-parties at home. Tramping along through the snow, we racked our brains thinking how to make the most of the meagre quantity of dogs' meat at hand.

The supply of kerosene for the primus stove promised to be ample, for none of it had been lost in the accident. We found that it was worth while spending some time in boiling the dogs' meat thoroughly. Thus a tasty soup was prepared as well as a supply of edible meat in which the muscular tissue and the gristle were reduced to the consistency of a jelly. The paws took longest of all to cook, but, treated to a lengthy stewing, they became quite digestible...Lying in the sleeping bag that day I dreamt that I visited a confectioner's shop. All the wares that were displayed measured feet in diameter. I purchased an enormous delicacy just as one would buy a bun under ordinary circumstances. I remember paying the money over the counter, but something happened before I received what I had chosen. When I realised the omission I was out in the street, and, being greatly disappointed, went back to the shop, but found the door shut and 'early closing' written on it...

[28 December] Our faithful retainer Ginger could walk no longer and was strapped on the sledge. She was the last of the dogs and had been some sort of a help until a few days before. We were sad when it came to finishing her off...We had breakfast off Ginger's skull and brains. I can never forget the occasion. As there was nothing available to divide it, the skull was boiled whole. Thus the right and left halves were drawn for by the old and well-established sledging practice of 'shut-eye', after which we took it in turns eating to the middle line, passing the skull from one to another. The brain was afterwards scooped out with a woooden spoon. On sledging journeys it is usual to apportion all foodstuffs in as nearly halves as possible. Then one man turns away and another, pointing to a heap, asks

Blandly titled 'Gathering ice for domestic use', this photograph (left) by Frank Hurley depicts the conditions at Base Camp. In winter, the only means of obtaining water was to melt ice over a stove, which necessitated regular forays outside the hut, even in the vilest weather.

'Whose?' The reply from the one not looking is 'Yours' or 'Mine' as the case may be. Thus an impartial and satisfactory division of the rations is made...

[30 December] Tramping over the plateau, where reigns the desolation of the outer worlds, in solitude at once ominous and weird, one is free to roam in imagination through the wide realm of human experience to the bounds of the great Beyond...One is in the midst of infinities – the infinity of the dazzling white plateau, the infinity of the dome above, the infinity of the time past simce these things had birth, and the infinity of the time to come before they shall have fulfilled the Purpose for which they were created... By 9. a.m. we had accomplished a splendid march of fifteen miles three hundred and fifty yards, but the satisfaction we should have felt at making such an inroad on the huge task before us was dampened by the fact that Mertz was not as cheerful as usual. I was at a loss to know the reason, for he was always such a bright and companionable fellow...

[31 December] Mertz said that he felt the dogs' meat was not doing him much good and suggested that we should give it up for a time and eat a small ration of the ordinary sledging food, of which we had still some days' supply carefully husbanded. I agreed to do this and we made our first experiment on that day. The ration tasted very sweet compared with the dogs' meat and was so scanty in amount that it left one painfully empty. The light was so atrocious for marching that, after stumbling along for two and a half miles, we were obliged to give up the attempt and camp, spending the day in sleeping bags. In the evening at 9.30 p.m. the sun appeared for a brief moment and the wind subsided. Another stage was therefore attempted but at considerable cost, for we staggered along in the bewildering light, continually falling over unseen sastrugi...

A team of huskies haul their master over flat ice. It was not often that Mawson encountered such perfect conditions. When he penetrated the Antarctic plateau he was faced by fields of sastrugi – corrugated waves of wind-frozen snow that made travel a nightmare.

[1 January] Mertz was not up to his usual form and we decided not to attempt blundering along in the bad light, believing that the rest would be advantageous to him.

He did not complain at all except of the dampness of his sleeping bag, though when I questioned him particularly he admitted that he had pains in the abdomen. As I had a continuous gnawing sensation in the stomach, I took it that he had the same, possibly more acute...

[5 January] The sky was overcast, snow was falling, and there was a strong wind. Mertz suggested that as the conditions were so bad we should delay another day.

Lying in the damp bags was wretched and was not doing either of us any good, but what was to be done? Outside the conditions were abominable. My companion was evidently much weaker than I, and it was apparently quite true that he was not making much of the dogs' meat...

[6 January] Mertz appeared to be depressed and, after the short meal, sank back into his bag without saying much. Occasionally, during the day, I would ask him how he felt, or we would return to the old subject of food. It was agreed that on our arrival on board the *Aurora* Mertz was to make penguin omelettes, for we had never forgotten the excellence of those we had eaten just before leaving the Hut...The skin was peeling off our bodies and a very poor substitute remained which burst readily and rubbed raw in many places. One day, I remember, Mertz ejaculated, 'Just a moment,' and reaching over, lifted from my ear a perfect skin-cast. I was able to do the same for him. As we never took off our clothes, the peelings of hair and skin from our bodies worked down into our under-trousers and socks, and regular clearances were made.

During the evening of the 6th I made the following note in my diary:

'A long and wearisome night. If only I could get on; but I must stop with Xavier. He does not appear to be improving and both our chances are going now.'

January 7. – At 10.a.m. I get up to dress Xavier and prepare food, but find him in a kind of fit. Coming round a few minutes later, he exchanged a few words and did not seem to realize that anything had happened. Obviously we can't go on to-day. It is a good day though the light is bad, the sun just gleaming through the clouds. This is terrible; I don't mind for myself but for the others...I pray to God to help us...

During the afternoon he had several more fits, then became delirious and talked incoherently until midnight, when he appeared to dall off into a peaceful slumber. So I toggled up the sleeping-bag and retired worn out into my own. After a couple of hours, having felt no movement from my companion, I stretched out an arm and found that he was stiff...For hours I lay in the bag, rolling over in my mind all that lay behind and the chance of the future. I seemed to stand alone on the wide shores of the world – and what a short step to enter the unknown future! My physical condition was such that I felt I might collapse in a moment. The gnawing in the stomach had developed there a permanent weakness, so that it was not possible to hold myself up in certain positions. Several of my toes commenced to blacken and fester near the tips and the nails worked loose. Outside the bowl of chaos was brimming with drift-snow and I wondered how I would manage to break and pitch camp single-handed. There appeared to be little hope of reaching the Hut. It was easy to sleep on in the bag, and the weather was cruel outside...

[9 January] I read the Burial Service over Xavier this afternoon. As there is little chance of my reaching human aid alive, I greatly regret the inability at the moment to set out the

detail of coastline met with for three hundred miles travels and observations of glacier and ice-formations etc.; the most of which latter are, of course, committed to my head. The approximate location of the camp is latitude 68° 2° S, longitude 145° 9° E. This is dead reckoning as the theodolite legs have been out of action for some time, splinted together to form tent-props...It was on January 11 – a beautiful, calm day of sunshine – that I set out over a good surface with a slight down grade. From the start my feet felt lumpy and sore. They had become so painful after a mile of walking that I decided to make an examination of them on the spot, sitting in the sun on my sledge. The sight of my feet gave me quite a shock, for the thickened skin of the soles had separated in each case as a complete layer, and abundant watery fluid had escaped into the socks. The new skin underneath was very abraded and raw. I did what seemed to be the best thing under the circumstances: smeared the skin with lanoline, of which there was a good store, and with bandages bound the skin soles back in place, as they were comfortable and soft in contact with the raw surfaces. Outside the bandages I wore six pairs of thick wollen socks, fur boots and a crampon over-shoe of soft leather. Then I removed most of my clothing and bathed in the glorious heat of the sun. A tingling sensation seemed to spread throughout my whole body, and I felt stronger and better...

January 17 was another day of overcast weather and falling snow. Delay meant a reduction in the ration which was low enough already, so there was nothing to do but go on...This is what happened, according to the following account in my diary:

'Going up a long, fairly steep slope, deeply covered with soft snow, broke through lid of crevasse but caught myself at thighs, got out, turned fifty yards to the north, then attempted to cross trend of crevasse, there being no indication of it; a few moments later found myself dangling fourteen feet below on end of rope in crevasse - sledge creeping to mouth – had time to say to myself, 'so this is the end', expecting the sledge every moment to crash on my head and all go to the unseen bottom – then thought of food uneaten on the sledge; but as the sledge pulled up without letting me down, thought of Providence giving me another chance. The chance was very small considering my weak condition. The width of the crevasse was about six feet, so I hung freely in space, turning slowly round. A great effort brought a knot in the rope within my grasp, and, after a moment's rest, I was able to draw myself up and reach another, and, at length, hauled myself on to the overhangin g snow-lid into which the rope had cut. Then, when I was carefully climbing out on to the surface, a futher section of the lid gave way, precipitating me once more to the full length of the rope

Exhausted, weak and chilled (for my hands were bare and pounds of snow had got inside my clothing) I hung with the firm conviction that it all was over except the passing. Below was a black chasm; it would be but the work of a minute to slip from the harness, then all the pain and toil would be over. It was a rare situation, a rare temptation - a chance to quit small things for great – to pass from the petty exploration of the planet to the contemplation of vaster worlds beyond. But there was all eternity for the last and, at its longest, the present would be but short. I felt better for the thought.

My strength was fast ebbing; in a few minutes it would be too late. It was the occasion for a supreme attempt. New power seemed to come as I addressed myself to one last tremendous effort. The struggle occupied some time, but by a miracle I slowly rose to the surface. This time I emerged feet first, still holding on to the rope, and pushed myself out, extended at full length, on the snow - on solid ground. Then came the reaction, and I could do nothing for quite an hour.

The Home of the Blizzard.

ERNEST SHACKLETON 1874-1922

Quest for survival in Antarctica

The 'Boss' tinkers with the binnacle, while one of the expedition dogs stares curiously at the camera. Shackleton advertised his voyage in the driest of terms. 'Men wanted for hazardous journey. Small wages, bitter cold, long months of complete darkness, constant danger, safe return doubtful. Honours and recognition in case of success.' Had the volunteers realized how haphazard his arrangements were they would probably have had second thoughts. Shackleton's plans relied on covering 15 miles per day on dog sled. The dogs were not huskies but a mixed bunch of mongrels whose bloodlines included everything from wolfhound to collie. Their Canadian handler dropped out at the last minute, leaving the crew to cope as best they could. Nobody knew how to handle them and only one man even knew how to ski. In the flurry of departure they also forgot to pack the dogs' worm tablets.

FOR A WHILE, DURING the first decade of the 20th century, Shackleton was odds-on favourite to reach the South Pole. He first visited Antarctica in 1901-4 with Scott and then led his own expedition in 1908-9. It was phenomenally successful, seeing the attainment of the South Magnetic Pole, the first ascent of Mt Erebus and a march by Shackleton that came within 100 miles of the Pole itself. When Scott and Amundsen captured the Pole in 1912, Shackleton primed himself for the next challenge. As he wrote: 'There remained but one great main object of Antarctic journeyings – the crossing of the South Polar continent from sea to sea.' The result was the Imperial Trans Antarctic Expedition of 1914. One party, aboard the Endurance , was to approach via the Weddell Sea while a second group laid depots from the Ross Ice Shelf on the other side of the continent. The Endurance was crushed, forcing Shackleton to evacuate ship. For several months he and his men survived on the ice before reaching a remote lump of rock and shingle called Elephant Island, from where he sailed in a small boat, the James Caird, to fetch help from South Georgia. Landing on the wrong side of the island he took two men on an epic ascent over its unknown mountains to the whaling station of Stromness. The group on Elephant Island were duly rescued, as were the men on the Ross Ice Shelf who had lost their ship and several men. The expedition returned to Britain in 1916, after two years absence, to devastating uninterest. In the turmoil of World War One, few people cared any longer for polar derring-do.

Although undoubtedly a great leader of men, Shackleton was a poor planner whose ambitions oustripped his capabilities. After the war he led a final expedition to Antarctica. It had no clear pupose and he died in 1922 of heart failure – probably caused by his previous exertions – to be buried at the South Georgia whaling station of Grytviken.

THE JOURNEY ABOARD THE JAMES CAIRD FROM ELEPHANT ISLAND TO SOUTH GEORGIA.

Real rest we had none. The perpetual motion of the boat made repose impossible; we were cold, sore and anxious. We moved on hands and knees in the semidarkness of the day under the decking...We had a few scraps of candle, and they were preserved carefully in order that we might have light at mealtimes. There was one fairly dry spot in the boat, under the solid original decking at the bows, and we managed to protect some of our biscuit from the salt water; but I do not think any of us got the taste of salt out of our mouths during the voyage...

The difficulty of movement in the boat would have had its humorous side if it had not involved us in so many aches and pains. We had to crawl under the thwarts in order to move along the boat, and our knees suffered considerably...The boulders that we had taken aboard for ballast had to be shifted continually in order to trim the boat and give access to the punp, which became choked with hairs from the moulting sleeping bags and finneskoe. The four reindeer-skin sleeping bags shed their hair freely owing to the continuous wetting, and soon became quite bald in appearance. The moving of the boulders was weary and painful work. We came to know every one of the stones by sight and touch, and I have vivid memories of their angular peculiarities even today. They might have been of considerable interest as geological specimens to a scientific man under happier condi-

tions. As ballast they were useful. As weights to be moved about in cramped quarters they were simply appalling. They spared no portion of our poor bodies. Another of our troubles, worth mentioning here, was the chafing of our legs by our wet clothes, which had not been changed now for seven months. The insides of our thighs were rubbed raw, and the one tube of Hazeline cream in our medicine chest did not go far in alleviating our pain, which was increased by the bite of the salt water. We thought at the time that we never slept. The fact was that we would doze off uncomfortably, to be aroused quickly by some new ache or another call to the effort. My own share of the general unpleasantness was accentuated by a finely developed bout of sciatica. I had become possessor of this originally on the floe several months earlier.

Our meals were regular in spite of the gales. Attention to this point was essential, since the conditions of the voyage made increasing calls upon our vitality. Breakfast, at 8 a.m., consisted of a pannikin of hot hoosh made from Bovril sledging ration, two biscuits, and some lumps of sugar. Lunch came at 1 p.m., and comprised Bovril sledging ration, eaten raw, and a pannikin of hot milk for each man...Tea, at 5 p.m., had the same menu. Then during the night we had a hot drink, generally of milk. The meals were the bright beacons in those cold and stormy days. The glow of warmth and comfort produced by the food and drink made optimists of us all. We had two tins of Virol, which we were keeping for an emergency; but, finding ourselves in need of an oil lamp to eke out our supply of candles, we emptied one of the tins in the manner that most appealed to us, and fitted it with a wick made by shredding a bit of canvas. When this lamp was filled with oil it gave a certain amount of light, though it was easily blown out, and was of great assistance to us at night...

Our boat took most of the seas more or less end on. Even then the crests of the waves often would curl right over us and we shipped a good deal of water, which necessitated unceasing baling and pumping. Looking out abeam, we would see a hollow like a tunnel formed as the crest of a big wave toppled over into the swelling body of water. A thousand times it appeared as though the James Caird must be engulfed; but the boat lived...

On the tenth night Worsley could not straighten his body after his spell at the tiller. He was thoroughly cramped, and we had to drag him beneath the decking and massage him before he could unbend himself and get into a sleeping bag. A hard northwesterly gale came up on the eleventh day and shifted to the southwest in the late afternoon. The sky was overcast and occasional snow squalls added to the discomfort produced by a tremendous cross-sea – the worst, I thought, that we had experienced. At midnight I was at the tiller and suddenly noticed a line of clear sky between the south and southwest. I called to the other men that the sky was clearing, and then a moment later I realised that what I had seen was not a rift in the clouds but the white crest of an enormous wave. During twenty-six years' experience of the ocean in all its moods I had not encountered a wave so gigantic. It was a mighty upheaval of the ocean, a thing quite apart from the big whitecapped seas that had been our tireless enemies for many days. I shouted, 'For God's sake, hold on! It's got us!' Then came a moment of suspense that seemed drawn out into hours. White surged the foam of the breaking sea around us. We felt our boat lifted and flung forward like a cork in breaking surf. We were in a seething chaos of tortured water; but

Endurance *trapped in the Weddell Sea. Frank Hurley, who took this photograph wrote, 'It is quite inconceivable, even to us, that we are dwelling on a colossal ice raft, with but five feet of ice separating us from 2,000 fathoms of ocean & drifting along under the caprices of wind and tide, to heavens knows where.'*

somehow the boat lived through it, half full of water, sagging to the dead weight and shuddering under the blow. We baled with the energy of men fighting for life, flinging the water over the sides with every receptacle that came to our hands, and after ten minutes of uncertainty we felt the boat renew her life beneath us. She floated again and ceased to lurch drunkenly as though dazed by the attack of the sea. Earnestly we hoped that never again would we encounter such a wave.

E. SHACKLETON, *South, 1919.*

HAVING CROSSED OVER TO SOUTH GEORGIA, SHACKLETON ARRIVED AT STROMNESS

Cautiously we started down the slope that led to warmth and comfort. The last lap of the journey proved extraordinarily difficult. Vainly we searched for a safe, or a reasonably safe, way down from the steep ice-clad

Percy Blackborrow with the carpenter's cat, Mrs Chippy. Aged 19, Blackborrow was the youngest member of the expedition and the only one not to have been chosen personally by Shackleton: he was a stow-away who had come aboard at Buenos Aires. Blackborrow survived the voyage but Mrs Chippy, alas, did not: after the Endurance *sank Shackleton ordered her to be killed in order to save food. The carpenter never forgave him.*

FAR LEFT
Leonard Hussey, the smallest member of the expedition, tussles with Samson, the largest dog. When Endurance *became trapped the dogs were moved from the upper deck to 'dogloos' on the ice. But as it became clear that the ship would never escape they were duly killed and made into 'dog pemmican'. 'This duty fell upon me and was the worst job I ever had in my life', wrote Frank Wild. 'I have known many men I would rather shoot than the worst of the dogs.'*

mountainside. The sole possible pathway seemed to be a channel cut by water running from the upland. Down through icy water we followed the course of this stream. We were wet to the waist, shivering, cold, and tired. Presently our ears detected an unwelcome sound that might have been musical under other conditions. It was the splashing of a waterfall, and we were at the wrong end. When we reached the top of this fall we peered over cautiously and discovered that there was a drop of 25 or 30 ft. With impassable ice cliffs on both sides. To go up again was scarcely thinkable in our utterly wearied condition. The way down was through the waterfall itself. We made fast one end of our rope to a boulder with some difficulty, due to the fact that the rocks had been worn smooth by running water. Then Worsley and I lowered Crean, who was the heaviest man. He disappeared altogether in the falling water and came out gasping at the bottom. I went next, sliding down the rope, and Worsley, who was the lightest and most nimble member of the party, came last. At the bottom of the fall we were able to stand again on dry land. The rope could not be recovered. We had flung down the adze from the top of the fall and also the logbook and the cooker wrapped in one of our blouses. That was all, except for our wet clothes, that we brought out of the Antarctic, which we had entered a year and a half before with well-found ship, full equipment, and high hopes. That was all of tangible things; but in memories we were rich. We had pierced the veneer of outside things. We had 'suffered, starved, and triumphed, grovelled down yet grasped at glory, grown bigger in the bigness of the whole.' We has seen God in his splendours, heard the text that Nature renders. We had reached the naked soul of man.

Shivering with cold, yet with hearts light and happy, we set off towards the whaling station, now not more than a mile and a half distant. The difficulties of the journey lay behind us. We tried to straighten ourselves up a bit, for the thought that there might be women at the station made us painfully conscious of our uncivilized appearance. Our beards were long and our hair was matted. We were unwashed and the garments that we had worn for nearly a year without a change were tattered and stained. Three more unpleasant-looking ruffians could hardly have been imagined. Worsley produced several safety pins from some corner of his garments and effected some temporary repairs that really emphasised his general disrepair. Down we hurried, and when quite close to the station we met two small boys ten or twelve years of age. I asked these lads where the manager's house was situated. They did not answer. They gave us one look – a comprehensive look that did not need to be repeated. Then they ran from us as fast as their legs would carry them. We reached the outskirts of the station and passed through the 'digesting-house', which was dark inside. Emerging at the other end, we met an old man, who started as if he had seen the Devil himself and gave us no time to ask any question. He hurried away. This greeting was not friendly. Then we came to the wharf, where the man in charge stuck to his station. I asked him if Mr. Sorlle (the manager) was in his house.

'Yes', he said as he stared at us.

'We would like to see him', said I.

'Who are you?' he asked.

'We have lost our ship and come over the island', I replied.

'You have come over the island?' he said in a tone of entire disbelief.

The man went towards the manager's house and we followed him. I learned afterwards that he said to Mr. Sorlle: 'There are three funny-looking men outside, who say they have come over the island and they know you. I have left them outside.' A very necessary precaution from his point of view.

Mr. Sorlle came to the door and said, 'Well?'

'Don't you know me? I said.

'I know your voice,' he replied doubtfully. 'You're the mate of the Daisy.'

'My name is Shackleton', I said.

Immediately he put out his hand and said, 'Come in. Come in.'

'Tell me, when was the war over?' I asked.

'The war is not over,' he answered. 'Millions are being killed. Europe is mad. The world is mad.'

E. SHACKLETON, *South*, *1919*.

The crew members that Shackleton left on Elephant Island while he sailed to South Georgia. They survived for months under a pair of upturned boats, cooking meals on a blubber stove the fumes of which covered their outfits with a layer of black grease. The conditions on Elephant Island were exceedingly squalid. Photographer Frank Hurley described the men as 'the most motley assemblage that ever was projected on plate'.

GEORGE MALLORY 1886–1924
Mystery on Everest

Fresh from fording a river, Mallory turns a pert cheek to the camera. His companions Howard Somervell and Arthur Wakefield enjoy the joke. The trek to Everest was almost as arduous as the business of climbing it. So inhospitable was the terrain that early expeditions resembled military campaigns, complete with lengthy baggage trains carrying food, fuel and accommodation.

EVER SINCE 1852, when British surveyors recognized Mount Everest (Peak XV on their maps) as the highest mountain in the world, climbers had had it in their sights. Not until 1921, however, did the assault begin in earnest. For four years British teams battered the slopes, each successive foray drawing closer to the summit. Members came and went but none was more persistent than a schoolteacher named George Mallory. Among the most experienced mountaineers of the day, famous for his elastic ability on rocks, Mallory was also a man of letters, a darling of London's literary elite. He set new altitude records on climb after climb and by 1924, having established a camp higher than any yet, he was ready for the final push. Accompanied by a strong but inexperienced youngster named Sandy Irvine, he left for the summit on the morning of 8 June. Mallory was confident that they could be there and back before nightfall – a view shared by an expedition member who spotted them moving fast, with just 800 feet to go. The two men never returned. Their fate remained a mystery until 1999 when an American expedition discovered Mallory's mummified corpse. He had fallen, but it was not possible to tell whether he had died before or after reaching the summit. Irvine's body has never been found, neither has the Kodak Vestpocket camera carried by Mallory. Until they are, the question remains open.

TRANSCRIPTS SENT FROM EVEREST DESCRIBE THE THREE SUMMIT ATTEMPTS OF 1924. THE WRITERS ARE CLIMBING LEADER 'TEDDY' NORTON, HOWARD SOMERVELL AND NOEL ODELL. NORTON: Camp III. East Rongbuk Glacier. June 8. I dictate the eighth dispatch from Camp III. I say dictate, as I am unable to write, as I am just recovering from an acute attack of snow-blindness... Geoffrey Bruce, jack-of-all-trades, is my secretary. Both of us having had a go at high altitudes feel that this particular work for the moment is exactly what suits us.

Above towers Everest, somewhat powdered with fresh snow, still and windless, and half-shrouded in that type of damp, stickly cloud which surely this time presages the advance of the monsoon proper. Every eye in camp is turned on the final pyramid. Expectation is at its keenest, for somewhere the final attempt, as it must inevitably be, is at this moment deciding the success or failure of the 1924 expedition...

Progress up the north ridge of Everest does not lend itself to description. It is a fight against wind and altitude, generally on rock, sometimes on snow, at an average angle of 45°. It will appeal to those who have ever tried mountain climbing above 23,000 feet. Camp V was to be situated on the east or sheltered side of the ridge at about 25,300 feet. At about 25,000 feet the endurance of the porters began to flag, and of eight only four made Camp V under their own steam. The remainder deposited their loads, unable to go on. While Mallory set to work to organise the camp, Bruce and one Lobsang, meriting the description of being one of the leaders of the 'Tigers,' made two trips back from the level of the camp and brought up the missing loads on their own backs. Whites cannot carry loads at these altitudes without impunity, and it is scarcely to be wondered at that Bruce's heart was strained, happily only temporarily, in this fine performance.

SOMERVELL: The altitude was beginning to tell severely on us. About 27,500 feet there was almost sudden change. A little lower down we could walk comfortably, taking three or four breaths for each step, but now seven, eight, or ten complete respirations were necessary for every single step forward. Even at this slow rate of progress we had to indulge in a rest for a minute or two at every 20 or 30 yards. In fact, we were getting to the limit of endurance...We agreed reluctantly that the game was up...So with heavy hearts, beating over 180 to the minute, we returned and retraced our steps; but slowly, for even downhill movement at this level is rather hard and breathless work, and both of us required frequent rests for regaining our breath and resummoning our energy. The view from the topmost point that we reached, and indeed all the way up, was quite beyond words for its extent and magnificence. Gyachang Kang and Chouyo, among the highest mountains in the world, were over 1000 feet beneath. Around them we saw a perfect sea of fine peaks, all giants among mountains, all as dwarfs below us. The splendid dome of Pumori, the most splendid of Everest's satellites, was but an incident in the vast array of peak upon peak. Over the plain of Tibet a distant range gleamed, 200 miles away. The view, indeed, was indescribable, and one simply seemed to be above everything in the world and to have a glimpse almost of a god's view of things...

We are now awaiting news of Mallory and Irvine, who to-day are making another attempt, hoping that they may reinforce the feeble summit air by artificially provided oxygen, and by its means be enabled to conquer the chief difficulty of reaching the

OVERLEAF
The 1924 party photographed by Captain Noel: back row, l. to r. Irvine, Mallory, Norton, Odell, Macdonald; front row, Shebbeare, Bruce, Somervell, Beetham. Asked why he was so determined to conquer Everest, Mallory replied: 'For the stone from the top for geologists, the knowledge of the limits of endurance for the doctors but above all for the spirit of adventure to keep alive the soul of man.' Then, flippantly, he added, 'Because it's there.'

Mallory and Irvine adjust their oxygen tanks as they leave for the North Col, in the last surviving photograph of the two men together. That they died in the summit attempt was certain; whether they reached their goal remains unknown. Norton, the climbing leader, penned an emotional obituary note: 'Together these two men went up the mountain for the last time, higher than ever man has been before. They were last seen, one giving a hand to the other, and then they were seen no more. Could either have wished for a better friend to hold his hand at the crossing into the unknown land beyond?'

summit. May the Genie of the Steel Bottle aid them! All of us are hoping that he may, for nobody deserves the summit more than Mallory, the only one of our number who has been at it for three years.

ODELL: On June 6, following an early breakfast of fried sardines, joyfully acclaimed and moderately partaken of, Mallory and Irvine left the North Col Camp for Camp V (25,000 feet) accompanied by five porters, with provisions and reserve oxygen cylinders...[On 7 June] Porters returning from Mallory that night [from Camp VI] were the bearers of a hopeful message in a note which said that they had only used the minimum of oxygen up to 27,000 feet, and that the weather was perfect for the job. The latter I could well appreciate, for, looking out that evening from the little rock ledge on which the tent was pitched at Camp V, I saw that the weather indeed seemed most promising for the morrow.

The situation of the camp was unique and the outlook a commanding one. Westward there was a savage, wild jumble of peaks, culminating in Ch Uyo (26,750 feet), bathed in pinks and yellows of most exquisite tints. Right opposite were the the gaunt cliffs of Everest north peak, intercepting a portion of the wide northern horizon, of a brilliant opalescence...Eastward, floating in the thin air, the snowy top of Kanchenjunga appeared, and lastly, the beautifully varied outlying Gyangkar Range. Sunset and after at that altitude were a transcendentant experience never to be forgotten.

At early morning of June 8 it was clear and not unduly cold at such an altitude. The two porters I had brought with me to Camp V complained of sickness and headache, and altogether I was not unthankful for an excuse to send them down to Camp IV at the North Col, for I especially wished to be free during an ascent I was to make for as wide a geological survey of the mountain face between Camps V and VI as possible. Soon after I had started on my task banks of cloud began to form, which periodically immersed one in gloom, but the wind remained quite light for such an exposed ridge. Now and then there would be an accompaniment of sleet and slight snow. I could see above me frequently during these squalls that there was a glow of light, indicating clearness at a higher altitude, and hoped that Mallory and Irvine were above the mist.

At 12.50, just after I had emerged in a state of jubilation at finding the first definite fossil on Everest, there was a sudden clearing of the atmosphere, and the entire summit ridge and final peak of Everest were unveiled. My eyes became fixed on one tiny black spot silhouetted on a small snowcrest beneath a rock-step in the ridge, and the black spot moved. Another black spot becamse apparent and moved up the snow to join the other on the crest...The first then approached the great rock-step and shortly emerged at the top; the second did likewise...the whole fascinating vision vanished, enveloped in cloud...

There was but one explanation. It was Mallory and his companion moving, as I could see even at that great distance, with considerable alacrity.

NORTON: Rongbuk base camp, June 14. There is no question of a resumption of hostilities on the mountain. Every one of the surviving climbers has shot his bolt. I have before me a medical report showing that each of us has a more or less dilated heart, besides various minor disabilities The trouble will right itself at the lower altitudes to which we are bound, but would probably be permanent if further high climbing were attempted...

We leave here with heavy hearts. We failed to establish success, for who will ever know if the lost climbers reached the summit before the accident which it may be assumed caused their death?...The price is out of all proportion to the results....Mallory was was

for three years the living soul of the offensive on Everest. I believe the thing was a personal matter with him, and was ultimately somewhat different from what it was to the rest of us…The fire within made him really great, for it caused his spirit constantly to dominate his body to such an extent that, much as I have climbed with him, I can hardly picture his ever succumbing to exhaustion…

Our one free day here before we finally leave this Base Camp of conflicting memories, so bleak and inhospitable after the sunny plains of Tibet, so homelike and cosy after the far bleaker glacier camps, is fully occupied. Every man that can be spared is at work arranging the loads for to-morrow's march, or employed on erecting a monument on one of the great conical morraine heaps which overlook the Base Camp to commemorate the names of those who lost their lives in the three Mount Everest expeditions.

The Mount Everest Dispatches, The Geographical Journal, Vol LXIV, No 2, 1924.

UMBERTO NOBILE 1885–1978

Zeppelins on top of the world

A crewmen in the rigging of the Norge, with flags to be dropped over the Pole. Amundsen and Ellsworth, who had been instructed to keep weight to a minimum, dropped modest pennants. Nobile, however, produced a gigantic Italian tricolour that had been stored in a heavy oak casket, and shoved it through the porthole to hearty cheers from his compatriots. Outraged, Amundsen commented that his tiny Norwegian flag looked like a handkerchief in comparison.

AN ITALIAN DIRIGIBLE DESIGNER, *umberto nobile was joint commander (with Roald Amundsen and Lincoln Ellsworth) of the* Norge *on its 1926 flight from Spitsbergen to Alaska via the North Pole. Spurred by this success, he undertook a series of flights to map the unknown sectors of the Arctic. In 1928, however, his airship* Italia *crashed on the ice off Spitsbergen: seven of the 16 crew were killed and an eighth died in mysterious circumstances while leading a party across the pack to fetch help. An international rescue team, comprising 18 ships, 22 planes and 1,500 men, converged on the region. One of the planes managed to extricate Nobile but overturned on the return journey, forcing its pilot to join the castaways. Several other planes also crashed, with the result that more people died rescuing the* Italia *survivors than had died on the* Italia *itself. Back in Italy, Nobile faced rumours of cannibalism and accusations of irresponsibility in allowing himself to be evacuated before the rest of his crew. Shunned in his homeland, he moved to the Soviet Union, where he participated in Stalin's megalomaniac scheme to build the world's largest dirigible. He later emigrated to the United States before finally settling in Spain.*

THE ITALIA'S CONTROL CABIN WAS TORN OFF WHEN IT CRASHED, TIPPING NOBILE AND SEVERAL OTHERS ONTO THE ICE. FREED OF THEIR WEIGHT, THE DIRIGIBLE ROSE BACK INTO THE AIR WITH SIX MEN STILL ABOARD.

I opened my eyes and found myself lying on the ice, in the midst of an appalling pack. I realized at once that the others had fallen with me.

I looked up to the sky. Towards my left the dirigible, nose in the air, was drifting away before the wind. It was terribly lacerated around the pilot-cabin. Out of it trailed torn strips of fabric, ropes, fragments of metal-work. The left wall of the cabin had remained attached. I noticed a few creases in the envelope...[I watched] as if fascinated, until the dirigible merged in the fog and was lost to sight.

It was only then that I felt my injuries. My right leg and arm were broken and throbbing; I had hurt my face and the top of my head, and my chest seemed all upside down with the violence of the shock. I thought my end was near...

Here and there one could see wreckage – a dreary note of grey against the whiteness of the snow. In front of me a strip of bright red, like blood which had flowed from some enormous wound, showed the spot where we had fallen. It was liquid from the glass [altimeter] balls...Beside me on the right Malmgren was still sitting silent in the same place, stroking his right arm. On his face, frowning and ashen pale, a little swollen from his fall, was a look of blank despair. His blue eyes stared fixedly in front of him, as if into the void. Lost in thought, he seemed not even to notice the other men around him...he got up. He could not stand erect, for his injured shoulder made him stoop...he turned to me and said in English: 'General, I thank you for the trip...I go under the water!'

So saying, he turned away. I stopped him: 'No Malmgren! You have no right to do this. We will die when God has decided. We must wait. Please stop here.'

I shall never forget the look he turned on me at that moment. He seemed surprised. Perhaps he was struck by the gentle and affectionate seriousness of my tone. For a moment he stood still, as if undecided. Then he sat down again...

Once the tent was ready they carried me there. The going was painful. More than once I had to set my teeth, not to cry out with the agony of my fractures. But at last they dragged me inside and laid me at the back of the tent, along the wall facing the entrance.

Then they carried in Cecioni and put him beside me...Then they gave me the news of Pomello's death. They had found him seated on the ice near the wreckage of his engine-boat. He had taken off one of his leather shoes. There was no sign of suffering on his face – no apparent injury.

Pomella was very dear to me; yet that tragic night his loss left me indifferent. It was not hardness of heart – but involuntarily I reflected that it was better for him to have died then and there and escaped the lingering death reserved for us...I envied him his lot.

Then having speculated a little about the fate of the other six we settled down to sleep. Nine men, huddled up together in that cramped space. A tangle of human limbs. Outside the wind was howling, and one could hear the canvas of the tent flapping with a lugubrious rhthym. Cecioni rambled on until weariness overcame him. It overcame me too, and I fell asleep.

U. NOBILE, *My Polar Flights, 1961.*

THREE MEN – MALGREM, MARIANO AND ZAPPI – VOLUNTEERED TO WALK OVER THE ICE TO FETCH HELP FROM SPITZBERGEN. MALGREM, WHO HAD BEEN BADLY INJURED IN THE CRASH, DIED EARLY ON. ZAPPI'S ACCOUNT, RELATED TO A JOURNALIST, TELLS HOW HE AND MARIANO WERE FINALLY RESCUED.

Mariano – it was the fourth day we had eaten nothing – entreated me once again to leave him so that I might reach the land. It was too late. Without food and in a weak condition, I considered that the attempt would not have the least chance of success. And so we resigned ourselves to die. The cold, the damp, and the wind were driving from our bodies the last remnants of strength. This agony lasted twelve days. We could no longer reasonably nourish any further hopes. Quietly we awaited the end.

On July 10 towards evening we suddenly heard overhead the fresh drone of engines. Stumbling out of our cave of ice, I waved wildly a strip of rag which had served us as a flag. I realized with surprise that the pilot had seen me, and a cry of joy broke from my lips. And, in fact, the machine began to make wide circles over our heads. Five times he swept round above our prison. I continued to wave the flag until the machine had disappeared in the mist...But the aeroplane did not return.

Desperation again swept over us. On the morning of the 12th the shrill blast from a siren violently startled both of us. At the time we were lying wrapped in the soaked blanket. I jumped up hastily, but at first saw nothing. Believing it to have been a sound produced by the movement of the ice, I lay down again. But then all of a sudden I seemed to see a trail of smoke. I climbed onto the highest point of our hummock...I summoned up my last remaining strength and waved the rag wildly. Another blast from the siren. All doubts vanished. The [icebreaker] had seen us.

'We are saved, Mariano. We shall see our families again, we shall see again our dear country.'

Another anxious half-hour went by, and then the vessel resolutely turned her bows towards our ice-floe. The cheers of the crew sounded in our ears like a song welcoming us back to life.

D. GIUDICI, *The Tragedy of the Italia, 1929.*

AUGUST COURTAULD 1904–59

Alone on the Greenland Ice Cap

THE SON OF A MILLIONAIRE INDUSTRIALIST, *Courtauld enrolled as a member of the British Arctic Aero Expedition. Its destination was Greenland; its aim was to study the Arctic's influence on European weather systems; and its leader was Gino Watkins, a man whose dedication was likened by his companions to that of Shackleton and Scott. (Like them, he too came to an untimely end, losing his life on a subsequent Greenland expedition.) Trapped for the winter, Watkins refused to call for assistance in the hope that the experience would yield valuable meterological information. Courtauld volunteered to man one of the more isolated weather stations. Beyond radio contact, and equipped with only the basics, he waited for the winter to pass. Snow covered his tent and crushed the igloos that contained his supplies. Stoically, he lit his pipe. 'There is nothing to complain of', he noted, 'unless it be the curse of having to go out into the cold winds every three hours to observe the weather.' He made a token effort to conserve food but, as he said, 'I prefer to eat my cake rather than have it. Carpe diem.' Eventually, the food ran out. So too, did his tobacco, whereupon he smoked tea leaves. When the fuel also failed, he smoked in the dark. The snow fell and fell until the only sign of his presence was a few inches of ventilator pipe protruding above the drifts. His parents mounted several air expeditions to save him but it was Watkins and two others who eventually sledged to his rescue. Courtauld was at first relieved, and then angry that so much money and effort should have been expended. His tribulations, as he told his fiancée, had been 'very mere'.*

COURTAULD PONDERS HIS SOLITARY EXISTENCE.

Why is it that men come to these places? So many reasons have been ascribed to it. In the old days it was thought to be lust for treasure, but the treasure is gone and still men wander. Then it was a craving for adventure. There is precious little adventure in sledging or sitting on an ice cap. Is it curiosity, a yearning to look behind the veil on to the mysteries and desolation of nature in her forlorn places? Perhaps, but that is not all. Why leave all whom we love, all good friends, all creature comforts, all mindly joys, to collect a little academic knowledge about this queer old earth of ours? What do we gain?...

Do we in fact morally bury ourselves in fleeing from the world? Do we simply rot or grow rank like some plant thrown over the garden wall? Or do we come nearer to reality, see more clearly the great purpose behind it all, in stripping our souls of the protection of our friends and in putting from us the pleasures of the body? How little the worries of the world seem to one in a situation such as this; how grand and awful the things that are here, the things that grip the heart and with fear, the forces that spin the universe through space. In leaving behind the transitory hopes and fears of pathetic humanity, does one become closer to the things that abide, the things that endure?...

The following pleasures I should like to have granted most, if wishing were any good. One, sitting in an armchair before dinner, in front of a roaring fire, listening to Mollie [his fiancee] playing and singing. Two: eight o'clock on a fine summer morning at sea, at the helm of a small boat, a fresh breeze blowing, all sail set, with Mollie and a smell of breakfast coming up to say good morning. Three: just having got into bed with clean sheets and ditto pyjamas. Four: bright autumn morning, eating an apple in the garden before break-

fast (an enormous one - kippers, poached eggs, kidneys and mushrooms, cold partridge). Five: getting into a hot bath...

As each month passed without relief, I felt more and more certain of its arrival. By the time I was snowed in I had no doubts on the matter, which was a great comfort to my mind. I will not attempt any explanation of this, but leave it as a fact, which was very clear to me during that time, that while powerless to help myself, some outer force was in action on my side and I wasn't fated to leave my bones on the Greenland ice cap.

N. WOLLASTON, *The Life of August Courtauld, 1980.*

OVERLEAF *Kayakers float in a berg-filled bay. Although equipped with an aeroplane, the expedition spent much of its time trying to make the thing work.*

AUGUSTE PICCARD 1884–1962

Into the stratosphere

The epitome of a mad scientist, Piccard (far right) bids farewell to the mill of friends and onlookers who saw him off on 27 May 1931. Having proved that his sphere could endure the airless stratosphere he used the same technology to explore the ocean. In 1953, when Hillary and Tenzing conquered Everest, Piccard equalled their highest above sea-level with a farthest below.

Piccard (right) and Kipfer don their dual-purpose aero-helmets. The baskets were used to store instruments and the cushions alleviated the discomfort of sitting

in a cast-iron sphere In the event of atmospheric 'bounce' the two could be combined as head protection.

ON 27 MAY 1931 *a balloon lifted off from Augsberg, Germany. Beneath it, in a pressurized aluminium capsule built to his own design, huddled Piccard and fellow physicist Paul Kipfer. The balloon reached a height of 16,142 metres, becoming the first manned craft to enter the stratosphere, before it came down on the Obergurgl Glacier in Austria. Piccard bettered this altitude in 1932 and subsequently made another 27 flights before turning to ocean exploration. Using the same technology that had taken him to near-space he built the bathyscaph Trieste, and in 1953 descended to a record depth of 3,139 metres. Seven years later his son Jacques took the Trieste to 10,917 metres – more than 11 kilometres below sea level. Piccard's twin brother Jean also made his name as a high-altitude balloonist; and his grandson Bertrand later followed family tradition by becoming the first person to circumnavigate the globe by balloon.*

ON THE DIFFERENCE BETWEEN SKY AND SPACE.

We live in the troposphere. It is here that all metereological phenomena take place. The sea-water evaporates; sucked up by the sun, it soars up to the sky, there to be seized by the winds. In their frantic whirlings they carry it over the oceans, over continents; never does it find peace. Sooner or later the water condenses, forms clouds, rain, snow or hail, and a sudden plunge ends its aerial journey. The winds, meanwhile, continue their aimless wanderings – sometimes as gentle breezes, sometimes as hurricanes, rising as cyclones, descending as anti-cyclones, whirling to the right, to the left. Never can a stable position be reached; it is an endless circle. This is where we have to live: in the troposphere...

Above this lies the stratosphere. There all struggling has ceased: there are no vertical movements. Each portion of air is satisfied with the position it has acquired; without altering its altitude, it pursues its journey at the mercy of the winds. No vertical motion introduces moisture, no condensation occurs. Nothing disturbs the clearness of the stratosphere, no mist, no cloud. It is unchangeable fine weather, an eternal peace. A bright sun rises over the horizon and travels the unsullied majesty of a purple sky. No sooner has it set in the evening than stars light up and sparkle as no earthly spectator has ever seen them.

This land of dreams, this paradise, is the stratosphere. Twenty minutes', half an hour's ascent in a free balloon separates us from it. That is all; but that is a great deal.

A. PICCARD, *Between Earth and Sky, 1950.*

PETER FLEMING 1907–71

Adventures in Brazil

IN 1932, WHILE LITERARY EDITOR of the Spectator, *Fleming saw an advertisement in* The Times *seeking volunteers for an expedition to find Colonel Percy Fawcett who had recently disappeared in the Matto Grosso. He answered, and was accepted. The party failed to locate Fawcett but gave Fleming material for a book,* Brazilian Adventure, *that broke new ground in exploration literature. He subsequently travelled through Tibet, China, Mongolia and the Caucasus, describing each trip with a wit that became his trademark. His facade of amateur insouciance concealed a steely determination. As one companion wrote, 'I appreciated Peter's brilliant intelligence, his faculty of being able to eat anything and sleep anywhere, and also his sure grasp of the kernel of any situation, of the essential point in any argument...[also] from what I knew of his life, he had been born under a lucky star.'*

RECRUITMENT FOR FLEMING'S BRAZILIAN EXPEDITION.

Roger [Pettiward] was walking along Gower Street. He had passed the School of Tropical Hygiene. He had passed the Royal Academy of Dramatic Art. In one minute, in less than one minute, he would have reached the Slade: would have spent the afternoon mixing blue and yellow and making green (or whatever it is that artists do): would never have heard of the expedition, for Roger is an inconstant reader of *The Times*.

By one of those coincidences which (as novelists are always careful to say) would hardly pass muster in a work of fiction, I came out in a great hurry from my office on the other side of Gower Street just as Roger passed. At Eton and Oxford I had known him only by sight. In the last three years I had met him three times. But here was a fine large chap with an eye for comedy: so I called across the street: 'Roger, come to Brazil.'

'What?' said Roger: playing, I dare say, for time.

'You'd better come to Brazil', I said, getting into a car.

'Why?' said Roger cautiously (or perhaps incautiously), also getting into the car. We set off down Gower Street: past the Royal Academy of Dramatic Art: past the School of Tropical Hygiene. I talked rapidly. At the end of Gower Street Roger got out.

'I'll let you know for certain on Monday', he said. But his fate was sealed.

Pure coincidence is a rare commodity. About three months later I was sitting over a fire in the middle of a chill night without a moon. A small river brushed quietly past our sandbank. Trees – too many trees – stood up all around us. No white man had ever come to this place before, and probably none would ever come again. Broadly speaking, we were as far as it was possible to be from anywhere. In his burrow, roofed over with branches against the mosquitoes, a one-eyed Brazilian snored with all the passion of the south. Roger was the only other person present. He also was asleep.

As I watched him, it suddenly occurred to me that here was the perfect, the flawless example of a pure coincidence.

If the Recording Angel, collecting advance data for his dossiers, had suddenly swooped down between the drought-sapped branches, woken Roger up, and said to him: 'Explain your conduct, please. I observe that you are sleeping – not all soundly, on account of the mosquitoes – beside a river which is marked on no map, inside one of the biggest unex-

Laden with rifles, Fleming strides through the Tapirape River. After splitting from the main party he and his companions found themselves boatless. Finding it easier to walk along the riverbed than struggle through the jungle on its banks, they spent two whole days in the water.

plored tracts in the word. I understand that you are looking for traces of a complete stranger whom you believe to have perished more than seven years ago. Would you mind telling me why you are doing this – what is the prime and fundamental cause of your being in so improbable a situation?' – If this question had been put to him, Roger could have given only one answer. He must have said: 'I am here, in the last analysis, because on the 20th of May last I walked down Gower Street at precisely the time I did. If I had been a minute earlier or a minute later – if I had not stopped to buy an evening paper, or if my shoe-lace had broken – I should not be here. You can't have anything more fundamental than that. I hope you are satisfied.' And the Recording Angel, too often embarrassed with a wealth of motive, a luxuriance of contributory circumstances, would have flown off well pleased with a case thus simple and explicit. Or so I figured, while the mosquitoes exulted over the victim of coincidence.

For me, the enrolment of Roger made the whole expedition at once more or less plausible. More, because here at last was a member with some techincal qualification for the

task at hand. (Roger had some knowledge of surveying, which he proceeded forthwith to increase at the Royal Geographical Society). Less, because two heads were better able than one to appreciate the hare-brained nature of our enterprise, and the childish inadequacy (so far) of our methods. For, in spite of our official plan, it was clear by this time that no one really knew where we were going or why we were going there, or whether it wouldn't perhaps be better to go somewhere else instead.

P. FLEMING, *Brazilian Adventure, 1933.*

A BUSH FIRE.

As usual, the open country on the other side [of the river] was less open than it looked. The scattered trees and the tall grass made a screen which the eye could not penetrate to any great depth. About 400 yards inland there was a thickish belt of low scrub, and on the edge of this stood a tree with a broad but curiously twisted trunk. This I climbed.

I stayed up it for half an hour, and in that half hour the world below me changed. A wind began to sing in the sparse leaves round my observation post. The sky darkened. Massed black cohorts of clouds assembled in the west and came up across the sky under streaming pennons. The wind rose until its voice was a scream; great weals appeared in the upstanding grass, and in the straining thickets the undersides of the leaves showed pale and quivering in panic. My tree groaned and bent and trembled. The sky grew darker still.

The earth was ablaze. That fire which the Indians had lit raced forward under the trampling clouds, and behind me, on the other side of the river, a long battle-line of flames was leaping out across the campo we had fired that morning. Huge clouds of smoke charged down the wind, twisting tormented plumes of yellow and black and grey. The air was full of fleeting shreds of burnt stuff. The fall of sparks threw out little skirmishing fires before the main body of the flames. A dead tree close beside me went up with a roar while the fire was still half a mile away.

There was something malevolent in its swift advance. The light thickened and grew yellow; the threatening sky was scorched and lurid. If there could be hell on earth, I thought, this is what it would look like. I remembered with a curious distinctness a picture which had made a great impression on me as a child: a crude, old-fashioned picture of a prairie fire in a book of adventure. Swung to and fro among the gesticulating branches of my tree, I saw again in memory every detail of that picture: the long grass flattened in the wind, the fierce and overstated glare of the approaching fire: and in the foreground a herd of horses in panic flight. I remembered that they were led – inevitably – by a grey: that a black horse in the right hand corner of the picture had fallen and would be trampled to death. I even recalled the place and time when I had first seen this picture: the dark winter afternoon, the nursery in which I was recovering from illness, the smooth brass rail on top of the high fender gleaming in the firelight, the shape of the little tree outside the window where half a coconut always hung for the tits. I realised with surprise how near the distant picture in that picture had been to the reality now before me, and how curiously the fascination exerted by the image had foreshadowed the fascination exerted by the reality.

There was indeed a kind of horrible beauty in the scene. A fury had fallen upon the world. All the sounds, all the colours, expressed daemonic anger. The ponderous and inky clouds, the flames stampeding wantonly, the ungovernable screaming of the wind, the murky yellow light – all these combined to create an atmosphere of monstrous, elemental crisis. The world would split, the sky would fall; things could never be the same after this.

The fire was almost on me now, but my retreat to the river was open and secure. Flames flattened and straining in the wind licked into the belt of scrub beside my tree; great gusts of heat came up from below and struck me. Little birds – why so tardily, I wondered – fled crying to the trees on the river bank. Two big kites warily quartered the frontiers of the fire, though I never saw either stoop. Presently one of them came and sat on a branch below me, so close that I could have hit him with a stick. He stayed there, brooding majestically, with his proud eyes, over the work of desolation. Every now and then he shrugged himself and fluffed his feathers: for fear, I suppose, that he might entertain a spark unawares. I felt oddly friendly towards him, as one might to a coastguard in a storm; his imperturbability, his air of having seen a good deal of this sort of thing in his time, were comforting. But a spark stung my naked back, and I swore. The kite looked at me in a deprecating way and dropped downwind to the next tree.

Then the storm broke. It opened first a random fire of huge and icy drops. I saw that we were in for worse and scrambled down the tree: not without regret, for I had seen a fine and curious sight and would willingly have watched for longer, the cataclysmic evening having gone a little to my head. But shelter of a sort was essential, and I found the best available under the trees on the river bank....

There began such a rain as I had never seen before. It fell in sheets and with ferocity. It was ice-cold. It beat the placid river into a convulsive stew. The world darkened; thunder leapt and volleyed in the sky. From time to time lightning would drain the colour and the substance from our surroundings, leaving us to blink timidly at masses of vegetation which had suddenly shown up as pale elaborate silhouettes, unearthly, ephemeral, and doomed. The rain beat land and water till they roared. The thunder made such noise in heaven as would shortly crack the fabric of the universe. The turmoil was almost too great to intimidate. It could not be with us that Nature had picked so grandiose a quarrel; her strife was internecine. Dwarfed into a safe irrelevance, dwarfed so that we seemed no longer to exist, we had no part in these upheavals. Roger and I smiled at each other across the loud waters with stiff and frozen faces.

Brazilian Adventure

Pistol at the ready, Fleming keeps an eye out for alligators. It was the privilege of the those on the leading boat to shoot anything they saw, every hit being greeted by, 'a wailing and ironic cry of "Viva o Brasil!" in tones of burlesque enthusiasm. This was one of the expeditionary jokes and never failed to please the men.' Nobody, including Fleming, could hit anything with the pistol but he was a dab hand with their .22 rifle. When forced to turn back he took a resentful shot at a passing alligator. 'This was probably the most phenomenal result ever produced with a rook rifle', he wrote. 'The peaceful river boiled. The alligator thrashed its head from side to side in agony. Then, as the tiny bullet touched (I suppose) its brain, it reared itself out upon the further bank and lay there, killed with a crumb of lead...We left it sprawling there, to mark the futile end of a hopeless quest. If those secret Indians came to our camp after we had gone (as I expect they did) I hope they were suitably impressed by a monster so mysteriously dead.'

FREYA STARK 1893–1993

Trekking in Arabia

AT THE AGE OF FIVE STARK *could speak three languages. At the age of twelve she lost an ear and much of her scalp when her hair became entangled in a machine. At the age of twenty she was working for the* Baghdad Times, *having studied literature at London University, survived a broken engagement, served as a nurse on the Italian Front in World War One, and learnt Arabic. This kaleidoscopic upbringing gave her a sense if not exactly of spirituality then of self that supported her through a lifetime of travel and exploration. As she wrote, 'Psychologists tell us that the impulse of sex is the fundamental mover of this world, and we are perhaps getting a little tired of hearing it so often. But there are two impulses stronger than desire, deeper than love of man or woman, and independent of it – the human hunger for truth and liberty. For these two, greater sacrifices are made than for any love of person; against them nothing can prevail, since love and life itself have proved themselves light in the balance...What with popular lectures, compulsory instruction and the belief that one is is educated if one can read and write, we sometimes forget that this hunger of our soul exists.' Her first expedition, at the age of thirty, took her through the 'forbidden territory' of Syria. A subsequent trek across Iraq and Iran established her reputation as an explorer. Later, she travelled throughout southern Arabia, covering routes that had been forgotten for centuries. Always going alone, save for the occasional servant, she survived imprisonment and disease to become one of the most insightful travel writers of the age.*

TOWARDS THE ALAMUT GORGE.

The path was narrow and red, eaten away at its riverside edge by floods and rains, unless it broadened out into swampy rice-fields, that quivered with mosquitoes and heat. Shut in by its mountain range from the Qazvin plain, the fertile and beautiful valley lay like a world of its own. Blue hills, ever fainter, settled to its shallow horizon on the west. Eastward, we were penetrating into the salty stretches of Rudbar on our left hand, a country uninhabited and lifeless as the moon. The Ma'dan Rud, a stream bitter as Acheron, fell before us from salt marshes through waste land. We crossed it, and came to a part of the track so narrow that Ismail had to unload the baggage and coax the mules one at a time round the corner, telling them the most distressing things about their parentage, punctuated with a stick from behind. I, meanwhile, sat with my head in my hands, looked at the flooded river below, and wondered at what was going on inside me to make me feel so ill.

We saw ahead of us the first pinnacles of the Alamut gorge, naked rock piled in chaos and rounded by weather, without a blade of grass upon it. Most of the bridges were washed away, but we found one, sagging in the middle but fairly solid, and crossed to the south bank of the Shah Rud below a village called Kandichal.

Here there was no salt in the ground, and a kinder nature appeared; we rode along an overhanging cliff, high above the brown snow-water. But here I felt too ill to continue. We came to a small solitary corrie where a whitewashed shrine or Imamzadeh slept peacefully in front of a sloping field or two of corn. A brook and a few tangled fruit trees were on one side of it in a hollow. A grey-bearded priest, dressed in blue peasant garb and black

skull cap, gave permission to stay; and Ismail put up my bed in the open, under a pear and sanjid tree overgrown with vines near the brook.

For nearly a week I lay there, not expecting to recover, and gazed through empty days at the barren Rudbar hills across the river, where shadows of the clouds threw patterns, the only moving things in that silent land. To look on its nakedness was in itself a preparation for the greater nakedness of death, so that gradually the mind was calmed of fear and filled with austerity and peace.

I lived on white of egg and sour milk, and had barley cooked in my water so that the taste might tell me if it were boiled, since the little stream running from the village on the hill was probably not as pure as it looked. It was an incredible effort to organise oneself for illness with only Ismail to rely on and the women of Kandichal, whose dialect was incomprehensible. One of them, called Zora, used to look after me for fourpence a day. With her rags, which hung in strips about her, she had the most beautiful and saddest face I have ever seen. She would sit on the grass by my bedside with her knees drawn up, silent by the hour, looking out with her heavy-lidded eyes to the valley below and the far slopes where the shadows travelled, like some Saint whose Eternity is darkened by the remote voice of sorrow in the world. I used to wonder what she thought, but was too weak to ask, and slipped from coma to coma, waking to see rows of women squatting round my bed with children in their arms, hopeful of quinine...

By the third day I was no better, and my heart began to give trouble. I decided to send Ismail and one of the mules across the mountain range to get a prescription from some doctor in Qazvin. This he did, and came back on the afternoon of the next day with a bottle of digitalis and a letter in English from some unknown well-wisher who 'hoped

OVERLEAF
A vertiginous path through the Wadi Du'an in Yemen. Stark's journey, made in 1935, was financed in part by royalties from her best-selling The Valley of the Assassins, *an account of her travels in Syria. Unfortunately, her expedition was brought to a premature close when she developed severe angina and had to be evacuated by the Royal Air Force to a hospital in Aden.*

that I now realized the gravity of my situation and would abandon this foolish idea of wandering unprotected over Persia.' I had, as a matter of fact, very nearly abandoned any idea of wandering altogether, and was envisaging eternity under the shadow of Sitt Zeinabar's tomb.

F. STARK, *The Valleys of the Assassins. 1934.*

IN THE HADHRAMAUT.

One man particularly I remember. After squatting on the sand beside his camels to wash his arms and legs and head and mouth, he stood to pray. One could not see in the late light that he had anything on at all (though in the middle of the prayer he did as a matter of fact loosen and hitch up his futah). He stood there with a pose graceful and sure, his beard and hair and lean unpampered limbs outlined against the sea – just a Man, with an indescribable dignity of mere Manhood about him. And when he had stooped to place his forehead on the ground, he came upright again with one spring of his body, as if it were made of steel.

Meanwhile, darkness stole down; the last sunset red and the first camp fire burned with the same colour; the straying parties by valley and shore grew fewer; the tribes gathered into the circles of their camels for the night. I had sat so long and so silently at my window that 'Awiz came in with the lamp without seeing me, and was concerned because the Emir had called and had been told that I was out...

I was charmingly looked after in the Sultan's guest house...When the evening came, and the sweet shrill cry of the kites, that fills the daylight, stopped, 'Awiz appeared with three paraffin lanterns, which he dotted about the floor in various places, and, having given me my supper, departed to his home. The compound with its dim walls, its squares of moist earth planted with vegetables and few trees, grew infinite and lovely under the silence of the moon. The gate of the city was closed now; a dim glow showed where the sentries beguiled their watch with a hookah in the guard house; at more or less hourly intervals they struck a gong suspended between poles, and so proclaimed the hour. And when I felt tired, I would withdraw from my verandah, collect and blow out the superfluous lanterns, and retire to my room. None of the doors shut easily, so I did not bother to lock them; I had refused the offer of a guard to sleep at my threshold, the precaution was so obviously unnecessary. As I closed my eyes in this security and silence, I thought of the Arabian coasts stretching on either hand: - three hundred miles to Aden; how many hundred to Muscat in the other direction? the Indian Ocean in front of me, the inland deserts behind: within these titanic barriers I was the only European at that moment. A dim little feeling came curling up through my sleepy senses; I wondered for a second what it might be before I recognized it: it was Happiness, pure and immaterial; independent of affections and emotions, the aetherial essence of happiness, a delight so rare and impersonal that it seems scarcely terrestrial when it comes.

F. STARK, *The Southern Gates of Arabia, 1936.*

Stark took this picture of a caravan in the Wadi-Hahdramaut during her second visit to the Yemen in 1937. The pictorial and written images she brought back from her expeditions made her famous in her own lifetime; but they were a mere adjunct to what she saw as the primary purpose of travel. Recalling her career, she wrote, 'The beckoning counts, and not the clicking of the latch behind you: and all through life the actual moment of emancipation still holds that delight, of the whole world coming to meet you like a wave.'

WILLIAM BEEBE 1877–1962

Exploring the deep

AS A NATURALIST, Beebe had long been intrigued by deep-sea life-forms. His studies being thwarted by the fact that most specimens either burst or turned to jelly when brought to the surface, he decided to visit them in their own habitat. To his aid came Otis Barton, a weathy inventor who developed in 1929 what he described as a 'bathysphere'. Little more than an enlarged diver's helmet, suspended by cable from a mother ship, the bathysphere was uncomfortable, cramped and cold. Nevertheless, it was sturdy enough to carry its occupants to unprecedented depths. During the 1930s Beebe and Barton used it for numerous descents, and recorded sights never seen before – such as a shrimp that 'exploded' in self-defence, and fish that carried their own lanterns. In 1934 they broke the half-mile barrier, an underwater record that would not be beaten for 15 years. At the time, Beebe was criticized by his peers for lack of scientific exactitude; he has since been recognized as one of the great pioneers of ocean exploration.

BARTON AND BEEBE MADE THEIR FIRST DESCENT IN 1930.

We were now very far from any touch of Mother Earth; ten miles south of the shore of Bermuda, and one and a half miles from the sea bottom beneath us. At 300 feet, Barton

Beebe peers through a glass 'eye' designed to withstand pressures of half a ton per square inch. The bathysphere had solid steel walls 45 centimetres thick and three minuscule portholes, one of which housed a searchlight. It looked, according to its creator, 'rather like an enormous inflated and slightly cock-eyed bull frog.' When packed with two people, a searchlight, scientific equipment and air-conditioning apparatus, the 121-cm wide sphere was 'as crowded as a sardine can'. In 1949 Barton invented an improved model, the 'Benthoscope', in which he sank to almost 1524 metres below sea level.

gave a sudden exclamation and I turned the flash on the door and saw a slow trickle of water beneath it. About a pint had already collected in the bottom of the sphere. I wiped away the meandering stream and still it came. There flashed across my mind the memory of gentle rain falling on a window-pane, and the first drops finding their way with difficulty over the dry surface of the glass. Then I looked out through the crystal-clear quartz at the pale blue, and the contrast closed in on my mind like the ever deepening twilight.

We watched the trickle. I knew the door was solid enough – a mass of four hundred pounds of steel – and I knew the inward pressure would increase with every foot of depth. So I gave the signal to descend quickly. After that, the flashlight was turned on the door-sill a dozen times during our descent, but the stream did not increase.

Two minutes more and '400 feet' was called out; 500 and 600 feet came and passed overhead, then 700 feet where we remained for a while.

Ever since the beginnings of human history, when first the Phoenicians dared to sail the open sea, thousands of thousands of human beings had reached the depth at which we were now suspended, and had passed on to lower levels. But all of these were dead, drowned victims of war, tempest, or Acts of God. We were the first living men to look out at the strange illumination: And it was stranger than any imagination could have conceived. It was of an indefinable translucent blue quite unlike anything I have ever seen

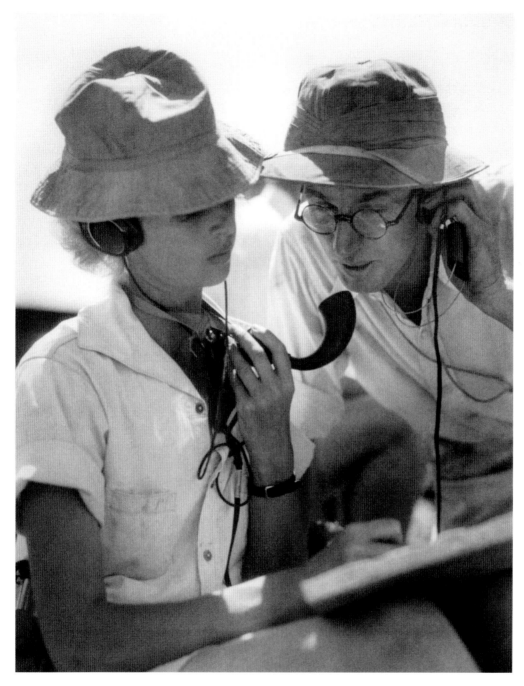

Beebe and Barton kept an open telephone line to the surface, through which they dictated their experiences to technical assistant Gloria Hollister – shown here, with her associate John Tee-Van. 'All our remarks were recorded by Miss Hollister', Beebe wrote, 'and when I read them later, the repetition of our insistence upon the brilliance, which yet was not brilliance, was almost absurd. Yet I find that I must continue to write about it, if only to prove how utterly inadequate language is to translate vividly, feeling and sensations under a condition as unique as submersion at this depth.'

in the upper world, and it excited our optic nerves in a most confusing manner. We kept thinking and calling it brilliant, and again and again I picked up a book to read the type, only to find that I could not tell the difference between a blank page and a coloured plate. I brought all my logic to bear, I put out of my mind the excitement of our position in watery space and tried to think sanely of comparative colour, and I failed utterly. I flashed on the searchlight, which seemed the yellowest thing I have ever seen, and let it soak into my eyes, yet the moment it was switched off, it was like the long-vanished sunlight – it was as though it had never been – and the blueness of the blue, both inside and outside our sphere, seemed to pass materially through the eye into our very beings. This is all very unscientific; quite worthy of being jeered at by optician or physicist, but there it was... I have seen strange fluorescence and ultra-violet illumination in the laboratories of physicists: I recall the weird effects of colour shifting through distant snow crystals on the high Himalayas, and I have been impressed by the eerie illumination, or lack of it, during a full eclipse of the sun. But this was beyond and outside all or any of these. I think we both experienced a wholly new kind of reception of colour impression. I felt I was dealing with something too different to be classified in usual terms.

After a few minutes I sent up an order, and I knew that we were again sinking. The twilight (the word had become absurd, but I could coin no other) deepened, but we still spoke of its brilliance. It seemed to me that it must be like the last terrific upflare of a flame before it is quenched. I found we were both expecting at any moment to have it blown out, and to enter a zone of absolute darkness. But only by shutting my eyes and opening them again could I realize the terrible slowness of the change from dark blue to blacker blue. On the earth at night in moonlight I can always imagine the yellow of sunshine, the scarlet of invisible blossoms, but here, when the searchlight was off, yellow and orange and red were unthinkable. The blue which filled all space admitted no thought of other colours.

We spoke very seldom now. Barton examined the dripping floor, took the temperatures, watched and adjusted the oxygen tank, and now and then asked, 'What depth now?' 'Yes, we're all right.' 'No, the leak's not increasing.' 'It's as brilliant as ever.'

And we both knew it was not as brilliant as ever, but our eyes kept telling us to say so. It actually seemed to me to have a brilliance and intensity which the sunshine lacked; sunshine, that is, as I remembered it in what seemed years ago.

'800 feet' now came down the wire and I called a halt. There seemed no reason why we should not go on to a thousand...and yet some hunch – some mental warning which I have had at half a dozen critical moments in my life – spelled bottom for this trip...Coming up to the surface and through it was like hitting a hard ceiling – I unconsciously ducked, ready for the impact, but there followed only a slather of foam and bubbles, and the rest was sky.

W. BEEBE, *Half Mile Down*, 1935.

IN 1934 BARTON AND BEEBE MADE THEIR DEEPEST DIVE YET.

At 11.12 a.m. We came to rest gently at 3,000 feet, and I knew that this was my ultimate floor; the cable on the winch was very nearly at its end. A few days ago the water had appeared blacker at 2,500 feet than could be imagined, yet now to this same imagination it seemed to show as blacker than black. It seemed as if all future nights in the upper world must be considered only relative degrees of twilight. I could never again use the word BLACK with any conviction.

I looked out and watched an occasional passing light and for the first time I realized how completely lacking was the so-called phosphoresence with which we are familar at the surface. There, whenever an ordinary fish passes, it becomes luminous by reflection from the lights of the myriads of the minute animals and plants floating in the water. Here each light is an individual thing, often under direct control of the owner. A gigantic fish could tear past the window, and if unillumined might never be seen.

My eyes became so dark-adapted at these depths that there was no possibility of error; the jet blackness of the water was broken only by sparks and flashes and steadily glowing lamps of appreciable diameter, varied in colour and of infinite variety as regards size and juxtaposition. But they were never dimmed or seen beyond or through any lesser mist or milky-way of organisms. The occasional evanescent, defence clouds of shrimps hence stand out all the more strongly as unusual phenomena...

'At 1,500 and again at 2,500 ft. this wholly unknown fish appeared suddenly in the beam of light', Beebe wrote. 'It was the colour of water-soaked flesh, toothless and lightless, with good eyes and long pectorals. I have called it Pallid Sailfin.'

OVERLEAF LEFT Little more than 2 cm long, a pair of juvenile Sabre-toothed Viperfish make short work of a Flammenwerfer Shrimp. The shrimp's defensive mechanism – a cloud of 'flame' that gave the impression of a small explosion – did not save it on this occasion.

OVERLEAF RIGHT A close up of the Sabre-toothed Viperfish's disproportionately large jaws. Its prey is a school of baby Ocean Sunfish – at this stage in their development little more than a pair of eyes surrounded by spines.

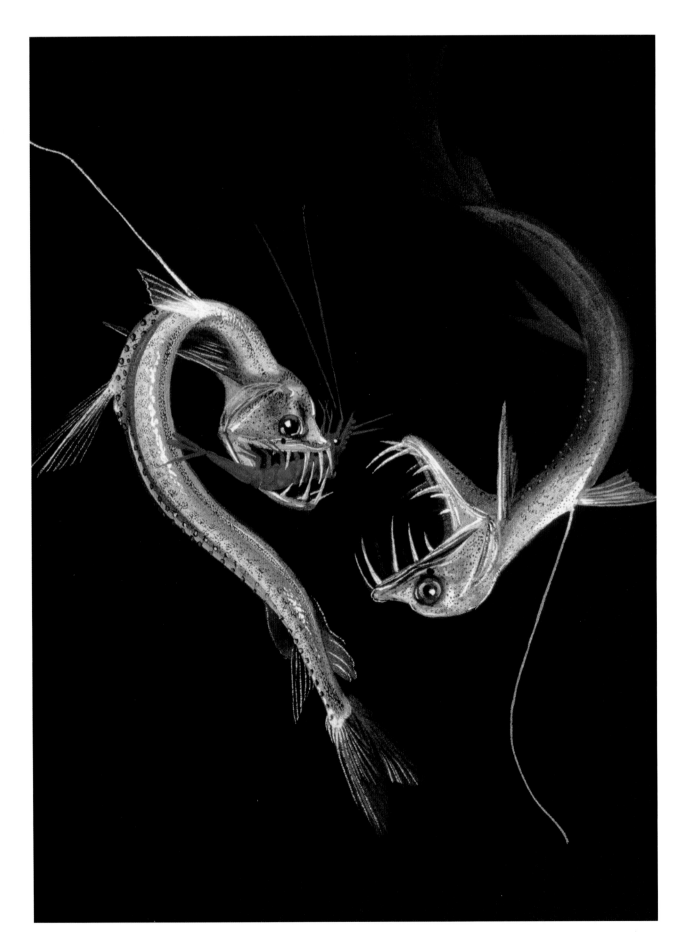

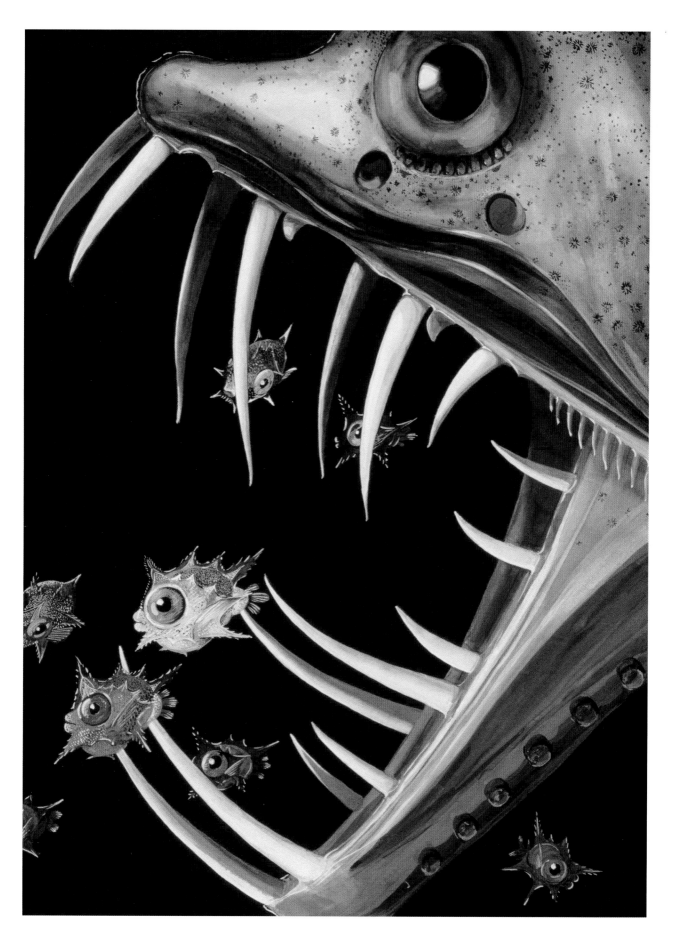

A second thing which occurred to me as I sat coiled in the bathysphere, more than half a mile down, was the failure of our powerful beam of light to attract organisms of any kind. Some fled at its appearance, others seemed wholly unconcerned, but not a single copepod or worm or fish gathered along its length or collected against the starboard window from which it poured...Even in this extremity of blackness I sensed the purity of the water, its freedom from sediment and roiling...there was no diffusion of light, no trails, no refraction. When sparks or larger lights moved they were as distinct as when they were motionless...Now and then I felt a slight vibration and an apparent slacking of the cable. Word came that a cross swell had arisen, and when the full weight of the bathysphere and cable came upon the winch, Captain Sylvester let out a few inches to ease the strain. There were only about a dozen turns of the cable left upon the reel, and a full half of the drum showed its naked, wooden core. We were swinging at 3,028 feet, and, would we come up? We would...

Before we began to ascend, I had to stop making notes of my own, so numb were my fingers from the cold steel of the window sill, and to change from my cushion to the metal floor, was like shifting to a cake of ice. Of the blackness of the outside water I have already written too much. As to pressure...I thought of a gondola 60,000 feet up in the stratosphere with a pressure of one pound to the square inch. And then through the telephone we learned that at this moment we were under a pressure of 1.360 pounds to each square inch, or well over half a ton. Each window held back over nineteen tons of water, while a total of 7,0126 tons were piled up in all directions upon the bathysphere itself. Yes, we had heard clearly, we were ready to be pulled up at once!

At 2,929 feet I heard a metallic twang through the phone, asked what it was, and got some noncommital answer. I found out later that one of the guy ropes used in spooling the incoming cable had suddenly given way with a terrific report – a ghastly shock to everyone on deck until they realized it was a rope and not the cable. Truly we in the bathysphere had the best of it at all times.

Whenever I sink below the last rays of light, similes pour in upon me. Throughout all this account I have consciously rejected the scores of 'as ifs' which sprang to mind. The stranger the situation the more does it seem imperative to use comparisons. The eternal one, the one most worthy and which will not pass from mind, the only other place comparable to these marvellous nether regions must surely be naked space itself, out far beyond atmosphere, between the stars, where sunlight has no grip upon the dust and rubbish of planetary air, where the blackness of space, the shining planets, comets, suns, and stars must really be akin to the world of life as it appears to the eyes of an awed human being, in the open ocean, one half mile down.

W. BEEBE, *Half Mile Down*.

A rogue's gallery from the abyss includes the Telescope-Eyed Fish (upper right), which Beebe likened to an aquatic baboon and the Shining-Toothed Angler (bottom right) whose grin, like that of the Cheshire Cat, was the last part of it to disappear.

RICHARD BYRD 1888–1957

By plane to the poles

DISCHARGED FROM ACTIVE *service in the US Navy due to leg injuries, Commander Byrd took to the air. As he declared: 'My one chance of escape from a life of inaction was to learn to fly.' On 9 May 1926 he made an airborne attempt at the North Pole. He claimed to have been successful but subsequent evidence suggests that, at best, he fell 150 miles short of his goal and, at worst, merely flew in circles once he was out of sight. In November 1929, however, he became the first person to fly to the South Pole. Five years later, sponsored by the car magnate Edsel Ford, he led a second expedition to Antarctica. It was remarkable for two things: its comprehensive survey of large tracts of unknown ice-cap; and Byrd's insistence on wintering alone on the Antarctic plateau. Theoretically, he was to man the meterological equipment at Bolling Advance Station but, as he explained, he had deeper motives: 'I wanted to sink roots into some replenishing philosophy...Out there on the South Polar barrier, in cold and darkness as complete as that of the Pleistocene, I should have time to catch up, to study and think and listen to the phonograph; and for maybe seven months, remote from all but the simplest distractions, I should be able to live exactly as I chose, obedient to no necessities but those imposed by wind and night and cold, and to no man's laws but my own.'*

Within a few months he was poisoned by carbon monoxide from a poorly-ventilated generator. The sickness persisted and eventually he had to radio for help. He was aware that, by summoning assistance before the end of winter, he was putting lives at risk. So were his saviours, who aborted several missions before finally rescuing him. 'That I miscalculated', Byrd later wrote, 'is proved by the fact that I nearly lost my life. Yet, I do not regret going. For I read my books – if not as many as I had counted on reading; and listened to my phonograph records – even when they seemed only to intensify my suffering; and meditated – though not always as cheerfully as I had hoped. All this was good, and it is mine. What I had not counted on was discovering how closely a man could come to dying and still not die, or want to die. That, too, was mine; and it is also to the good. For that experience resolved proportions and relationships for me as nothing else could have done; and it is surprising, approaching the final enlightenment, how little one really has to know or feel sure about.'

AT BOLLING ADVANCE BASE, WITH RELIEF AT HAND.

That Thursday night I really grasped how far I had fallen. In the diary I wrote: '...These early morning [radio] schedules are killing. They leave me without strength to go through the day. Tremendously difficult to get even a little sleep. There are strange nagging pains in my arms, legs, shoulders, and lungs...I'm doing everything possible to hold out. Could I but read, the hours would not seem half so long, the darkness half so oppressive, and my minor misfortunes half so formidable.

Across the room, in the shadows beyond the reach of the storm lantern, were rows of books, many of them great books, preserving the distillates of profound lives. But I could not read them. The pain in my eyes would not let me. The phonograph was there, but the energy to crank it had to be saved for the business of living. Every small aspect of the shack bespoke my weakness: the wavering, smoking flame in the lantern and the limp

OVERLEAF
*An Eskimo child plays
the harmonica for an
American camerman.
Sponsored by the
National Geographic
Society, the 1925
MacMillan expedition
to Greenland – in which
Byrd commanded the
naval unit – obtained
valuable data and
specimens as well as
providing the first film
of Eskimo life.*

A view over
Antarctica, taken on
Byrd's 1933-35
expedition. Byrd was
reportedly terrified of
flying. It was also said
that he drank heavily,
and that his 1929 South
Polar flight was
accomplished with only
the aid of a bottle. His
immurement at Bolling
Advance Base was
considered by some as
a publicity stunt - and
by others as an excuse
to drink himself silly
before drying out.
Neverthless, to most he
was a national hero.

outlines of the clothing on the walls; the frozen cans of food on the table, the slick patches of ice on the deck, the darker stains of spilt kerosene, and the yellowed places where I had vomited; the overturned chair beside the stove which I hadn't bothered to pick up, and the book – John Marquand's *Lord Timothy Dexter of Newburyport,* which lay face down on the table.

June 8 – I am endeavouring to set forth, day by day, the way I live. I am steadfastly holding to a routine designed to give me the best chance of pulling through. Though the mere thought of food is revolting, I force myself to eat – a mouthful at a time. It takes me two or three minutes just to get down a single mouthful. Mostly I eat dehydrated vegetables – dried lima beans, rice, turnip tops, corn, and canned tomatoes – which contain the necessary vitamins – occasionally cold cereals slaked with powdered milk. When I feel up to it, I cook fresh seal meat.

The uncertainty of my existence rises from the realisation, when I blow out the candles at night, that I may lack the strength to get up on the morrow. In my stronger moments I fill the oil tank supplying the stove. I use kerosene exclusively now. Its fumes seem less injurious than those from the solvent. I no longer carry the tank into the tunnel as at first. My only container holds just one gallon, and I must make four trips into the tunnel to fill the tank and supply fuel for my lantern. I creep a bit, then rest a bit – over an hour at the job this morning. I froze my hand rather badly. Little by little I've added to the food stores on the shelves within reach of my bunk. They are my emergency cache. The last thing I do when I turn in is to make sure that the lantern is full of oil. If some morning I cannot get out of my bunk, I shall have enough food and light at hand to carry on for a while.

What baffles me is that I have no reserve strength whatever. Climbing the ladder to go topside, I must rest at every other rung. The temperature today was only 40° below zero; but, though I was clad in furs, the cold seemed to shrivel my bones. It's been blowing pretty steadily from the southeast, and I can't seem to keep any heat in the shack. At night the pains in my body nag incessantly. Sleep is what I need most, but it seldom comes. I drift into a torpor, lighted up by fearful nightmares. Mornings it's a tough job to drive myself out of the sleeping bag. I feel as if I had been drugged. But I tell myself, over and over again, that if I give in – if I let this stupor claim me – I may never awaken.

R. BYRD, *Alone, 1938.*

THOR HEYERDAHL 1914–2002

Kon-Tiki's Pacific voyage

IT WAS ON AN ANTHROPOLOGICAL expedition to the Marquesas Islands, in 1937, that Heyerdahl noticed similiarities between Polynesian and South American cultures. Wondering whether the South Pacific might have been settled from the Americas, he decided to put his theory to the test. In 1947, with five companions, he left Peru aboard a balsa-wood raft, the Kon-Tiki. One hundred and one days and 6920 kilometres later they arrived triumphantly at Tuamoto Island. In 1970, to prove that the ancient Mediterranean civilizations could have reached America long before Columbus, he crossed the Atlantic in the Ra II, built of papyrus reeds. Subsequently, aboard the Tigris, he showed that these primitive craft could also manoeuvre against the wind and were therefore capable of making return journeys. Undertaken with the bare minimum of modern equipment, on vessels constructed with the most basic of materials, Heyerdahl's voyages were not only remarkable in their own right but shed light on humankind's earliest exploration of the planet.

THE LOW-LYING QUARTERS OF THE KON-TIKI GAVE ITS CREW A VIVID ACQUAINTANCE WITH MARINE LIFE IN THE PACIFIC.

Our neighbourly intimacy with the sea was not fully realised by Torstein till he woke one morning and found a sardine on his pillow. There was so little room in the cabin that Torstein was lying with his head in the doorway and, if anyone inadvertently trod on his face when going out at night, he bit him in the leg. He grasped the sardine by the tail and confided to it understandingly that all sardines had his entire sympathy. We conscientiously drew in our legs so that Torstein should have more room the next night, but then something happened which caused Torstein to find himself a sleeping-place on the top of all the kitchen utensils in the wireless corner.

It was a few nights later. It was overcast and pitch dark, and Torstein had placed the paraffin lamp just by his head, so that the night watches could see where they were treading when they crept in and out over his head...About four o'clock Tortsein was woken by the lamp tumbling over and something cold and wet flapping about his ears. 'Flying fish', he thought, and felt for it in the darkness to throw it away. He caught hold of something long and wet that wriggled like a snake, and let go as if he had burned himself. The unseen visitor twisted itself away and over to Herman, while Torstein tried to get the lamp alight. Herman started up too, and this made me wake thinking of the octopus that came up at night in these waters. When we got the lamp alight, Herman was sitting in triumph with his hand gripping the neck of a long thin fish which wriggled in his hands like an eel. The fish was over three feet long, as slender as a snake, with dull black eyes and a long snout with a greedy jaw full of long sharp teeth. The teeth were sharp as knives and could be folded back into the roof of the mouth to make way for what it swallowed. Under Herman's grip a large-eyed white fish, about eight inches long, was suddenly thrown up from the stomach and out of the mouth of the predatory fish, and soon after up came another like it. These were clearly two deep water fish, much torn by the snake-fish's teeth. The snake-fish's thin skin was bluish violet on the back and steel blue underneath, and it came loose in flakes when we took hold of it.

Bengt too was woken at last by all the noise, and we held the lamp and the long fish under his nose. He sat up drowsily in his sleeping bag and said solemnly:

'No, fish like that don't exist.'

With which he turned over quietly and fell asleep again.

Bengt was not far wrong. It appeared later that we six sitting round the lamp in the bamboo cabin were the first men to have seen this fish alive. Only the skeleton of a fish like this one had been found a few times on the coast of South America and the Galapagos Islands; ichthyologists called it Gempylus, or snake mackerel, and thought it lived at the bottom of the sea at a great depth, because no one had ever seen it alive. But if it lived at a great depth, this must at any rate be by day, when the sun blinded the big eyes. For on dark nights Gempylus was abroad high over the surface of the seas; we on the raft had experience of that.

A week after the rare fish had landed in Torstein's sleeping bag, we had another visit. Again it was four in the morning, and the new moon had set so that it was dark, but the stars were shining. The raft was steering easily, and when my watch was over I took a turn along the edge of the raft to see if everything was shipshape for a new watch. I had a rope around my waist, as the watch always had, and, with the paraffin lamp in my hand, I was walking carefully along the outermost log to get round the mast. The log was wet and slippery, and I was furious when someone quite unexpectedly caught hold of the rope behind me and jerked till I nearly lost my balance. I turned round wrathfully with the lantern, but not a soul was to be seen. There came a new tug at the rope, and I saw something shiny lying writhing on the deck. It was a fresh Gempylus, and this time it had got its teeth so deep into the rope that several of them broke off before I got the rope loose. Presumably the light of our lantern had flashed along the curving white rope, and our visitor from the depths of the sea had caught hold in the hope of jumping up and snatching an extra long and tasty tit-bit. It ended its days in a jar of formalin.

The sea contains many surprises for him who has his floor on a level with the surface, and drifts along slowly and noiselessly. A sportsman who breaks his way through the woods may come back and say that no wild life is to be seen. Another may sit down on a stump and wait, and often rustlings and cracklings will begin, and curious eyes peer out. So it is on the sea too. We usually plough across it with roaring engines and piston strokes, with the water foaming around our bows. Then we come back and say that there is nothing to see far out on the ocean.

Not a day passed but we, as we sat floating on the surface of the sea, were visited by inquisitive guests which wriggled and waggled about us...When night had fallen, and the stars were twinkling in the dark tropical sky, the phosphoresence flashed around us in rivalry with the stars, and single glowing plankton resembled round live coals so vividly that we involuntarily drew in our bare legs when the glowing pellets were washed up round our feet at the raft's stern. When we caught them we saw that they were little brightly shining species of shrimp. On such nights we were sometimes scared when two round shining eyes suddenly rose out of the sea right alongside the raft and glared at us with an unblinking hypnotic stare...These were often big squids which came up and floated on the surface with their devilish green eyes shining in the dark like phosphorus. But sometimes they were the shining eyes of deep water fish which came up only at night and lay staring, fascinated by the glimmer of light before them. Several times, when then sea was calm, the black water round the raft was suddenly full of round heads, two or three feet in diameter, lying motionless and staring at us with great glowing eyes. On other nights balls of light three feet and more in diameter would be visible down in the water, flashing like electric lights turned on for a moment.

T. HEYERDAHL, *The* Kon-Tiki *Expedition, 1950.*

OVERLEAF
Ra II wallows perilously in the Atlantic. Constructed using traditional methods by South American Indians from Lake Titicaca, the ship sank at a disspiriting rate of four inches per day. 'Toward evening the sea runs high and choppy', wrote Heyerdahl, 'white wave crests rush past in the violent wind. The sea pours in on every side, forward and aft...We lie already lower in the water than I had expected...The situation is somewhat dismal.' Five weeks into the voyage, however, its reed hull stopped absorbing water. Waterlogged but still afloat, the vessel successfully completed its journey.

WILFRED THESIGER 1910–90

Travels in southern Arabia

BORN IN ADDIS ABABA, *Thesiger spent most of his life trying to escape Western civilization. He travelled throughout the Islamic world, from Afghanistan to Morocco, and became the first man to fully explore the Unknown Quarter of Arabia. His philosophy was best expressed on a journey through the Sahara: 'I was exhilarated by the sense of space, the silence, and the crisp clearness of the sand. I felt in harmony with the past, travelling as men had travelled for untold generations across the deserts, dependent for their survival on the endurance of their camels and their own inherited skills.' From 1968 to 1994 he lived with the Samburu in northern Kenya before failing eyesight forced him to retire to Britain. Rejecting the combustion engine in all its forms he was, in his own words, 'the last explorer in the tradition of the past'. His crisp, poetic journals were augmented by the equally fine black and white photographs that he took on his travels.*

TRAVELLING THROUGH ARABIA.

Our flour was finished, but that evening Musallim produced from his saddle-bags a few handfuls of maize, which we roasted and ate. It was to be the last food we had until the others returned from Liwa three days later. They were three interminable days and nights.

I had almost persuaded myself that I was conditioned to starvation, indifferent to it. After all, I had been hungry for weeks, and even when we had had flour I had had little inclination to eat the charred or sodden lumps which Musallim had cooked. I used to swallow my portion with even less satisfaction than that with which I eventually voided it. Certainly I thought and talked incessantly of food, but as a prisoner talks of freedom, for I realised that the joints of meat, the piles of rice, and the bowls of steaming gravy which tantalised me could have no reality outside my mind. I had never thought then that I should dream of the crusts which I was rejecting.

For the first day my hunger was only a more insistent feeling of familiar emptiness; something which, like a toothache, I could partly overcome by an effort of will. I woke in the grey dawn craving for food, but by lying on my stomach and pressing down I could achieve a semblance of relief. At least I was warm. Later, as the sun rose, the heat forced me out of my sleeping-bag. I threw my cloak over a bush and lay in the shade and tried to sleep again. I dozed and dreamt of food; I woke and thought of food. I filled myself with water, and the bitter water, which I did not want, made me feel sick. Eventually it was evening and we gathered round the fire, repeating, 'Tomorrow they will be back.'; and thought of the supplies of food which bin Kabina would bring with him, and of the goat which we should eat. But the next day dragged out till sunset, and they did not come.

I faced another night, and the nights were worse than the days. Now I was cold and could not even sleep, except in snatches. I watched the stars; some of them – Orion, the Pleiades, and the Bear – I knew by name, others only by sight. Slowly they swung overhead and dipped down towards the west, while the bitter wind keened among the dunes. I remembered how I had once awakened with hunger during my first term at school and cried, remembering some chocolate cake which I had been too gorged to eat when my mother had taken me out to tea two days before. Now I was maddened by the thought of the crusts which I had given away in the Uruq al Shaiba. Why had I been such a fool? I

Thesiger's party crosses
the Empty Quarter of
Saudi Arabia in 1948.
*'For me', Thesiger
wrote, 'exploration is a
personal venture. I did
not go to the Arabian
desert to collect plants
or make a map: such
things were incidental...
I went there to find
peace in the company of
desert peoples. I set
myself a goal on these
journeys, and although
the goal itself was unim-
portant, its attainment
had to be worth every
effort and sacrifice.'*

could picture the colour and texture, even the shape, of the fragments which I had left.

In the morning I watched Mabkhaut turn the camels out to graze, and as they shuffled off, spared for a while from the toil which we imposed upon them, I found that I could only think of them as food. I was glad when they were out of sight. Al Auf came over and lay down near me, covering himself with his cloak; I don't think we spoke. I lay with my eyes shut, insisting to myself, 'If I were in London I would give anything to be here.' Then I thought of the jeeps and lorries with which the Locust Officers in the Najd were equipped. So vivid were my thoughts that I could hear the engines, smell the stink of petrol fumes. No, I would rather be here, starving as I was than sitting in a chair, replete with food, listening to the wireless, dependent upon cars to take me through Arabia. I clung desperately to this conviction. It seemed infinitely important. Even to doubt it was to admit defeat, to forswear everything to which I held.

I dozed and heard a camel roaring. I jerked awake, thinking, 'They have come at last', but it was only Mabkhaut moving our camels. The shadows lengthened among the sand-hills; the sun had set and we had given up hope when they returned. I saw at once that they had no goat with them. My dream of a large hot stew vanished. We exchanged the formal greetings and asked the formal questions about the news. Then we helped them with the only camel which was loaded. Bin Kabina said wearily, 'We got nothing...We have two packages of bad dates and a little wheat...'

The past three days had been an ordeal, worse for the others than for me, since, but for me, they could have ridden to the nearest tents and fed. However, we had not suffered the final agonies of doubt. We had known that the others would bring us food. We had thought of this food, dreamt of this food. A feast of rich and savoury meat, the reward of our endurance. Now all we had was this. Some wizened dates, coated with sand, and a mess of boiled grain. There was not even enough of it. We had to get back across Arabia, travelling secretly, and we had enough food for ten days if we were economical. I had eaten tonight, but I was starving. I wondered how much longer I could should be able to face this fare. We must get more food...

[Further minimal supplies having been obtained] While we were leading our camels down a steep dune face I was suddenly conscious of a low vibrant hum, which grew in volume until it sounded as though an aeroplane were flying low over our heads. The frightened camels plunged about, tugging at their head-ropes and looking back at the slope above us. The sound ceased when we reached the bottom. This was 'the singing of the sands'. The Arabs describe it as a roaring, which is perhaps a more descriptive word. During the five years that I was in these parts I only heard it half a dozen times. It is caused, I think, by one layer of sand slipping over another. Once I was standing on a dune-crest and the sound started as soon as I stepped on to the steep face. I found on this occasion that I could start it or stop it at will by stepping on or off this slip-face.

Near Rabadh, Musallim suddenly jumped off his camel, pushed his arm into a shallow burrow, and pulled out a hare. I asked him how he knew it was there, and he said that he had seen its track going in and none coming out. The afternoon dragged on until we reached the expanse of small contiguous dunes which gave these sands the name of Rabadh. There was adequate grazing, so we stopped on their edge. We decided to eat the rest of our flour, and Musallim conjured three onions and some spices out of his saddle-bags. We sat round in a hungry circle watching bin Kabina cooking the hare, and offering advice. Anticipation mounted, for it was more than a month since we had eaten meat...We sampled the soup and decided to let it stew just a little longer. Then bin Kabina looked up and groaned, 'God! Guests!'

Coming across the sands towards us were three Arabs...We greeted them, asked the news, made coffee for them, and then...dished up the hare and the bread and set it before them, saying with every appearance of sincerity that they were our guests, that God had brought them, that today was a blessed day, and a number of similar remarks. They asked us to join them but we refused, repeating that they were our guests. I hoped that I did not look as murderous as I felt while assuring them that God had brought them on this auspicious occasion.

W. THESIGER, *Arabian Sands, 1959.*

OVERLEAF
The great gale of 1954 bends palm trees in the marshes of southern Iraq. The storm was so fierce that the desert to the west was covered by six feet of floodwater and Baghdad itself was threatened. Amidst a disaster that over-whelmed most of Iraq, life continued much as usual in the marshes. (Maybe the area had divine protection – it is thought by some authorities to have been the site of the Garden of Eden.) Describing his travels in the Middle East, Thesiger wrote, 'No man can live this life and emerge unchanged. He will carry, however faint, the imprint of the desert, the brand which marks the nomad; and he will have within him the yearning to return, weak or inconsistent according to his nature. For this cruel land can cast a spell which no temperate clime can match.'

MAURICE HERZOG 1912–

The summit of Annapurna

BY 1939, WHILE STILL IN HIS TEENS, Herzog had already established himself as one of the world's more adventurous climbers. It was not until after World War Two, however, that he realized his full potential. In 1950, he led an expedition to Annapurna, the tenth-highest mountain in the world, unmapped, unclimbed and so inaccessible that it took him two months just to find it. He reached its summit at 2 PM on 3 June, accompanied by Louis Lachenal, thus completing the first ascent of a peak higher than 8000 metres. The two men, and their companions Gaston Rebuffat and Lionel Terray, suffered fearfully on the return journey. Herzog lost his gloves and became frostbitten in both hands; he subsequently became frostbitten in both feet too. Lachenal, similarly, became frostbitten. Both men were permanently crippled by the experience and never again climbed to their full ability. The expedition was hailed as an extraordinary example of team-work and perseverance, as well as a landmark in mountaineering history. Herzog's journal was an instant best-seller and he became an international icon. When his climbing career was at an end, he was eventually made France's Minister of Sport.

DESCENDING FROM THE SUMMIT, HERZOG'S MEN WERE FORCED TO SPEND A NIGHT ON THE SLOPES OF ANNAPURNA.

Time passed but we had no idea of it. Night was approaching, and we were terrified, though none of us uttered a complaint. Rebuffat and I found a way we thought we remembered, but were brought to a halt by the extreme steepness of the slope – the mist turned it into a vertical wall. We were to find, next day, that at that moment we had been almost on top of the camp, and that the wall was the very one that sheltered the tents which would have been our salvation...

Night had suddenly fallen and it was essential to come to a decision without wasting another minute; if we remained on the slope, we would be dead before morning. We should have to bivouac. What the conditions would be like, we could guess, for we all knew what it meant to bivouac above 23,000 feet...

[By sheer luck they discovered a crevasse] The intense cold of this minute grotto shrivelled us up, the enclosing walls were damp and the floor a carpet of fresh snow; by huddling together there was just room for the four of us. Icicles hung from the ceiling and we broke some of them off to make more head room and kept little bits to suck – it was a long time since we had had anything to drink.

That was our shelter for the night. At least we should be protected from the wind, and the temperature would remain fairly even, though the damp was extremely unpleasant. We settled ourselves in the dark as best we could. As always in a bivouac, we took off our boots; without this precaution the constriction would cause immediate frost-bite. Terray unrolled the sleeping-bag which he had had the foresight to bring, and settled himself in relative comfort. We put on everything warm that we had, and to avoid contact with the snow I sat on the cine-camera. We huddled close up to each other, in search for a hypothetical position in which the warmth of all bodies could be combined without loss, but we could not keep still for a second.

We did not open our mouths – signs were less of an effort than words. Every man withdrew into himself and took refuge in his own inner world. Terray massaged Lachenal's feet; Rebuffat felt his feet freezing, too, but he had sufficient strength to rub them himself. I remained motionless, unseeing. My feet and hands went on freezing, but what could be done? I attempted to forget suffering, to forget the passing of time, trying not to feel the devouring and numbing cold which insidiously gained upon us...

Terray generously tried to give me part of his sleeping-bag. He had understood the seriousness of my condition, and knew why it was that I said nothing and remained quite passive; he realized that I had abandoned all hope for myself. He massaged me for nearly two hours: his feet, too, might have frozen, but he did not appear to give the matter a thought. I found new courage

Maurice Herzog, binoculars in hand, on a reconnaissance of Annapurna. Frostbite would later claim all his fingers and all his toes.

simply in contemplating his unselfishness; he was doing so much to help me that it would have been ungrateful of me not to go on struggling to live. Though my heart was a lump of ice itself, I was astonished to feel no pain. Everything material about me seemed to have dropped away. I seemed to be quite clear in my thoughts and yet I floated in a kind of peaceful happiness. There was still a breath of life in me, but it dwindled steadily as the hours went by. Terray's massage no longer had any effect upon me. All was over, I thought. Was not this cavern the most beautiful grave I could hope for? Death caused me no grief, no regret – I smiled at the thought...

[Come daybreak] A ghastly light spread through our grotto and we could just vaguely make out the shapes of each other's heads. A queer noise from a long way off came down to us - a sort of prolonged hiss. The noise increased. Suddenly I was buried, blinded, smothered beneath an avalanche of new snow. The icy snow spread over the cavern, finding its way through every gap in our clothing. I ducked my head between my knees and covered myself with both arms. The snow flowed on and on. There was a silence. We were not completely buried, but there was snow everywhere. We got up, taking care not to bang our heads against the ceiling of ice, and tried to shake ourselves. We were all in our stockinged feet in the snow. The first thing to do was find our boots.

Rebuffat and Terray began to search, and realized at once that they were blind. Yesterday they had taken off their glasses to lead us down, and now they were paying for it. Lachenal was the first to lay hands upon a pair of boots. He tried to put them on, but they were Rebuffat's. Rebuffat attempted to climb up the shoot down which we had come yesterday, and which the avalanche had followed in its turn...

We were still groping for our things. Terray found his boots and put them on awkwardly, unable to see what he was doing. Lachenal helped him, but he was all on edge

and fearfully impatient, in striking contrast to my immmbility. Terray then went up the icy channel, puffing and blowing, and at last reached the outer world. He was met by terrible gusts of wind that cut right through him and lashed his face...

At the bottom of the crevasse there were still two of us looking for our boots. Lachenal poked fiercely with an ice-axe. I was calmer and tried to proceed more rationally. We extracted crampons and an axe in turn from the snow, but still no boots.

Well – so this cavern was to be our last resting-place! There was very little room – we were bent double and got in each other's way. Lachenal decided to go out without his boots. He called out frantically, hauling himself up on the rope, trying to get a hold or to wriggle his way up, digging his toes into the snow walls. Terray from outside pulled as hard as he could: I watched him go; he gathered speed and disappeared.

When he emerged from the opening he saw the sky was clear and blue, and he began to run like a madman, shrieking, 'It's fine, it's fine!'

I set to work again to search the cave. The boots had to be found, or Lachenal and I were done for. On all fours, with nothing on my hands and feet, I raked the snow, stirring it round this way and that, hoping every second to come upon something hard. I was no longer capable of thinking – I reacted like an animal fighting for its life.

I found one boot! The other was tied to it – a pair! Having ransacked the whole cave I at last found the other pair. But in spite of all my efforts I could not find the camera, and gave up in despair. There was no question of putting my boots on – my hands were like lumps of wood and I could hold nothing in my fingers; my feet were very swollen – I should never be able to get boots on them. I twisted the rope round the boots as well as I ould and called up the shoot:

'Lionel...boots!'

There was no answer, but he must have heard, for with a jerk the precious boots shot up. Soon after the rope came down again. My turn. I wound the rope round me; I could not pull it tight so I made a series of little knots. Their combined strength, I hoped, would be enough to hold me. I had no strength to shout again; I gave a great tug on the rope, and Terray understood.

At the first step I had to kick a niche in the hard snow for my toes. Further on I expected to be able to get up more easily by wedging myself across the tunnel. I wriggled up a few yards like this and then I tried to dig my hands and feet into the wall. My hands were stiff and hard right up to the wrists and my feet had no feeling up to the ankles; the joints were inflexible and this hampered me greatly.

Somehow or other I succeeded in working my way up, while Terray pulled so hard he nearly choked me. I began to see more distinctly and so knew that I must be nearing the opening. Often I fell back, but I clung on and wedged myself in again as best I could.

My heart was bursting, and I was forced to rest. A fresh wave of energy enabled me to crawl to the top. I pulled myself out by clutching Terray's legs; he was just about all in and I was in the last stages of exhaustion. Terray was close to me and I whispered:

'Lionel...I'm dying!'...

I knew the end was near, but it was the end that all mountaineers wished for – an end in keeping with their ruling passion. I was consciously grateful to the mountains for being so beautiful for me that day, and as awed by their silence as if I had been in church. I was in no pain, and had no worry. My utter calmness was alarming...

At this moment Lachenal shouted: 'Help! Help!'

Obviously he didn't know what he was doing...Or did he? He was the only one of the four of us who could see Camp II down below. Perhaps his calls would be heard. They were shouts of despair, reminding me tragically of some climbers lost in the Mont Blanc massif whom I had endeavoured to save. Now it was our turn. The impression was vivid: we were lost.

I joined in with the others: 'One...two...three...Help!'...We tried to shout all together, but without much success; our voices could not have carried more than ten feet. The noise I made was more of a whisper than a shout. Terray insisted that I should put my boots on, but my hands were dead...Terray resolutely got out his knife, and with stumbling hands slit the uppers of my boots back and front. Split in two like this I could get them on, but it was not easy and I had to make several attempts. I lost heart – what was the use of it all anyway since I was going to stay where I was? But Terray pulled violently and finally he succeeded. He laced up my now gigantic boots, missing out half the hooks. I was ready now. But how was I going to walk with my stiff joints?...

I remained sitting in the snow. Gradually my mind lost grip – why should I struggle? I would just let myself drift. I saw pictures of shady slopes, peaceful paths, there was a scent of resin. It was pleasant – I was going to die in my own mountains. My body had no feeling – everything was frozen.

'Aah...aah!'

Was it a groan or a call?...Barely 200 yards away Marcel Shatz, was coming slowly towards us like a boat over the surface of the the slope. I found this vision of a strong and invincible deliverer inexpressibly moving. I expected everything of him. The shock was violent, and quite shattered me. Death clutched at me and I gave myself up.

When I came to again the wish to live returned and I experienced a violent revulsion of feeling. All was not lost! As Schatz came nearer my eyes never left him for a second – twenty yards – ten yards – he came straight towards me. Why? Without a word he leant over me, held me close, hugged me, and his warm breath revived me.

I could not make the slightest movement – I was like marble. My heart was over-whelmed by such tremendous feelings and yet my eyes remained dry.

'Well done, Maurice. It's marvellous!'

M. HERZOG, *Annapurna*, 1952.

EDMUND HILLARY 1919–
TENZING NORGAY 1914–86

The conquest of Everest

Hillary and Tenzing take a mug of tea on their return from the summit. 'Some day Everest will be climbed again', wrote expedition leader John Hunt. ' And there are many other opportunities for adventure, whether they be sought among the hills, in the air, upon the sea, in the bowels of the earth, or on the ocean bed; and there is always the moon to reach. There is no height, no depth, that the spirit of man, guided by a higher Spirit, cannot attain.' Hillary described the conquest in less grandiose terms: 'In some ways I believe I epitomise the average New Zealander: I have modest abilities, I combine these with a good deal of determination, and I rather like to succeed.'

IN 1953 THE BRITISH EVEREST *expedition, led by John Hunt, launched its attack on the world's highest peak. The summit team comprised a handful of climbers who were to attack the mountain in pairs from a camp on the South Col. Among them were Hillary and Tenzing. The former was a New Zealand bee-keeper who had first visited the Himalayas in 1951, since when he had completed 11 ascents above 6096 metres. The latter was a Nepalese sherpa who had attacked Everest in 1935 and had subsequently participated in four expeditions during one of which, in 1952, he had come within 300 metres of the summit. After the first pair had failed, Hillary and Tenzing left camp on the morning of 29 May. They attained the summit at 11.30 am. The news reached Britain on the day of Queen Elizabeth II's coronation, to widespread jubilation. Later, there was acrimony as to who stood first on the peak, who helped who over various difficult passages, and whether Everest had been conquered in the name of Britain, India or Nepal. Tenzing Norgay was magnanimous in victory: 'All those who had gone before were in my thoughts – sahibs and Sherpas, English and Swiss – all the great climbers, the brave men, who for thirty-three years had dreamed and challenged, fought and failed, on this mountain, and whose efforts and knowledge and experience had made our victory possible.' Hillary was more abrupt: 'Well, we knocked the bastard off!'*

HILLARY'S NARRATIVE OF THE CONQUEST.
The ridge continued as before. Giant cornices on the right, steep rock slopes on the left. I went on cutting steps on the narrow strip of snow. The ridge curved away to the right and we had no idea where the top was. As I cut around the back of one hump, another higher one would swing into view. Time was passing and the ridge seemed never-ending...I was beginning to tire a little now. I had been cutting steps continuously for two hours, and Tenzing, too, was moving very slowly. As I chipped steps around still another corner, I wondered rather dully just how long we could keep it up. Our original zest had now quite gone and it was turning more into a grim struggle. I then realized that the ridge ahead, instead of still monotonously rising, now dropped sharply away, and below I could see the North Col and the Rongbuk glacier. I looked upwards to see a narrow snow ridge running up to a snowy summit. A few more whacks of the ice-axe in the firm snow and we stood on top.

My initial feelings were of relief – relief that there were no more steps to cut – no more ridges to traverse and no more humps to tantalize us with hopes of success. I looked at Tenzing and in spite of the balaclava, goggles and oxygen mask all encrusted with long icicles that concealed his face, there was no disguising his infectious grin of pure delight as he looked all around him. We shook hands and then Tenzing threw his arms around my shoulders and we thumped each other on the back until we were almost breathless. It was 11.30 a.m. The ridge had taken us two and a half hours, but it seemed like a lifetime. I turned off the oxygen and removed my set. I had carried my camera, loaded with colour film, inside my shirt to keep it warm, so I now produced it and got Tenzing to pose on top for me, waving his axe on which was a string of flags – United Nations, British, Nepalese and Indian. Then I turned my attention to the great stretch of country lying

below us in every direction...The most important photograph, I felt, was a shot down the North ridge, showing the North Col and the old route which had been made famous by the struggles of those great climbers of the 1920s and 1930s. I had little hope of the results being particularly successful, as I had a lot of difficulty in holding the camera steady in my clumsy gloves, but I felt that they would at least serve as a record...Meanwhile, Tenzing had made a little hole in the snow and in it he placed various small articles of food - a bar of chocolate, a packet of biscuits and a handful of lollies. Small offerings, indeed, but at least a token gift to the Gods that all devout Buddhists believe have their home on this lofty summit. While we were together on the South Col two days before, Hunt had given me a small crucifix which he had asked me to take to the top. I, too, made a hole in the snow and placed the crucifix beside Tenzing's gifts.

I checked our oxygen once again and worked out our endurance. We would have to move fast in order to reach our life-saving reserve below the South Peak. After fifteen minutes we turned to go...We both felt a little tired, for reaction was setting in and we must get off the mountain quickly. I moved down off the summit on to our steps. Wasting no time we cramponed along our tracks, spurred by the urgency of diminishing oxygen. Bump followed bump in rapid succession. In what seemed almost miraculous time, we reached the top of the rock step. Now, with the almost casual indifference of familiarity, we kicked and jammed our way down it again. We were tired, but not too tired to be careful. We scrambled cautiously over the rock traverse, moved one step at a time over shaky snow sections and finally cramponed up our steps and back on to the South Peak.

Only one hour from the top! A swig of sweetened lemonade refreshed us and we

A yawning crevasse on
the West Cwm of
Mount Everest. At the
bottom of the highest
mountain horseshoe in
the world, the 'Valley of
Silence' as it is known,
gave Hillary and
Tenzing their first full
view of Everest's peak.
Three kilometres long
and three-quarters of a
kilometre wide, the
Cwm's array of
fearsome gorges still
deters climbers – as
does, on a still day, its
near suffocating heat.

turned down again. Throughout the climb we had a constant nagging fear of our return down the great snow slope, and as I led down I packed each step with as much care as if our lives depended on it, as well they might. The terrific impression of exposure as we looked straight down on to the Kangshung glacier, still over 9,000 feet below us, made us move with the greatest caution, and every step down seemed a step nearer safety. When we finally moved off the slope onto the ridge below, we looked at each other and without speaking we both almost visibly shrugged off the sense of fear that had been with us all day...

As we approached Camp IV, tiny figures appeared from the tents and slowly drifted up the track. We made no signal but wearily moved down the track towards them. When only fifty yards away, Lowe with characteristic enthusiasm gave the 'thumbs-up' signal and waved his ice-axe in the direction of the summit. Immediately the scene was galvanized into activity and our approaching companions, forgetting their weakness, ran up the snow towards us. As we greeted them all, perhaps a little emotionally, I felt more than ever before that very strong feeling of friendship and co-operation that had been the decisive factor throughout the expedition.

What a thrill it was to be able to tell them that all their efforts amongst the tottering chaos of the Icefall, the disheartening plunging up the snowy inferno of the Western Cwm, the difficult technical ice work on the Lhotse Face and the grim and nerve-racking toil above the South Col had been fully rewarded and that we had reached the top.

To see the unashamed joy spread over the tired, strained face of our gallant and determined leader was to me reward enough in itself.'

E. HILLARY, QUOTED IN J. HUNT, *The Ascent of Everest*, 1953.

HUNT'S ACCOUNT OF HILLARY AND TENZING NORGAY'S RETURN.

At 2 p.m., just after the Indian Wireless News bulletin had informed the world that we had failed, five men could be seen at the top of the shallow trough about 500 yards above the camp. Some of us started out at once, Mike Westmacott and myself ahead, while our Sherpas crowded outside their Dome tent, no less eager than the rest of us to know the result. But the approaching climbers made no sign, just plodded on dejectedly towards us; they did not even wave a greeting. My heart sank. In my weak state, this plod up the track was already an effort; now my feet felt like lead. This must be failure; we must now think of that third and last attempt.

Suddenly, the leading man in the party – it was George Lowe – raised his axe, pointing unmistakably towards the distant top of Everest; he made several vigorous thrusts. The others behind him were now making equally unequivocal signs. Far from failure, this was IT! They had made it!! Feelings welled up uncontrollably as I now quickened my pace – I still could not muster the strength to break into a run, and Mike Westmacott was now well ahead. Everyone was pouring out of the tents; there were shouts of acclamation and joy. The next moment I was with them: handshakes – even, I blush to say, hugs – for the triumphant pair. A special one for Tenzing, so well merited for him personally, this victory, both for himself and for his people.

Amid much chatter, we escorted them into camp, where the Sherpas, grinning broadly, crowded round, shaking Ed warmly by the hand, offering a more respectful, indeed reverent welcome to Tenzing, their great leader. We all went into the Mess tent to hear the great story. Devouring an omelette, draining mugfuls of his favourite lemonade drink, Ed Hillary described the events of 28th and 29th May in graphic yet simple terms.'

J. HUNT, *The Ascent of Everest*.

TENZING NORGAY'S RETROSPECTIVE.

I spent only one night at Camp Four. Half of it was celebration, half rest. The next morning my only thought was to get down off the mountain, and in one day I descended the cwm and the icefall, all the way to base camp...Now I am free, I kept thinking. I have been freed by Everest...At base camp, too, I stayed only one night, and then, in another single day, I went thirty-five miles down the glacier and valleys to Thamey, to see my mother. I told her we had had success, and she was very happy. Staring up into my face, she said to me, 'Many times I have told you not to go to this mountain. Now you don't have to go again.' All her life she had believed that there was a golden sparrow on top of Everest, and also a turquoise lion with a golden mane; and when she asked me about them I was sorry to have to disappoint her. But when she asked if I had seen the Rongbuk Monastery from the top I was able to say yes – and this pleased her...

Since the climbing of Everest all sorts of questions have been put to me, and not all of them have been political. From the people of the East there have been many that have to do with religion and the supernatural. 'Was the Lord Buddha on the top?' I have been asked. Or 'Did you see the Lord Siva?' From many sides, among the devout and orthodox, there has been great pressure upon me to say that I had some vision or revelation. But here, again – even though it may be disappointing to many – I can tell only the truth; and this is no, that on the top of Everest I did not see anything supernatural or feel anything superhuman. What I felt was a great closeness to God, and that was enough for me. In my deepest heart I thanked God. And as we turned to leave the summit I prayed to him for something very real and very practical – that, having given us our victory, He would get us down off the mountain alive.

T. NORGAY, *Man of Everest, 1955.*

VIVIAN FUCHS 1908–99

First crossing of Antarctica

IN 1957, FUCHS LED *a british-commonwealth expedition to complete what Shackleton had left unfinished in 1916 – the traverse of Antarctica via the South Pole. In concept and in application it was an updated version of Shackleton's own plan: the main party was to approach from the Weddell Sea, while another laid supplies from the Ross Ice Shelf towards the Pole. The Weddell Sea party, under Fuchs, was equipped with three massive Sno-Cats, several 'Weasels' (smaller vehicles, with caterpillar tracks, developed in World War Two), a set of dog teams whose job was to reconnoitre the immediate landscape and vast amounts of dynamite with which to produce a seismic chart of the continent. Meanwhile, the support group, led by Everest hero Edmund Hillary, was given a fleet of tractors to lay a string of food depots from the Ross Ice Shelf. Both teams were in regular radio contact and were supported by planes from the Royal Air Force. Fuchs ground his way steadily to the South Pole, but he could not claim primacy. Having deposited his last cache of supplies, Hillary drove his tractors the final distance, reaching the Pole several days before him. The expedition succeeded admirably, not only making the first overland crossing of Antarctica but plotting for the first time its underlying landmass. When Fuchs returned home in 1958, however, he found his achievement overwhelmed by the Suez Crisis. After so many glamorous failures at the South Pole, it seemed that victory had become a non-event. Marginalized not only by world events but by his own success – nobody died, everything went more or less to plan – Fuchs nevertheless remained an elder statesman of British exploration.*

APPROACHING A CREVASSE FIELD 320 KILOMETRES INTO THE ANTARCTIC PLATEAU.
In my opinion the next ten miles are going to make or break the expedition, for we may well lose vehicles over the ground close ahead. With crash-helmets, safety straps and roped vehicles we have taken all the precautions we can...

[Crossing a snow bridge] David S. was standing on the far side, I on the near side of the crevasse, while Geoffrey and David P. were driving. As they moved across I heard a tremendous rumble and the snow beneath me quaked, making me want to move rapidly to some other place, but as I had no idea where the noise originated, I stood where I was. As the vehicles continued to move slowly, I saw a cloud of snow rising in the air from an immense crater which had appeared only six feet to the left of the Weasel. It was about 20 feet across and 40 feet deep, with dark and deep caverns descending to unknown depths. For a long time clouds of snow dust rose from it and drifted away, the whole thing appearing as though a bomb had fallen. The hole was large enough to have swallowed Sno-Cat, Weasel, sledge and all, but with amazing good fortune the bridge broke to the left of the vehicles and not under them! [Scouting the terrain] has been a very slow task, but some of the monstrous caverns which we have discovered beneath the innocent surface have certainly justified the work. Some of them would have accepted a double-decker bus, and there is no doubt that we should have lost at least one Weasel if we had not spent so much time on the ground...As vehicles rumble over the booming crevasses below, it is with a sense of some considerable relief that each driver reaches the far side.'
V. FUCHS, *The Crossing of Antarctica*, 1958.

JACQUES COUSTEAU 1910–97

Underwater discoveries

Cousteau prepares for a dive. Even in his old age he pursued a sport that, as he said, made him 'feel like an angel'. During his lifetime he produced fifty books, two encyclopaedias, several films and more than 100 documentaries – an output that made him a household name across the planet. In later years his fierce advocacy of green issues earned him the nickname 'Captain Planet'.

TRAINED IN THE FRENCH NAVY *during world war two, Jacques Cousteau was a pioneer of underwater exploration. He invented not only the scuba lung but also a number of submarine vessels that enabled researchers to stay farther down for longer than ever before. His research ship,* Calypso, *became famous during the 1950s and 1960s for its relentless investigation of the ocean's mysteries. It was remarkable, too, for its intrinsically Gallic lifestyle. 'Calypso carried a one-ton stainless steel wine tank', Cousteau wrote, 'which amused foreign oceanographers, some of whom travel on wretched craft with without a drop aboard. Calypsonians may drink as much as they like: average daily consumption per capita has been about a pint.' Never a man to scorn publicity, Cousteau made numerous films and documentaries about his work. Although unremarkable by modern standards, his expeditions were ground-breaking at the time.*

DAWN, THE RED SEA, DECEMBER 1951.

Sharks had been in sight throughout the dive. As I progressed deeper, they turned faster, making my eyes dizzy as I tried to keep them under scrutiny. There were one or two in every direction, and now they were closing in. Some swam straight towards me with vacant eyes and then withdrew. When I reached 150 feet, I glanced up. A dozen torpedo-shaped shadows were outlined against the viridescent ceiling. I looked down. Fifty feet below pale sharks were strolling on a sand slope. I sighted my forgotten companions, naked and far from our boat, surrounded by Red Sea sharks of whose traits we knew nothing. It struck me that our situation was untenable.

Out of the roving pack, the biggest shark, an animal about twelve feet long, came with seeming deliberation towards the professor. I was thirty feet from Drach and the shark was approaching him at ankle level. The sight of a man ogling a reef while Carcharhinus sniffed his legs was utterly revolting. I rushed towards them, grunting as loudly as I could through the mouthpiece, but despairing of the outcome. Drach heard nothing. When I was ten feet from them, the big shark wheeled ponderously and swam away. I patted Drach's shoulder and tried to explain by signs what had happened. He looked at me severely, and turned back to the reef. He did not wish to be disturbed again.

The scholar's sang-froid was contagious. I felt strangely reassured about everything. I sank lower, relaxed and receptive. At a depth of two hundred feet the cliff broke off into a forty-five degree incline of grey soil. I was disappointed that the pageant was ending in this dull, lifeless bank. At second look, I found the slope extended only fifty feet out to another blue horizon, another drop-off. I was on a corniche laden with fossils and waste fallen through the ages from the bustling metropolis above.

I hovered, contemplating the brink ahead. I stretched my arms and legs in space and greedily inhaled a lungful of thick, tasty air. Between the sibilants of my air regulator, I heard rhythmc grating sounds and cycles of bubbles rustling overhead. Other human beings were alive near by. Their commonplace respirations took on a cosmic significance. I was being seized by depth rapture. I knew it and I welcomed it as a challange to whatever controls I had left.

The gray bank two hundred feet down was the boundary of reason; over the precipice

lay madness. Danger became voluptuous. My temples pounded. Extending my arms like a sleepwalker, I stroked my fins and glided over the edge of beyond.

Hundreds of white walking sticks were sticking out of a vertiginous wall. I dropped slowly along a torment of life forms. Witches heads stared at me. Pale gelatinous tumours grew on giant sponges ornate with spiders' webs. As far down as I could see, untold populations clung along that wall. They were denied to me. I trimmed off 250 feet down.

I heard a distant mechanical sigh, one of my companions opening his air-reserve valve. I paused. Now I must soar out of here, pick up my friends, and obey the law of sun and air that rules my kind. Now? Why now?

I stole another minute, clutching a white sea whip, and looked down longingly. Then I knew I had an appointment with the second reef. I swore I would design, build and operate devices that would deliver to me the sunken ridges of the silent world.

J. COUSTEAU, *The Living Sea*, 1963.

OVERLEAF
Cousteau's team cross the equator beneath the waves of the Indian Ocean. In previous centuries those who had never crossed the 'Line' were subject to an embarrassing initiation ritual. On the Calypso they merely had to take a dive. The ship's motor launch obligingly trailed a stream of yellow-green dye to mark the zero parallel.

WALLY HERBERT 1934–

On foot across the Polar pack

HERBERT MADE HISTORY IN 1968-9 when, equipped with dog-sleds, he led an expedition from Alaska to the North Pole, to become the first man to have indisputably reached the pole on foot. Then, supported by air-drops, he continued across the ice until he reached Spitsbergen, thereby completing the first, 6,115-kilometre traverse of the Arctic pack. His record-breaking achievement was overshadowed by the Apollo moon-landing, but Herbert was interested less in publicity than in exploration. During the course of forty years he travelled 37,000 kilometres through the polar regions, mapped 119,140 square kilometres of unknown Antarctic territory and spent several years with the Inuit of Greenland accompanied by his wife and young family. His name is immortalized in an Antarctic range and a mountain in the Arctic.

HERBERT AND HIS TEAM WERE THREATENED BY POLAR BEARS.
We seemed to be travelling and travelling but making no progress. The distraction, however, was the polar bears and we killed three during those three days. Sometimes they would come down-wind, but usually they approached us from behind and they just kept coming. There was one occasion when a polar bear came in sight and Fritz was in an awkward position: he was trying to cross a stretch of very tricky ice, weak, sloppy ice, with rotten small pans in the middle of it, and suddenly a polar bear came along. The dogs of course took off and dragged the sledge into the water...It was pulled out with a great deal of difficulty. And all this time the polar bear kept on coming, and Fritz didn't know what to do: whether to shoot it with a gun, shoot it with a camera, or try and rescue the sledge. All the other dog teams were going berserk and it was absolute chaos...Fritz and Ken fired a couple of shots, but it wouldn't go away. It just kept coming. It didn't actually attack – it just kept walking. You've got to shoot them sometimes otherwise they would come right on and hit you, and there is no knowing how close they will come before they turn around and walk away – if they do walk away at all.

To kill a polar bear, you had first to knock him over. We never went for a head shot in these situations. We would always have at least two guns aimed at him at the same time, or even three, and we didn't take any chances. This wasn't a sport, it was the real thing. We were killing to protect ourselves and the dogs...

Polar bears normally travel on all fours. They will rise up on their hind legs occasionally, when they are some distance off, just to look over the pressure ridges. They are very fearsome but very beautiful, too. When they are some distance off they are magnificent beasts, but when they come closer and closer, they do become very menacing. They just amble towards you with a completely fearless expression on their faces. Almost casually, they look over their shoulders and don't seem particularly interested in you at all, but they keep heading in your direction. They don't look you in the eye and come towards you; they casually close the distance...

We couldn't take chances, and we dropped this particular one about fifteen feet away. That's as close as I want to be to a polar bear, and from that time we decided that we would shoot all polar bears that came within twenty feet, though we always tried to scare them off. We tried several techniques. There was one occasion when all four of us, with

three guns between us, walked towards the polar bear, making a lot of noise and shouting and so on. But he kept coming. As we were walking towards him we were closing the distance that much quicker. It was ridiculous. We should really have been going the other way...

It seemed a shame, having shot a polar bear, even in self-defence, to leave it there, so we felt obliged to chop it up for dog food. It took about a couple of hours and was very hard work for all four of us. But the dogs now began to associate the walking polar bear with the meat and, from that time on, it was impossible to hold them whenever a polar bear came in sight. They just went wild and were very difficult to control.

W. HERBERT, *Across the Top of the World, 1969.*

OFF SPITSBERGEN, THE TRANS-ARCTIC EXPEDITION WAS HELICOPTERED TO ITS SUPPORT SHIP. The helicopters could only stay on the ground for a maximum of about five minutes. They couldn't switch the engines off for some reason I never fully understood. The temperature wasn't very low at the time, but presumably they felt safer if they kept the blades going...Everything was panic and flap and bustle, and everyone was rushing around shouting 'Hurry up!'

I felt, I must admit, a little hostile towards the first man that greeted me. He wore a bone-dome helmet and a satanic beard, and his name...was 'Beest'. Later, on board ship, we were to become great friends, but on the ice he wanted me to rush. I didn't want to rush. I hadn't rushed for eighteen months, but his helicopter was sitting there, whirring away, kicking up an awful racket and blowing everything about. I found out later that they were so close to the maximum range at which they could operate with a heavy load that to have stayed an extra five or ten minutes on the ice could have been disastrous.

Dogs don't seem to mind being put in an aeroplane providing the engines are not running - but try putting dogs on a helicopter when the rotors are whizzing round and the whole machine is shaking! One has literally to wrestle them in and stand at the door fighting them back, until eventually, overcome by their fear, they cower on their bellies and start dribbling all over the floor.

Fritz, Allan and Kent were carried away and I was left with only a sledge, a tent and my team of dogs...When everything was ready, I sat on the sledge and had a smoke. It was a wonderful feeling being all by myself out there. For the first time in sixteen months I was further than five miles from the nearest man. This was something to be savoured. I just sat there and smoked, not thinking about anything in particular but just feeling good. I was neither sad about what I was leaving, nor excited about what I was going to. It was a sort of suspended state.

The helicopters came back, and the stillness and purity of the Arctic were shattered with noise and tainted with evil engine smells. So this was civilisation. It hurt the ears. It was an intrusion. People were screaming at me, yelling, laughing, inviting me to parties. I had to rush. I had to lift dogs, push them into helicopters. Lift sledges. Crawl in after the dogs and pacify them during the flight. Occasionally I took a glance out of the window – the ice below was really broken up, an absolute mess...I was going back to something I was unsure of. Everything was confused and happening too quickly. The helicopter banked and for a moment or two I could see the ship. It was framed in the window. It looked very small. I could see as we were coming in that the hangar on the flight deck was full of people.

We hovered over the deck for a second or two, then settled. The doors were flung open and the noise flooded in. Wind from the rotors was whipping the film of water on the flight deck, beating it slippery. I was pushing the dogs out of the helicopter door and they were all scared. Their legs were kicking before they hit the deck and they took off as soon as their claws scratched the steel. There were sailors grabbing the dogs and disappearing with them, and I didn't bother. I knew that once the dogs were outside, someone was going to look after them, so I just hurled them out of the door and followed them. I jumped down on to the flight deck with a hell of a thud. Bloody hell, it was hard – the thud resonated all through the ship.

There was a great sea of faces directly ahead – a huge crowd of strangers, and so much wind from the rotors and noise from the engines, I couldn't tell whether the sailors were shouting as I was swept in amongst them. Everyone seemed to be smiling – I could hear voices – and feel my hand being shaken. I was confused and too many emotions came crowding in at once. At that moment, I only knew that my journey was over.

Across the Top of the World.

Herbert and his huskies career over the pack ice. Despite being supported by air-drops, the Trans-Arctic team relied for its survival on the speed and strength of their huskies. On a later expedition to the east coast of Greenland Herbert paid oblique tribute to their sturdiness: 'For 10 hours we drove our two teams of dogs into a blizzard. The wind was too strong for us to set up our tent, so we were forced to feel our way in pitch darkness along the eastern shore...The last two miles of the 20-mile journey were among one of the most frightening experiences of my life. Avataq and I literally crawled those miles on our hands and knees, roped to our dogs and to each other to avoid losing contact in the blinding storm.'

EDWIN BUZZ ALDRIN 1930–
NEIL ARMSTRONG 1930–
MICHAEL COLLINS 1930–

Footsteps on the Moon

IN 1969, FOLLOWING A DECADE *of breakneck development, America's space programme climaxed with the launch of* Apollo 11. *The rocket took off on 16 July and four days later it was positioned off the moon. While Collins stayed aboard the spacecraft, Aldrin and Armstrong steered the Lunar Module Eagle to the surface. Their stay was brief, but in the two and a half hours they were outside the Eagle they were able to collect valuable soil samples, run and jump in low gravity and, weirdest of all, to see their home planet. 'Earth hung in the black sky', wrote Aldrin, 'a disk cut in half by the day-night terminator. It was mostly blue, with swirling white clouds, and I could make out a brown landmass, North Africa and the Middle East. Glancing down at my boots, I realised that the soil Neil and I had stomped through had been here longer than any of those brown continents. Earth was a dynamic planet of tectonic plates, churning oceans, and a changing atmosphere. The moon was dead, a relic of the early solar system.' They returned to Earth on the 24th, having completed one of the shortest, most expensive, yet most momentous journeys in the history of exploration.*

ON 20 JULY, 1969, THE EAGLE TOUCHED DOWN.

Neil rocked his hand controller in his fist, changing over to manual command. He slowed our descent from 20 feet per second to only nine. Then, at 300 feet, we were descending at only three and a half feet per second. As Eagle slowly dropped, we continued skimming forward.

Neil still wasn't satisfied with the terrain. All I could do was give him the altimeter call-outs and our horizontal speed...We scooted across the boulders...At 200 feet Neil slowed the descent again. The horizon of the moon was at eye level. We were almost out of fuel.

'Sixty seconds,' Charlie warned.

The ascent tanks were full, but completely separate from the descent engine. We had 60 seconds of fuel remaining in the descent stage before we had to land or abort. Neil searched the ground below.

'Down two and a half,' I called. The LM moved forward like a helicopter flaring out for landing. We were in the so-called dead man's zone, and we couldn't remain there long. If we ran out of fuel at this altitude, we would crash into the surface before the ascent engine could lift us back toward orbit. 'Forward. Forward. Good. Forty feet. Down two and a half. Picking up some dust. Thirty feet...'

Thirty feet below the LM's gangly legs, dust that had lain undisturbed for a billion years blasted sideways in the plume of our engine.

'Thirty seconds,' Charlie announced solemnly, but still Neil slowed our descent.

The descent engine roared silently, sucking up the last of its fuel supply. I turned my eye to the ABORT STAGE button. 'Drifting right,' I called, watching the shadow of a footpad probe lightly touching the surface. 'Contact light.' The horizon seemed to rock gently and then steadied. Our altimeter stopped blinking. We were on the moon. We had about 20 seconds of fuel remaining in the descent stage. Immediately I prepared for a sudden abort, in

A memorable footprint. Aldrin noted that 'I watched the toe of my boot strike the surface. The gray dust shot out with machinelike precision, the grains landing nearly equidistant from my toe. I was fascinated by this...The legs of my spacesuit were smeared with sooty dust...When we removed our helmets back inside the Eagle, there would be no way we would be able to keep from breathing some of [it]. If strange microbes were in this soil, Neil and I would be the first guinea pigs to test their effects.' The dust – which eventually proved germ free – had the texture of gritty charcoal and smelled of fireworks.

case the landing had damaged the Eagle or the surface was not strong enough to support our weight.

'Okay, engine stop,' I told Neil, reciting from the checklist. 'ACA out of detent.'

'Got it,' Neil answered, disengaging the hand control system. Both of us were still tingling with the excitement of the final moments before touchdown.

'Mode control, both auto,' I continued, aware that I was chanting the readouts. 'Descent engine command override, off. Engine arm, off...'

'We copy you down Eagle,' Charlie Duke interrupted from Houston.

I stared out at the rocks and darkness of the moon. It was as stark as I'd ever imagined it...the horizon curved into blackness.

'Houston,' Neil called, 'Tranquility Base here. The Eagle has landed.'...

We were supposed to do a little house-keeping in the LM, eat a meal, and then try to sleep for seven hours before getting ready to explore the surface. But whoever signed off on that plan didn't know much psychology – or physiology, for that matter. We'd just landed on the moon and there was a lot of adrenaline still zinging through our bodies. Telling us to try to sleep before the EVA was like telling kids on Christmas morning they had to stay in bed until noon. I decided to begin a ceremony I'd planned with Dean Woodruff, my pastor at Webster Presbyterian Church. He'd given me a tiny Communion kit that had a silver chalice and wine vial about the size of the tip of my little finger. I asked 'every person listening in, whoever and wherever they may be, to pause for a moment and contemplate the events of the past few hours, and to give thanks in his or her own way.' The plastic note-taking desk in front of our DSKY became the altar. I read silently from the Dean's Communion service – I am the wine and you are the branches... – as I poured the wine into the chalice. The wine looked like syrup as it swirled around the sides of the cup in the light gravity before it finally settled at the bottom.

Eagle's metal body creaked. I ate the tiny Host and swallowed the wine. I gave thanks for the intelligence and spirit that had brought two young pilots to the Sea of Tranquility...

Seven hours after we touched down on the moon, we depressurized the LM, and Neil opened the hatch. My job was to guide him as he backed out on his hands and knees onto the small porch...When he reached the ladder attached to the forward landing leg, he moved down carefully...

'I'm at the foot of the ladder,' Neil said, his voice slow and precise. 'The LM footpads are only depressed in the surface about one or two inches.' The surface was a very fine-grain powder. 'I'm going to step off the LM now...'

From my window I watched Neil move his blue lunar overshoe from the metal dish of the footpad to the powdery gray surface.

'That's one small step for...man, one giant leap for mankind.'

Lunar gravity was so springy that coming down the ladder was both pleasant and

HORNET + 3

tricky. I took a practice run at getting back up to that high first step, and then I hopped down beside Neil.

'Isn't that something?' Neil asked. 'Magnificent sight out here.'

I turned around and looked out at a horizon that dropped steeply away in all directions. We were looking 'down sun,' so there was only a black void beyond the edge of the moon...pebbles, rock fragments, and small craters covered the surface. Off to the left, I could make out the rim of a larger crater. I breathed deeply, goose flesh covering my neck and face. 'Beautiful, beautiful,' I said. 'Magnificent desolation.'

Stepping out of the LM's shadow was a shock. One moment I was in total darkness, the next in the sun's hot floodlight. From the ladder I had seen all the sunlit moonscape beyond our shadow, but with no atmosphere, there was absolutely no refracted light around me. I stuck my hand out past the shadow's edge into the sun, and it was like punching through a barrier into another dimension...

Neil leaned toward me... 'Isn't it fun?' he said.

I was grinning ear to ear, even though the gold visor hid my face. [We] were standing together on the moon.

E. ALDRIN & M. McCONNELL, *Men From Earth, 1989.*

President Richard Nixon applauds the Apollo 11 crew in their quarantine chamber aboard USS Hornet. They splashed down eight days, three hours and eighteen minutes after leaving Cape Kennedy. On arrival, they were given sterile overalls and consigned to a carefully ventilated chamber that was then flown to Ellington Air Base. Twenty-one days later they were let free – on the premise that moon germs had the same the same life cycle as earth germs and that even if they didn't nobody cared.

RANULPH FIENNES 1945–

The Trans-Global Expedition

Blobs amidst the polar gloom, Fiennes's skidoos forge over the ice on his Transglobe Expedition of 1979-82. The Transglobe Expedition followed the Greenwich Meridan for 56,330 kilometres around the globe and produced a startling array of scientific observations from the meterology of the Arctic, to the zoology of Africa and the katabatic winds of Antarctica. This expedition was a success; but some of Fiennes's others were not. Still, as he said, 'Know when to turn back and live to fight another day. Better to be a live donkey than a dead lion.'

ARMY OFFICER AND ARISTOCRAT, *Ranulph Fiennes became one of the late 20th century's most peristent explorers. He undertook numerous expeditions to Africa and Antarctica, but his most famous exploit was the Trans-Global Expedition of 1981-82 which involved a circumnavigation of the globe not side to side but top to bottom, taking in the Sahara, both poles and the North West Passage. At the outset Fiennes was a relative greenhorn, with little experience of polar conditions. Once he returned he had a comprehensive – and often unpleasant – acquaintance of ice. A professional explorer in the tradition of Amundsen he continually sought new barriers to overcome. 'Why did I choose such a way of life?' he wrote. 'I didn't really; it just sort of came about. Things worked out that way.'*

ON THE DIFFICULTIES OF POLAR TRAVEL.

Each time an ax struck, bits of ice flew about. But so little ice for so much activity. Feather-soft snow lay over the cracks in between ice blocks, and we kept falling into these. On one occasion Charlie disappeared up to his shoulders. On another, one of my boots became stuck in a cranny. We laughed weakly at each other. What else could we do? To strike a stance from which to use the ax gainfully it was often necessary first to dig out a flat platform. Otherwise the act of swinging the ax had us sliding all over the place. The exertion meant taking deep breaths of freezing air, and this created a burning sensation in the chest...

The twin aches of hunger and thirst always travelled with us. The hunger was each day with coffee for breakfast and nothing but deep-frozen Mars bars or a packet of pelletlike Rollos and eight sweets aptly called Fox's Glacier Mints. The Mars bars were great once you managed to gnaw a piece off small enough to close your mouth over and suck. But they were also tooth killers. By the end of the following June when we returned to London, we had among the six of us lost a total of nineteen fillings. Oliver had been trained to take out teeth and fill up holes, but despite the professional-looking set of dental instruments, which he would show Charlie and me with loving pride from time to time and despite the unpleasantness of our gaping holes, neither of us approached him to undertake molar repairs of any sort.

The thirst was fourteen hours in the arid atmosphere of a polar desert with nothing to drink but little balls of snow. Little lollipops of ice looked nicer but I avoided them after once cutting a thin sliver off a big block. I put it in my mouth. There was a fizzling noise and stinging sensation. I felt around with my mitt and removed the ice. I tasted blood. For days afterward my tongue remained raw where the ice had burned it.

R. FIENNES, *To the Ends of the Earth, 1983.*

WHILE TRAVELLING ACROSS THE ARCTIC PACK, FIENNES FELL THROUGH THE ICE.

The ice felt spongy at first, then more like rubber. Without warning it began to move. A few feet ahead black water gushed up and spread rapidly over a wide area. I stopped at once but the water rushed past me, covering my boots and, perhaps because of its weight or my involuntary movements, the whole mass of new ice began to rise and fall as though a motor boat had passed by. The undulating movement of a swell approached in slow motion...as it passed under me the ice rind broke up beneath my boots and I began to sink.

Afraid of disturbing the ice further, I kept rigid, like a mesmerized rabbit.

As the water closed over my knees the remaining layer of crust broke, and I sank quietly and completely. My head could not have been submerged more than a second – the air trapped under my wolfskin acted as a life jacket. At first I had no thoughts but to get out fast. But the nearest solid floe was thirty yards away. Instinctively I shouted for the others, then remembered they were a good half-mile away on the other side of who knew how many slabs and ridges.

I leaned both arms on the new ice that hung suspended under two or three inches of water, then kicked with my boots to lever my chest up onto this fragile skin. I succeeded and felt a rush of hope. But the thin skin broke beneath me and I sank again.

I tried several more times. Each time I clawed and crawled until half out, and each time I sank I was weaker.

My mind began to work overtime but not constructively. Perhaps a passerby might see me and throw a rope. Realization hit like a bombshell. There would be no passerby.

Was it deep? A vivid picture of the Arctic Ocean's floor mapped in the National Geographic magazine flashed to mind and gave me a sort of watery vertigo. Yes, it was deep. Deep. Directly under my threshing feet was a cold drop to the canyons of the Lomonosov Ridge between fourteen and seventeen thousand feet below. I vaguely remembered that sailors on the Murmansk convoys reckoned on survival in the waters of the North Sea for about one minute before the cold got them. And this thought brought back the words of an SAS lecturer on survival: 'Never struggle, don't even try to swim, just float and keep as still as you can. Give the water trapped in your clothes a chance to warn up a bit, then keep it there.'

So I tried doing nothing except paddle my arms to keep afloat. But, from a great distance it seemed, I sensed a numbness in my toes. My inner boots filled up, my trousers were sodden. Only in the wolfskin could I feel myself. Inside the gloves there was no sensation in my fingers. And all the while my chin inside the parka hood was sinking slowly lower as the clothes became heavier.

It might work in the Mediterranean or even in the North Sea but not here. I felt a rising panic. I must get out now or never. I smashed at the ice with one arm while the other thrashed wildly to keep my head above water.

The seconds seemed like minutes and the minutes like hours. The precarious platform of ice rind was too strong to smash with one arm. Only with the weight of my chest could I crack it, a few inches at a time, and my strength was draining quickly. My arm slapped down on a solid chunk, inches thick, suspended in the skein like a layer of clay in quicksand. I levered my chest onto it. It held. Then my thighs, and finally my knees.

For a second I lay gasping on this island of safety, but once out of the water the cold and the wind zeroed in. It was minus 38 degrees Fahrenheit that morning with a seven-knot breeze. At 20 degrees below zero with a nineteen-knot wind, dry exposed flesh freezes in one minute.

Moving my stomach and wriggling legs and arms like a turtle in soft sand I edged to the nearest floe with the nilas [newly formed ice] bending and pulsating under me as though it was alive. But it held. Standing up I watched the water dribble out of boots, trousers and sleeves. When I moved I heard the trousers crackle as they froze. The shivering began, and I could not control it. I tried press-ups but five had always been my limit in the best of times. I slumped over to my Skidoo. The air movement was bitter on my face and legs. It would be foolish to walk back to the others. My Skidoo had stalled. I couldn't start it again without taking off my thick outer mitts. This I couldn't do; the leather had gone rigid and shrunk.

For fifteen, twenty minutes I plodded round and round my Skidoo with a sodden heavy jog, flapping my arms in wheeling windmills and shouting all the while.

Then Ol arrived....

After that, all was action. I got on the back of his Skidoo and we went back slowly to where Charlie was stopped with an overturned sledge. They quickly erected the tent, started the cooker, cut my boots and wolfskin off with a knife and between them found bits and pieces of spare clothes to replace my soaked ones. Soon the wet items were strung dripping above while tea brewed and Ol rubbed the blood back into my fingers and toes.

I had been damn lucky.

To the Ends of the Earth.

In 1992 Fiennes (right) and Dr Mike Stroud slog across Antarctica on the first unassisted traverse of the continent. Dragging loads of 226 kilograms apiece, they took ninety-seven days to cross from one side to the other. When they used wind sails Stroud was exultant:

'Compared with the toil of manhauling, to be pulled forward at high speed was a delight so intense that to ignore it, merely because it was difficult and dangerous, was nigh impossible.' A less enthusiastic Fiennes wondered: 'How would I explain Mike's death to his wife and mother?'

BERTRAND PICCARD 1900–

Around the world by balloon

BORN INTO A LONG LINE *of explorers – his father Jacques reached a record depth under-water in 1960; his grandfather Auguste took a balloon to the stratosphere in 1931 – Piccard determined to follow family tradition by becoming the first person to fly a balloon non-stop round the globe. His first attempts in 1997 and 1998 were hampered by technical fail-ures and political obstructions. On 1 March 1998, however, accompanied by British co-pilot Brian Jones, he took off from his native Switzerland aboard the* Breitling Orbiter 3. *Flying south to Africa, the balloon caught an eastward jet stream and on the morning of 20 March passed its starting point, landing a day later in Egypt. Piccard drew a telling comparison between their circumnavigation and the Apollo moon landing. 'When Neil Armstrong stepped on the moon, he was happy to be so far away', he wrote. 'When we stepped onto the desert, we were happy to put our footprints back on earth.'*

DURING THE JOURNEY PICCARD SWUNG BETWEEN EXULTATION AND DESPAIR.
High above the red vastness of the Sahara, the silver bubble of the Breitling Orbiter 3 balloon feels absolutely motionless. Only our instruments tell us we are moving: 85 miles an hour. Yesterday Brian and I climbed out the hatch. As he fixed a problem with the burners, I used a fire ax to break off ten-foot long icicles that had formed on both sides of the capsule, watching them tumble and turn as they fell toward the impossibly empty sands of Mali below. After closing the hatch, we repressurized the capsule, fired our burners, and climbed back to our cruising altitude of 23,000 feet. Now, sitting in our cockpit in front of our navigation instruments, we smile at each other. After flying south-west for three days, we have entered the jet stream at last. For the first time...we can finally say that our trip around the world has started...

[Over the Pacific] All around us the clouds seem alive. Every morning small cumulus clouds appear next to the balloon, growing little by little until they become fearsome cumulonimbus storms, able to tear the fragile skin of our balloon in their turbulence. As if guided by an invisible hand, we weave among the thunderclouds, which dissolve every night in the coolness of glorious sunsets...The immense expanse of ocean has become a mirror in front of which it is impossible to fool myself. I feel naked with my emotions, my fears, and my hopes. We'd like to be farther on in our flight, but all we can do is accept being where we are, drifting in a lazy wind over the biggest ocean on the globe.

After six days of flight over the Pacific...we enter a powerful jet stream. Now, at 33,000 feet, we are delighted to race towards Mexico at 115 miles an hour. The typical cirrus clouds of the jet streams accompany us, their ice crystals glistening in the bright sunlight. But the euphoria lasts only 24 hours. At this altitude the outside temperature is minus 58°F, our burners use a lot more propane, and our cabin heater becomes less effi-cient. The water reserves inside the capsule have turned to ice.

Cold and exhausted, Brian and I begin to pant in the overdry air of the cabin. Worse, we watch, powerless, as our speed drops. Somehow we have been ejected out of the jet stream over Mexico and are flying the wrong way, southeast toward Venezuela.

Wearing oxygen masks, Brian and I take turns sleeping as much as we can to regain

strength. Completely out of breath, I phone my father and my wife with tears in my voice. My dream is falling apart, I tell them. So close to our goal! I decide to risk everything. We will fly as high as the balloon can take us, no matter how much propane it takes, to try to get into a jet stream...At 35,000 feet my eyes are fixed on the instruments, and I can barely believe what I see: Degree by degree, our flight curves northeast...[by march 19] we are halfway across the ocean, flying at 105 miles an hour...We cross the coast of Africa during the night, and when the sun rises on March 20, we are just a few hours away from Mauritania. These are the longest hours of my life. Western Sahara stretches in front of my eyes. I am happy to see red sand desert again.

At 9.54. a.m. Greenwich Mean Time Brian and I look at our maps incredulously: After having flown 26,050 miles, we have reached the finish line at 9°27 west longitude, where we first headed east...But for us nothing has changed. We are above the same desert we left from, and have yet to find a suitable place to land. The fuel has held out, so, for the thrill of it as much as for a less remote landing, we fly another 2,380 miles, at speeds exceeding 130 miles an hour, reaching Egypt.

During the last night, I savor once more the intimate relationship we have established with our planet. Shivering in the pilot's seat, I have the feeling I have left the capsule to fly under the stars that have swallowed our balloon. I feel so privileged that I want to enjoy every second of this air world. During our three weeks of flight, protected by our high-tec cocoon, we have flown over millions of people suffering on this Earth, which we were looking at with such admiration. Why are we so lucky?...

Very shortly after daybreak on March 21, after 19 days, 21 hours, and 47 minutes in the air, Breitling Orbiter 3 will land in the Egyptian sand, Brian and I will be lifted away from the desert by helicopter, and we will immediately need to find words to satisfy the public's curiosity. But right now, muffled in my down jacket, I let the cold bite of the night remind me that I have not yet landed, that I am still living one of the most beautiful moments of my life. The only way I can make this instant last will be to share it with others. We have succeeded thanks to the winds of providence. May the winds of hope keep blowing around the world.

B. PICCARD, *National Geographic Magazine, September 1999.*

Breitling Orbiter 3 hovers above the Alps at the start of its circumnavigation. Fifty-five metres tall, the balloon supported an 5.4-metre long pressurized capsule containing oxygen and food to support its occupants for four weeks. Theoretically capable of sustaining life at 12,192 metres, the capsule was equipped with bottled oxygen, an air-recycling system, propane tanks and an array of solar panels. When Breitling Orbiter 3 *descended in North Africa it was caked with ice and at the limit of its endurance. 'We clasp hands and give each other a hug', Piccard wrote. 'We have achieved the craziest of our crazy dreams, the first non-stop flight around the world in a balloon.'*

INDEX

PICTURE CREDITS